THE GATES OF WRATH

The Fourth Instalment of the
Chronicles of Martindale

by

John Blaylock

This Book Is Dedicated
To The Memory
Of
Robert S. Abley

(Historian *Extraordinaire*)

1939 - 2014

Text copyright 2015
This edition 2024

John Blaylock

All Rights Reserved

Prologue:-
September 1862

Geoffrey Hodge, the curate of St. John's, Church, Kirkby saw off the last of his Evensong congregation and as it was a fine evening decided to smoke a cheroot. For tobacco of any kind wasn't allowed in the vicarage, this due to the Reverend Marshall's lung condition, so he went to sit on the churchyard wall to enjoy his smoke in peace.

However, he soon saw that Manners, the verger, was already ensconced there, "Don't mind if I join you, Tom?" Asked the curate.

Manners much preferred his own company, though in recent years he had become used to the curate sharing his idyll.

"Aye, take a seat," he invited, shuffling along the well-worn stones of the wall.

Hodge climbed up, took out a cheroot and lit it. Previously he had preferred a pipe, but since the Crimean War these small cigars had become very popular, especially as they provided a good smoke without the fiddle and mess a pipe required.

"You should try these," suggested Geoffrey Hodge, as the small cigar began to draw.

"I'll stick t'me pipe," replied the verger shortly.

Hodge was soon blowing smoke rings into the still air as he gazed down at the town of Martindale which lay spread out below him.

As it was a Sunday, the collieries, ironworks and factories were quiet, which reduced the noise and fug of the place considerably.

"Very still down there to-day," the curate offered eventually.

"Wants t'be if ye ask me, far too much happenin' doon there for my likin'," grumbled the old man.

The curate nodded his agreement though; funnily enough, he was now attracted to Martindale, for a start it was far livelier than Kirkby could ever be.

"Martindale's interesting in its own way."

"Aye, it is, if ye like fighting every night and murders even. Why, that Love fellow came back from who knaws where, killing people."

"He's the one who set Martin Hall afire, did he not?"

"Aye, he did that and ruined poor Frank Turner's whole body – not t'mention his terrible scarred face."

"Married to the eldest of the Lander girls too, I believe," added Hodge.

"Distress never arrives by itsel'," commented the verger shortly.

Hodge decided it would be wiser to keep his own opinion of Mrs Abigail Turner to himself, especially as she was the daughter of the Rector of Holy Innocents, a fellow clergyman.

"Aye, poor Frank's also had the misfortune t'marry the most shrewish woman t'be found anywhere in that town."

Manners was too old and long-serving to worry about his comments reaching the ears of Mrs Abigail Turner.

Geoffrey Hodge nodded gently, feeling sorry for the sufferings of the badly scarred Mr Turner.

Manners puffed steadily away at his pipe, his head turned towards the sinking sun.

"Still, the Turner family have done very well out of Martindale," the curate ended a long silence between them with what he hoped would lead to a more cheerful conversation.

"They're not simple farm folk no more," Manners nodded as he spoke.

"I suppose most folk do well down there," commented the curate, again in a positive tone of voice.

"Aye, then there's Miss Bellerby, marries Mister Schilling who then sends himself off t'war. Far away in America too, he could just as easily have fought in one of our wars, we've plenty to spare."

The verger couldn't believe any man in charge of his senses could bear to leave Blanchwell and Miss Caroline for any reason whatsoever.

"Though Schilling's very much against slavery, as are we all."

"Our navy does that already," grumbled the older man.

The curate again tried to move the conversation on to a more positive track, "Though there's much good to be found down in Martindale too."

"I canna' think o' much."

"Why, there's the only theatre for miles around," Hodge was becoming desperate to avoid the ruination of a beautiful evening.

"Aye, but then that actor feller was taken away by the bailiffs. Left the Fisher woman at the altar."

"Oh, no, Tom, he didn't do that," defended the curate.

"Theatre will shut wi' out Villiers."

"Mrs Esprey will see that the place is kept going," Hodge spoke with a confidence he didn't have.

"Theatre or no, the place doon there will end badly," prophesied Manners gloomily as he pointed the stem of his pipe towards the New Gomorrah.

The curate managed a short laugh, "Why, it prospers greatly, not a man lost his job during the recent recession."

"Aye, thanks to Sir Charles Martin, but there's still that Wright fellow to think on, I hear he's richer than ever since he's been an' gone to America."

"He's a very powerful man, there's no doubting that," replied Hodge who then added, "And his daughter is a Marchioness now, or so I've been told."

"Ha," the verger's laugh was more in the manner of an exclamation, "Her second husband didn't last much longer than her first."

"Yes, I've heard some scarcely believable stories about her marriage."

"Buried her husband alive, or so some say," returned the verger.

The curate shivered at the thought.

"Aye, well, Lady Elysia Martin; as she once was, has a lot of money behind her, that'll keep her safe," pronounced Manners.

"She has even more now, or so I believe."

"Money," the verger swung his right arm in an arc that encompassed the town below him, "Money brought all this about and money will see the end o' it."

"Lack of money, perhaps."

"Aye, no money'll mean no town, it'll wilt away t'nothing. A ghost town it'll become."

Geoffrey Hodge finished his smoke, flicked away the stub of his cheroot and said, "That's always possible these days, but there is wealth a plenty down there at the moment."

"It'll run away t'sand, you just remember what I said when it happens."

"I'm sure you're right, Tom," Hodge decided to give up the fight for positivity as he clambered from the wall and set off for the vicarage two hundred yards away.

"Lovely evening, though," called the verger cheerily.

"It was till now," muttered Hodge to himself.

PART ONE

Chapter One

28th December 1862

Captain Helmuth Schilling, commanding Company 'J' of the Seventeenth Pennsylvania Cavalry, found his mouth so dry that his tongue was sticking to the roof of it, and his feet were so cold that he could no longer feel any constituent part of them.

Then, from behind him, he heard the whinnying of a horse, "Go tell them to keep the damn horses quiet," he whispered vehemently to Andy Jackson who lay nearby.

The ex-slave nodded before he crept away from the edge of the wood where J company was deployed, with each trooper peering nervously into the freezing mist.

For the umpteenth time, Helmuth checked the workings of his favourite revolver, the one which always sat most comfortably in his hand and the cylinder of which always spun with a deeply satisfying, well oiled, smoothness.

"I think I can hear 'em comin' up, captain," Sergeant Crittenden spoke in his calm, unhurried way.

Helmuth listened intently and could just about detect the sound of oncoming horses.

Was this Jeb Stuart's or Hampden's lot? He asked himself.

"Maybe it's local farmers visiting friends for New Year?" Suggested Crittenden.

"Maybe, though it sounds as though the hooves have been muffled," replied Helmuth slowly, taking a tighter grip on the butt of his revolver.

The sergeant nodded in agreement, "I doubt farmers'd bother with that."

"Pass the word on, no one's to fire until I do," ordered Captain Schilling keeping his voice as steady as he could.

The company commander heard his order being passed in whispers from man to man down the hundred yards or so of the company line.

"It's Rebs right enough, sir," Crittenden nodded towards the point where the road from the ford emerged between the trees which lined the Occaquon River.

"Get ready to fire," Captain Schilling's voice croaked to a halt as he began to feel the restless movement of his troopers along the skirmish line. He instinctively knew that his inexperienced men were easing themselves away from the enemy and towards their horses.

A long plume of gun smoke spread along the bushes and trees to their left front and the sound of musketry crashed into their ears.

"They're behind us boys...," the cry was more of a scream than a shout and was taken up by many men of the Seventeenth.

Helmuth was finding it hard to believe that the panicky voice was that of his second-in-command, Lieutenant Eldred Matheson.

The soldiers of J Company, who were already jumpy began to desert their positions in ever greater numbers.

Helmuth brought himself erect, "*Hold on boys…,*" he shouted, "Stay where you are, the Rebs haven't hurt a single one of us yet."

His words had no appreciable effect on his men who were hurrying towards their picketed horses, now making no attempt to conceal their movements.

Helmuth's mind became rapidly concerned for his own safety as a second; well directed, enemy volley came from the tree line opposite him.

A swarm of rifled musket balls filled the air with the sound of many angry bees as they passed just over his head.

This firing was followed by the clatter of horsemen riding at high speed, accompanied by the usual Rebel yells, these having the effect of speeding his own men on their way to the rear.

The enemy cavalry now burst through the trees and began to deploy along the road.

Seeing that his line was disintegrating, he ran towards the horses in an attempt to hold up those of his troopers who were seeking to put distance between themselves and the enemy.

"Jameson.., Garland..., Schmitd...," Schilling yelled, waving his pistol above his head, "Stop, stop boys, they've not shot at you yet, time enough to panic when they do."

His troopers paused momentarily, but then a further rattle of musketry drowned his words and his soldiers rode on, each man not daring to look him in the face.

Helmuth watched them go before turning to see a calm and slowly moving Andy Jackson bringing his mount to him, accompanied by Crittenden.

"This war's to be a long 'un, sir, if this is the best we can do," the ex-slave commented as he handed over the reins.

Helmuth shook his head wistfully, "It appears you're right, Andy, all we can do is follow 'em. Once they've stopped running and thought about what they've done, maybe they'll hold better the next time."

"If there is a next time," put in Sergeant Crittenden, shaking his head slowly.

*****

The commander of J Company stared hard at his soldiers who had been brought to attention before him. They stood in silence awaiting the wrath which was about to descend upon them and which they knew was fully deserved.

"You do understand, I trust, that yesterday morning you brought shame upon yourselves, your regiment, your State and the Union Army?"

"Warn't just us, cap'n," someone called out.

"Whole regiment skedaddled," another voice joined in.

"*DAMN YOU ALL, I'LL HAVE SILENCE,*" Helmuth glowered, his eyes seemingly lighting up red with anger.

Then he calmed himself down again, "You are right, the whole regiment did run for it, but it was our company which set them off. Who's to say that they wouldn't have stood firm if it hadn't been for our panic."

He looked along the line, pausing for a second at random faces and daring them to contradict him.

After a long silence, his voice rang out again, strong, clear and commanding, "However, what you did discover yesterday was that killing Johnnie Reb with your mouth is much easier than dealing with him on the field-of-battle."

A low murmur of agreement passed along the line.

"Yesterday morning; hopefully, you learned not to panic when a few minnie balls fly over your heads. I do not expect you to become battle-hardened overnight, but becoming *real* soldiers is a goal we must work for if we're to get the better of Johnie Reb."

Many of the troopers were now nodding in agreement and there was a buzz of agreement from them.

"To this end we are going to drill harder and for longer than we ever have before. Once we're done, the next time we meet Stuart's or any other damn Rebel general's boys we'll show them what we're made of."

Helmuth was then pleased to hear a subdued rumble of enthusiasm coming from his men. He waited until the ranks became quiet again and then spoke in much softer tones, "I know you're mostly plain country boys from Adams County, but you can ride as well as the Rebs and shoot as straight as they can too, so we'll put this morning behind us and move on."

The rank-and-file muttered their mutual agreement with their commanding officer's sentiments.

Once more Captain Schilling gazed sternly at the company assembled before him, before ordering Sergeant Crittenden to exercise the company in the rapid deployment of a skirmish line.

*****

After calling for his junior officers, Helmuth repaired to his tent and took the very late breakfast that Andy Jackson had ready for him.

As he ate, lieutenants Matheson and Gibson arrived and as was usual they slumped into the camp chairs arranged before the captain's table.

Eldred Matheson stretched his legs out before him and put both hands behind his head, "God, I'm whacked. What a day."

"I'm with you there, brother," supported Carter Gibson.

"GET UP AT ONCE. How dare you enter without so much as a salute or a howdy-do," Helmuth's voice was harsh and menacing.

Both junior officers jumped to their feet, completely surprised.

"But.., but Helmuth…," began Gibson.

"Damn you both, remember I am the commanding officer of this company and I will be respected as such in future."

"Coming all regimental now, British influence, I suppose, well…," then Matheson's voice trailed away as he saw the grim expression on Helmuth's face.

"We lacked discipline yesterday morning and our line gave-way for no reason at all."

"They were firing at us, Captain," muttered Matheson.

"We couldn't stand alone, nobody could have," Gibson supported his brother officer.

"Every one of us ran, who is to say which of us broke first," said Matheson pointedly.

Helmuth's gaze became tightly fixed on his second-in-command, "You'd be best advised to keep your mouth shut, Mr Matheson, for your voice was the first one I heard spreading panic."

Matheson tried to make reply, but found his throat blocked and his eyes opened wide as; in his mind, he suddenly found himself back in his father's study after he'd been thrown out of Princeton.

Helmuth continued his voice dangerously low and his eyes became mere slits, "I am sure, Mister Matheson, that it was you who began the rout with your shout of *They're behind us boys*."

Matheson's face became crimson, he shook his head, "Dammit, sir, I'll have satisfaction, I'm an officer and a gentleman," he began violently but his voice died away soon thereafter.

"Yesterday, you showed yourself to be a coward, which is a much greater fault in an officer than it is in a trooper," Helmuth's tone was grim.

"I.. Agh... It..," Eldred Matheson blustered toward silence.

"They were on us I stayed as long as I dared," Gibson tried to defend himself.

"You ran too, Carter, and not long after me," claimed Matheson, pointing his finger accusingly at his brother officer.

Gibson's head dropped, "We all ran, the cap'n took to his heels pretty soon," then his words trailed away too.

"Yes," agreed Helmuth, "I *did* run and I'm truly ashamed of it. I trust you gentlemen also regret your actions and have become determined to do better next time."

"Yes, sir," Gibson was first to reply, in a hang-dog kind of way.

"Well, Lieutenant Matheson, speak up, for your commission is in danger and shame awaits you," Helmuth's voice was a steely as he could make it.

"If you say so,   sir," the reply came slowly and was begrudged.

After allowing them pause for thought Helmuth nodded to the chairs, "Sit down, gentlemen and have some coffee, we need to consider what's best to do next."

He waited until they had settled and then continued, "It is said that the Seventeenth Pennsylvania Cavalry are the regiment that *charged furiously to the rear*. This being so, it is our duty to force the rest of the Division to change their low opinion of us."

Chapter Two

Tom Harrington was greeted by his hostess, Lady Glencora Keyes, looked around the room and found himself to be astonished at how much this New Year's Day *soiree* must have cost her.

"Sandy Keyes must have enjoyed a big win," he muttered to himself before making his way to the stocked buffet tables.

"Tom, how wonderful to see you," he looked around to see an expensively turned out Elysia Scott-Wilson hurrying towards him.

He took her hand and kissed it, "Why, Elysia, I don't know how long it is since we met."

Elysia, Marchioness of Studland, kissed his cheek, "Oh, no one invites me anywhere these days. I'm a fallen woman, don't you know, and just because of my divorce," she pulled in her cheeks and pouted her lips.

"I'm surprised Glencora invited you here, she's as much of a snob as the rest of them."

Elysia laughed gently and swept her arm around the room at the plentiful food, the bottles of fine wine and the fresh hothouse flowers which flourished in every corner.

"Lady Keyes was unable to resist my offer to pay for this, at least not after Sandy lost such a packet at Newmarket."

"Money will breach most barriers eventually," surmised Tom.

"Too true, my dear and I have lots of it."

Tom glanced around, he'd heard that Elysia was currently in charge of the Wright fortune, "Your 'pa not here?"

"No, he's still in America and finding it much to his liking. He has dozens of enterprises underway though is mainly involved in financing the manufacture of the tens-of-thousands of boots the Union Army needs."

Tom laughed to himself, "He'll be selling them to the Confederates too, at twice the price, I shouldn't wonder."

"How enterprising and so like my dear papa."

"They'll be shoddy boots, no doubt, so both armies will end up fighting in bare-feet."

Elysia laughed and then looked around the room before asking, "Isn't Lydia with you?"

Tom Harrington smiled broadly, "No, she's back at Glossom Park, we're expecting our first child."

Elysia clapped her hands lightly, "Oh, how wonderful," she cried and then her face clouded and she forced a single tear from each eye.

The Member of Parliament tensed himself for he knew Elysia's tears were always contrived and it became plainly evident that she required something of him.

"I'm sorry, Tom," she began, patting dry her cheek with a minute lace-handkerchief, "Forgive me, for I'm so, so unhappy."

"Really?" Tom's tone expressed his doubt, "You don't look it."

"Once Lydia has given you children, then you'll be able to imagine just how heartrending it is not to be able to see them, to watch them grow, to…," she finished with a sniffle.

"You have Warren," Tom pointed out.

"Of course and I love him, I do so love him. Though I've not seen Albert and Alexandrina for nearly five years. By now they won't recognise their *own* mama," she choked back a sob and the handkerchief was brought into play again.

Tom shrugged his shoulders, whatever it was that Elysia wanted he hoped she'd soon get to the point.

"Tom," she wheedled, "Would you do me a very great favour?"

"As long as it doesn't cost me too dear."

Elysia laughed, "Why, no, it's a very simple request really," she paused, her eyes glinting and startlingly bright, "Would you take a letter to Charles for me?"

"Why don't you post it?"

"I would, but I fear he would not read it, he may not even open it."

"I don't see that I can help you with this."

"Please Tom, please, I need you to persuade him to read my letter and to consider its contents carefully."

Tom shook his head, "He's my best friend, Elysia and there has been so much conspiracy and skulduggery directed against him I doubt he'll take a request on your behalf very kindly."

"All the events you speak of were not of my making. I was completely unaware of the scheme to steal away Bertie and Drina."

"Then how do you know of it?"

"Miss Kleist has told me everything and I explained to her that what she had done was very wrong."

Tom Harrington shook his head slowly, "You ask a lot of me, Elysia, I risk losing an old and valuable friend."

Elysia opened her eyes wide and made them sparkle, "Why, Tom," she spoke in velvety tones, "After all, are we not old friends too? Did we not have a romantic connection once?"

"A long time ago," Tom's tone was flat and neutral, "Though I don't believe I can help you with this."

Elysia's tone then became business-like, "Tell me," she queried, "presently, how close to a post in the government are you?"

"I know people, I have some influence with them."

"How would you like much greater influence? How would you like a juicy worm with which to bait your hook?" She put in sharply.

"Of course I would, for I'd be no worse a booby as a minister than some of those already in post."

"Have you heard that old Jack Somerville is on his death-bed? The current Member of Parliament for Winterbourne?"

"No, I hadn't heard that," Tom's mind filled with possibilities and then he finished quickly, "though I am already safely ensconced at Glossop."

"True, though suppose you were able to approach one of your most influential connections and tell him that Winterbourne was available to a candidate of his choice?"

Tom's eyes lit up signalling his interest.

"What then? Surely, some powerful man will be looking for a place for a younger son or a nephew?"

"Yes, indeed, that would be very useful," Tom's brain clicked into gear and began to hum away.

"Then you'll approach Charles with the letter I mentioned?"

"How can I be sure that you will deliver what you promise?" Tom's eyes narrowed.

"I'll hand you a document; signed and sealed by me, offering to leave the selection of the Abbey's candidate in your hands."

It took very little time for the Member for Glossop Park to make up his mind, "We shall exchange letters, then."

*****

John Fisher groaned wearily as he heard the sound of weeping coming from the next room.

"She's gone from crying to howling," he complained quietly to himself as he entered, expecting there to be at least a cup of tea poured for him.

As her brother sat down, Roberta Fisher took her handkerchief from her eyes for a moment and sniffed loudly, "Has the post arrived?" She asked.

"Yes, though there's nothing in it for you."

His reply brought forth an extended bellow, followed by what appeared to be a hopeless struggle for breath and then came a prodigious downpour of tears.

"Roberta, Mr Villiers was taken from us nearly three months ago, you can't continue like this for ever can you? Surely, not."

"How can my own brother be so... so very heartless. To think, my sweetheart dragged from the very bosom of my love," screamed Roberta who then she set to bawling again.

"But Bobbity, they actually took Villiers from the Martin Arms," corrected the schoolmaster, "your bosom was not present."

The Sirens themselves couldn't have shrieked any louder than Miss Fisher did, she beginning with a slow groan which developed over long seconds to a screech of eardrum shattering proportions.

Fisher let her run out of breath before he began to complain, "You'll have to forget Mr Villiers and address your other duties. I need you to run my household properly, supply meals, see that the laundry and cleaning is done...," his voice trailed off as he decided he had already been as firm with his sister as he could ever dare to be.

"*Ahh... Ohhh....,*" she began to shriek again with its sound filling the room.

The schoolmaster gave up and looked around in vain for something to have for his breakfast.

"Look, Bobbity, it's not *my* fault the bailiffs took Villiers away the day before your wedding, and after all he did owe a great deal of money."

The siren stopped, began again and then stopped, "You could have covered his debts," she accused.

"Though Bobbity it was four-hundred and fourteen pounds, sixpence halfpenny."

"You could have signed a bill for it, to give him time to settle what he owed," she accused, her voice becoming ever more strident.

The only answer that Fisher could manage was a long, splutter of exasperation.

Roberta began to wag a finger towards her brother, "I'll *never* forget about this, never, *never* and I'll go on about it for as long as I wish – which will be a long, *long* time."

Fisher groaned and swallowed half-a-cup of cold, well stewed tea.

*****

Lieutenant Eldred Matheson collapsed on to his camp bed and searched beneath it for the bottle of whiskey he habitually kept there. He took a long slug and then offered it to Carter Gibson.

"No thanks, Dred, I just want to put my head down, I'm whacked."

"Damn Schilling, he's been on my back all day, nothin' I ever do is right for him."

"The Captain's fair though, he's just desperate to put the company to rights… and the colonel's on his back."

Matheson snorted, "Why can't he give me a break though? We're in the same army ain't we?"

"We haven't lived down Occaquon yet, the entire regiment is a laughingstock."

"I don't see why we should be, for the whole army's not done a lot better," commented Matheson.

"Anyway, Schilling just wants us to be steady the next time we face the enemy," replied Gibson.

"He's come back from England full of British ideas, discipline, discipline and *discipline*. He'd like the whole company to be made of red-coated stuffed shirts," complained Dred Matheson.

"Yes, but it's all got a point, ain't it? We can change formation much more quickly now and our shooting is definitely faster and more accurate. Even you can't deny this," Gibson supported his company commander to the obvious annoyance of his companion.

Matheson took a further long swallow of spirit, wiped his mouth and then said, "Married an English woman, didn't he? She'll be a fine lady, I figure, filling his head full of what's proper to do an' what's not proper to do, in that damned supercilious way they have over there."

"I've seen her picture, she sure is a looker."

Again, Matheson took to his bottle, "Well, I'm sick of Mr Schilling and if he don't quit riding me he'd better look out behind him when we're next in action."

Carter Gibson got to his feet, "I expect this is just the drink talking."

"*Aww*, sit down, sonny and remember you're junior to me," Eldred Matheson raised his hands, "It's just the way I was feeling, me having been ridden so hard."

Gibson sat down, though his companion's words had not settled easily on him, "Ok, but don't come up with anything like that again."

"Forget it. I'll not be putting up with Schilling for much longer anyway, my uncle Jefferson Stanley, is on Hooker's staff and my pa's written to ask him to find a place for me there. My new posting will drift through any day now, I expect."

"There may not be a place for you," put in Carter Gibson, who was rather envious that a coveted staff-officer billet might go to one not worthy of it.

Matheson laughed, "My pa's a Philadelphia lawyer and he's got Uncle Jeff out of trouble more than once, so he owes us."

"Well, when you're riding high with Joe Hooker, spare a thought for me."

"I won't," replied Matheson airily before he slumped back on to his bed, put his hands behind his head and seemed to fall asleep immediately.

*****

"I thought you'd be far too busy to visit Durham at this time of year, especially with a new baby to coo over," remarked Sir Charles Martin as he led Tom Harrington into the library for an after-lunch coffee.

Harrington smiled broadly, "Yes, she's a delight."

"Vanessa's to be the name, is it not?"

"Yes, that's right."

"Newly born daughter, though you've still found time to travel all the way to Durham to see me?" Charles was curious.

"Yes, it's true I am very busy," the Member for Glossop Park looked a little shamefaced as he spoke.

Charles raised his eyebrows, "Obviously, there's something on your mind."

Wordlessly, Harrington pulled from his pocket an envelope and placed it on the table which stood between them.

Charles' eyes narrowed, "That's in Elysia's hand."

"It is."

"Then how were you persuaded to deliver it and not the postman?"

Harrington sighed, "She wanted to be sure that you would read it."

The owner of Martin Hall picked up the wafer, turned it over and then threw it back down. "I've no desire to hear or read anything from my ex-wife."

Tom shook his head, "Look, Charles, I'm aware that Elysia leaves deep wounds behind her and I know what a troublesome, devious, bitch she can be, but she seemed very sincere when last I met her."

"Sincere?" Charles almost spluttered coffee out as he spoke.

"Trouble is, she asked a favour of me and you know how I melt in the gaze of a pretty face."

"Tom, I am sure that you are aware of the succession of nefarious schemes directed against myself and my people in recent times by Wright."

"The nurse trying to steal the children, you mean?"

The baronet's face reddened, "Much more than that, Tom, much, much more. Did you know that Wright plotted to take my life? Were you aware that four of my people were attacked and one of them killed?"

"I'd heard about young Russell, but didn't connect Wright with it," Tom paused for a while and then continued, his voice expressing his puzzlement, "Why on earth would Hannibal Wright want to be rid of you?"

"I can't say anything about that."

"I suppose he was annoyed about the divorce, even though Elysia seems to have fallen on her feet – as usual."

"The divorce meant nothing to him. No, he wished to be rid of me because of what the evidence I have against him."

"Concerning what?" Tom was really curious now.

"I can't say, though it's very serious business. Please don't question me further."

The Member of Parliament nodded, "Very well, Charles, but did these event involve Elysia? She claims not to have known of the attempt to steal away your children."

"A likely tale."

"She insists that she only knows what Fraulein Kleist has told her of it."

"And you believe her?" Charles was incredulous.

"Wright himself has always been fully in charge of his own affairs and Elysia's more interested in hats, shoes and dresses than conspiracies. You know, she could be telling the truth."

Charles considered for a moment, "What has she written?"

"I believe it's to do with Albert and Alexandrina."

"Missing her children? She was joking, of course."

"Like it or not, it appears that she has changed,"

"What about her other child? Warren isn't it? Warren Marquis of Studland," Charles' voice trailed off and when he spoke again his tone curious, "And what about the unborn child, the one she tried to pass off as mine?"

"I've no idea," the Member of Parliament shook his head.

"Dead in a ditch somewhere, I shouldn't be surprised," Charles spoke hotly.

Tom shrugged his shoulders and after a long pause spoke again, "Well, anyway, I said I'd bring her letter to you and I have done so."

Charles picked up the envelope again, "I'm surprised my oldest friend has delivered this."

"You are and have always been my best friend, but I could see no harm in carrying out Elysia's request."

The coal-owner thought for a long half-minute and then said, "I'll discuss it with Marian and should she agree, then I'll read it. Report this to my ex-wife."

*****

Caroline Schilling had taken up water-colouring once more and was working on a picture of the garden from the viewpoint of the dining room when she was interrupted by her butler.

"From America, ma'am, thought you'd wish to read it immediately," he nodded as he offered her the silver platter upon which the letter lay.

"Thank you," she smiled before taking her mail and ripping open the envelope.

Near Occaquon, Virginia,
January 3rd, 1863

My Dearest,

We had our first taste of action on the 28th December and I'm sorry to say we did not cover ourselves in glory. However, none of my company were killed, wounded or even scratched which is a good thing, I suppose.

We're back in camp and expecting to be sent north to join the main-body of the Army of the Potomac.

This war isn't going well, as our generals leave a lot to be desired, many being mere politicians who know only how to strut around like peacocks.

Still, I'm sure Lincoln will find us a proper general soon. He must, he really <u>must</u>. He could do worse than you – remember how you out-flanked the slave-chasers!

On a more positive note, I have managed to acquire (don't ask how, but at a cool $45 a piece!) a dozen Spencer repeating carbines, which I have *given to the best shots in my company. These will increase our volume of fire considerably when we next meet the Rebs. In which case, hopefully, the enemy will believe us to be a much larger force than we actually are and persuade them to avoid us.*

I am adapting splendidly to the outdoor life and my every need is seen to by the excellent Andy Jackson – who is desperate himself to take-up arms against the slave owners he so despises.

I trust you are well and little Julia thrives back at Blanchwell. I used to make fun of your desire to return there, but now I've been away from that haven of tranquillity for four months, I fully understand what made you so desperate to return. How I wish I could once more have sight of the ancient church atop the ridge and see the woods full of bluebells this spring. Even the bustle, noise and smell of Martindale would be well received by my ears, nose and eyes!

Please give my regards to the Coven and to Charles, Richard and Colonel Esprey.

The good colonel gave me much excellent advice which I intend to follow to the letter. I've even packed my sabre away, it being next to useless in a modern war. However, I keep so radical an opinion to myself whenever I mess with my fellow officers, some of whom can't wait to lead a charge to glory. Dying' being the probable outcome of such a desire.

Thank-you for your regular, amusing and loving letters, they help to keep my spirits up and maintain my concentration on achieving the final destruction of slavery in my homeland.

As this war could go on for years yet, I must accept the possibility that I may never return.

Should I fall, then please keep a place for me in your heart, even if it were not to be a central one.

With Every Last Ounce of My Love,

Helmuth

Caroline's could not hold back her tears. How could he believe
he didn't dwell in the depths of her heart?

"How have I come to allow him to feel this? I have sent him off to war believing he was *not* central to my life?" She took herself to task.

Then she sat down heavily and began to wipe away her tears, at the same time whispering fiercely to herself, "What a stupid, *stupid*, woman I have been."

Then, once she had settled down, she took her pen to send Helmuth as instant a response as three and a half thousand miles would allow.

*****

"When do you suppose it'll be safe to return to Martindale so you can pay me?" Asked Solomon Vasey, a fellow thespian of Roderick Villiers.

The actor-manager shook his head sadly, "I know not, Solly, old fellow, I wish I did."

"Then I'm not to be reimbursed for my role in your escape? Were my accomplices not spectacularly good? Would they not have taken in a judge of the High Court? Come, tell me, explain yourself."

"They were excellent, they were indeed, there's no doubt of that," Villiers thought for a while before continuing, "I would even have said they were magnificent if the word had not become so overused."

"Why, they were even accosted and threatened with violence from several colliers and other assorted ruffians when they escorted you away from that awful town."

"I know, Solly, I know and I'm very grateful to them and especially to you for arranging it so well."

"I had to pay them in advance you know," Vasey was annoyed at his own foolishness.

"You did everything asked of you and my gratitude will be eternal," Villiers's voice dropped to a velvety whisper.

Vasey shook his head in annoyance, for every time he had anything to do with Roddy Villiers either he hadn't been paid or if he had the money was short. Failing this, he had been let down in some other way.

"It won't do, Villiers, we can't stay here without money – the landlord is becoming quite insistent."

"A moonlight flit, perhaps?"

"This would appear to be our only option. Though where could we find safe refuge as we're both so well known here?"

"Perhaps we could gather a troupe of our old companions and set out along the Queen's highway to entertain all who'll pay us a penny or two."

Vasey groaned, "Are you mad? Winter's full on and we'd find ourselves up to our knees in slush. What we require is a safe harbour, a sweet port wherein we can anchor securely and enjoy the pleasures of the shore."

"Just because you spent a year on the Irish Sea packets it doesn't give you the right to turn lyrical.

I'm the poet here, if anyone is," replied Villiers quickly.

Solomon threw up his hands, "I should have known better than to become entangled in your schemes again."

"Perhaps we should try our luck in America," pondered Villiers slowly.

"Why don't we just go to the moon and be done with it," interrupted Solly sharply.

After a further few moments of thought, Villiers came to a decision, "I suppose I'll have to write the letter sooner than I intended."

"To whom? Lizzie Harper?"

Villiers considered seriously for a few seconds and then said, "No. No, I don't think so, I have someone else in mind."

*****

Thomas Leakey, otherwise known as the Deacon, entered the New Church Asylum For Orphans and delicately removed his gloves. He looked about the empty hall and then bawled out, "BOY."

There came a scurrying from beneath the stairs and a ragamuffin soon stood quivering before him, "Yes, sir, yes, sir, I'm 'ere, sir... I wasn't asleep."

Leakey, smiled down at the child's terrified face and patted his shoulder, "There, there," he comforted silkily.

Signs of relief crossed the orphan's face and he made the beginnings of an uncertain smile.

The Deacon nodded slowly his approval, "Here, take my gloves, hat and coat," he ordered.

"Yes, sir," the child jumped forward eagerly.

"Good, boy," again Leakey's tone was soft.

The inmate of the orphanage did as he'd been directed and then returned, his face still showing great relief.

Leakey continued to smile, he stretched out his hand and chucked the child beneath the chin.

The little boy beamed and half-closed his eyes.

Then the Deacon, with all his power, punched the little waif's head, knocking him to the floor.

The infant shrieked and began to cry.

The office door was flung open and Jemmy Cruikshank; the warden, appeared, "What's goin' on here? What's this bloody racket about," he became silent as soon as he saw the Deacon had returned.

Leakey crossed to the boy, who was curled up on the floor, and kicked him. He waited a second or two and then kicked him again, but even more violently.

The child began to howl in pain and fear.

"Shut up boy, or worse'll come to you," the Deacon's voice was full of intent.

The howling stopped immediately, to be followed by well subdued sobs.

"Come in, Deacon," welcomed Cruikshank.

"Mitchin here is he? Twiss has come too I expect. What about Losser, is he with us?" Leakey enquired.

"Yes, they're all here. We've been awaiting you," Cruikshank said as he ushered his visitor forward.

"Good," nodded the Deacon after he'd checked that his underlings were indeed present, "You've visited the Keogh woman, I presume?"

"Yes, two of us spent an hour wi' her," replied Jemmy Cruikshank.

"More like two," put in Grubby Mitchin.

"Well, what did she have to say?"

The warden thought for a moment before replying, "The Martindale people were a party of.. What was it? Seven?"

"Six," corrected Grubby.

"Aye, six," Cruikshank sat back with a well-satisfied smile on his face.

"Well, who were they you idiot. I need their names."

"Let's see," pondered the warden, "Sir Charles Martin led them."

"Aye, he's a baronet," Grubby smiled, for he, had a fondness for a lord.

"Then there's a big, scarred, ugly man," the warden recalled Mrs Keogh's words.

"Aye, she sez he wears a funny hat an' has a beard," Grubby, supplied further details.

"Turner is his name, he's Sir Charles' agent – an important man in Martindale, so Kathy made out," added Cruikshank.

The Deacon nodded, "Carry-on, gentlemen, you are doing well."

"Then there's Geordie Cook, a little fellow of no account an' his wife, a fat lass wi' a sharp mind."

"Sharp mind, that's what Kathleen said," confirmed Grubby, nodding his agreement.

"She runs a pie-shop that's doin' very well," mused Cruikshank.

"*Ha*, I suppose this is the origin of the tasty pies with the glossy gravy," said Leakey more or less to himself.

"That pie George baked looked t'be a good 'un to me," said Grubby, shaking his head sadly at the thought of its loss.

"Damned thing was thrown in my face," the Deacon looked hard at Grubby who's head dropped.

"Then there's the other two," put in Cruikshank slowly, not wishing to upset his visitor.

"They're the two I'm most interested in," Leakey words were delivered in icy tones.

"Aye, well, the one that sat on Grubby was a Jack Nicholson, he's a collier and well known in the town. Top hewer and has the reputation of being a hot-head," continued the warden of the orphanage.

"He only got the better o' me 'cos he took me by surprise," Grubby defended himself.

"The slowest member of the entire sloth family would move quickly enough to catch you by surprise," sneered the Deacon.

"The other one, the one that…," noticing the look on Leakey's face Cruikshank dried up.

"Come on man, out with it, for his is the name I really want."

"It's Dunnett, Joseph Dunnett, he's Sir Charles' gamekeeper."

"Dunnett, eh," mused the Deacon.

"Aye, that's him," reasserted Cruikshank.

Leakey's eyes sought out Twiss, "Well, Peter, I expect you'll have a couple more stout fellows in mind for our expedition?"

"Aye, Deacon, sir," replied Twiss stoutly, "Carver and Cutter, they're ready."

"And willing, I trust."

"Yes, sir, more than ready," confirmed Twiss.

Listening to all of this, Losser knew for certain that neither of the lads mentioned were enthusiastic. They were as keen as he was himself, which wasn't very. Though he thought it best to say nothing which might upset either Leakey or Twiss.

The Deacon considered for a moment and then instructed, "Good, then we shall depart for Martindale in a month or so."

"All of us?" Asked an appalled Jemmy Cruikshank.

"Of course, all of us. Were we not *all* brought low by these assailants?"

"Well, I can't go," pleaded Jemmy, "I've t'look after this place. It won't run itsel' yer know."

Thomas Leakey considered for a few seconds and then said, "Very well, you may remain here."

"Maybe I'll be needed here as well... Help Jemmy, like," Losser plucked up all that remained of his courage, which fled as soon as he saw the icy stare directed at him by the Deacon.

"You shall join my merry band," Leakey ordered coldly.

"Aye, sir," Losser's eyes blinked rapidly as he spoke.

"Good, then that's settled," said Leakey.

"Ye'll have some dinner, sir?" Enquired Cruikshank.

"No, I shall dine out, somewhere quiet where I may think."

"Ye'll not be needing me then, sir?" Asked Grubby.

"No, but make sure my bed is well aired," ordered the Deacon before leaving.

Grubby and Losser exchanged glances of fear and desperation as they heard the front doors close.

"D'ye think," whispered Losser, looking furtively towards the doorway, afraid that Leakey might pop in again like a jack-in-the-box, "D'ye believe... The Deacon's gone off his head a bit, y'know, since...?"

"He's been fixed on nowt else," said Mitchin.

"He's always been strange, like," muttered Jemmy Cruikshank.

"He just doesn't like folk getting the better of him," put in Twiss.

Losser continued gazing at the office door, "I don't want t'go to Martindale. Why, they'll murder us there for the way young George was treated," he half whispered.

"You'll all be seen as strangers straight away," Cruikshank spoke with the casualness of one who has not been asked to risk life-and-limb.

"Aye, they will that. Mind, this time, I'll be ready for Nicholson, I'll chew him up an' spit out his bones," promised Grubby, though with little real conviction in his voice.

"I'm not goin'," said Losser quickly, balancing on the balls of his feet as though he were preparing to speed off immediately.

Twiss grabbed Losser's arm and nearly pulled him over, "You'll be there with the rest of us 'cos you're too afraid to do anything else."

Losser pulled himself free, "I will get away from here," he shouted.

"Where else would you find a place? Ye'll have t'go wi' the rest o' them," Jemmy Cruikshank spoke dismissively.

"He's right," backed up Mitchin, "We'll just have t'go and try to keep out o' the way of trouble."

"Though what's the Deacon expecting of us? Carry-out killings or something?" Losser's concern could be heard in his voice.

"What's a killing or two matter," Twiss's mouth twisted into a smile.

"They'll matter right enough if we get caught," returned Losser, his face contorted by worry.

"The Deacon will plan it so we won't be taken."

Mitchin shook his head sadly, "Anyway, the Deacon owns us all, if it weren't for him none o' us would have a place to begin with."

"*And what a place it is*," Losser now saw the orphanage in its true-light and didn't much like what he saw.

He'd been an inmate since the age of two and had been badly bullied, until he was big enough to play the role himself.

"Aye, but it's all we have," replied Grubby.

"What about the Guardians?" Queried Losser, "Can they not have Leakey out?"

"He has the lot o' them in his pocket, he owns them," said Cruikshank.

"Why, he owns us if it comes t'that," muttered Losser, whose confidence had seeped away to next to nothing after the beating he had taken in the railway goods-yard.

All three stood silent, full of their own thoughts, before the warden spoke again, "Aye, though what would we do if he cast us aside?"

"Aye, what could we do," Grubby spoke dolefully.

The room was silent for a minute or so and then Cruikshank turned to Losser, "Right, get the boys t'dinner, mutton stew wi' plenty o' grease," he ordered.

*****

"I won't read this, if you think it best not to," said Charles as he lay in bed with his wife.

Marian looked up from her book and smiled, "Surely, no one can resist an unopened letter."

"Then you think I should see what Elysia wants of me?"

"It's your letter, Charles, to do with as you think best."

Charles considered for a moment or two and then tore open the envelope and began to read its contents aloud.

Dear Charles,

You must wonder how I dare to write to you after all which has happened between us. For I understand that my family and my self have done you much wrong, for which I have no excuse to offer apart from my youth and girlish silliness.

In the first place I should never have agreed to marry you, though at the time my head was filled with the idea of becoming a country lady.

I soon found such a life to be so unutterably tiresome that I made my pregnancy the excuse for fleeing from it. This led to other misdemeanours, of which you are now fully aware.

However, I beg you to believe that I never consented to the stealing away of your children by Frau von Kleist and I was shocked when she told me of it.

No doubt, as; hopefully, you are reading this, you will be thinking what can this woman possibly want of me now?

It is quite simply that; due to the love a mother bears for her children, I desperately wish to see Albert and Alexandrina. For the thought often saddens me that I may never be able to gaze upon their sweet faces again.

I beg you to grant me even the briefest of access to them. I will submit to any condition you may wish to apply in order to ensure their safe return to Martin Hall and no doubt Mr Digby will be able to produce a water-tight, legally binding document which I will happily sign in the presence of my lawyer, Mr Hill.

I was hoping that you would let me meet with Bertie and Drina in Durham over the course of a day or two, or even allow them to travel to Winterbourne for a week or so during the summer.

I wish you to understand that I am now a grown; and I believe, a mature woman. A mother who wishes no finer favour than the opportunity to be; however briefly, reunited with her children once more.

Should you worry over any influence my papa may have over them, I can assure you that he is currently in the United States and is likely to remain there for many months to come. In addition, I can faithfully promise that should he return unexpectedly, he shall not have any access to our children.

Yours most sincerely and hopefully,

Elysia Scott-Wilson

Charles looked at his wife, "Well, she didn't sign it Elysia, Marchioness of Studland, that's not like her to say the least."

Marian nodded, "She seems very sincere. I can understand how she misses her children, why, should Robert be suddenly whisked away…"

"My dear, you are without doubt an angel working here on earth," whispered Charles as he turned to kiss his wife.

"Though perhaps a gullible one, is that not what you're thinking?"

Charles laughed, "No, not gullible, though perhaps you're too caring for your own good. Think of the rough time Elysia meted out to you when she was last in charge here."

"She had no wish to lose her husband and she was right to suspect us."

"Yet, she'd only returned to Martin Hall in an attempt to deposit a cuckoo in my nest."

"No doubt she was desperate and anyway I suspect Sir James may have had a hand in the plan."

"I wish to believe her, I truly do, though I don't know how I can," said Charles after a thoughtful pause.

"She *is* the mother of Drina and Bertie and I know how miserable I'd feel were I in her position."

"Strange though, that she's never shown much interest in the twins until now. What can she be planning?"

"Why not take her letter at face-value, as a plea from a mother to see her children. Anyway, she will be bound by a legal document to return Bertie and Drina to us."

Charles turned and kissed his wife lightly on the lips before saying, "You're too kind, Marian," then he paused before saying flatly, "Elysia hasn't a maternal nerve in her body.

"It seems as though she's matured, Charles and...,"

"She's a devious bitch," Charles cut off his wife.

"You should never refer to the mother of your children as a *bitch*," Marian admonished her husband gently.

Again Charles kissed his wife, "Of course, that was very intemperate of me."

"Elysia is the mother of two of your brood and I'm sure that Drina and Bertie will wish to see her as much as she wishes to see them."

"Then you'd allow Elysia to have her way?"

"What harm can there be in it? Legally you'll have them tied to you with knots as tight as Digby can make them."

Charles nodded and yawned, patting his fingers across his mouth, "Yes, I suppose you're right, though I'll sleep on it."

Chapter Three

As Thomas Leakey dozed on the Darlington train he was dragged back to full awareness when his mind suddenly filled with nightmarish images of his recent debasement. In his dream he could hear the *swish* of the descending strokes as they came down upon his defenceless posterior, "*No.., No.., Stop,*" he cried aloud before he'd woken up enough to still his tongue.

"Are you well, sir," enquired a female voice.

Leakey eyed the speaker coldly, a woman he took to be of farming stock.

"I have somethin' warming in my pocket," offered a man who was obviously her husband.

Leakey smiled weakly, "I'm sorry to have disturbed you. It was nothing, merely a passing fancy."

"Gentleman of the Cloth, I see," the farmer pointed at Leakey's collar.

"Yes," replied the Deacon shortly, preparing to distance himself from his travelling companions as quickly as he could.

"Can I take it ye have a church an' flock t'administer to somewhere in Durham County?" the wife picked up where her husband had left off.

"No, I've never been before," again, Leakey's reply was short and sharp. He closed his eyes again, hoping that they would take the hint and leave him in peace.

The farmer's wife shook her head sadly, "We're in want of decent, God-fearing folk where we live,"

"Aye, ever since the miners and ironworkers came," backed up her husband.

Leakey's light-blue, though dull eyes brightened slightly, "I am sorry, but I took you to be good country-folk. Is this not the case?"

The farmer spoke up, "No, bless ye, sir. You were correct in your first reading o'us. I'm John Parkin, a tenant of Mr Helmuth Schilling, recently gone off to the war in America."

"An American landowner, here? Is this not unusual?"

"Well, his wife has connections wi' us goin' back a long time. Miss Caroline Bellerby; as she was, came back from America as Mrs Schilling."

"Yes, the Parkins have been the tenants of Coldstream Farm for generations, have they not, my love," as she spoke the wife patted her husband's knee.

"Well, how can colliers and ironworkers much affect you?" Asked Leakey, bringing them back to the point.

"Our nearby town, sir, Martindale by name, is full of 'em."

"A Godless place, Reverend," the farmer's wife's tone became funereal.

"Strong drink! Fighting! Venal sin! They're all t'be found there in good measure," added the farmer.

"Aye, they're there in plenty," backed up his wife.

"Martindale, I believe I have heard of the place. Would the landowner be a Sir Charles Martin?"

"Why, bless ye sir, he is. 'Tis he who started the whole thing off, let me see, that would be… Five years ago."

"No, John, no, it was *nine* years ago this spring comin'," rectified the wife.

"Aye, Betsy, I stand corrected, it was the year the bottom meadow was flooded by the stream not being able to get into the river, so swollen was it."

"It is my intention to visit Martindale soon, for I should like to see at first-hand the working of a raw, new town. I may well have some business there."

"Oh, there's plenty of labourers to be found, they being needed by two collieries, and a big iron works…"

"There's steel too," interrupted the wife.

"Aye, steel, there is that. Much of it goes into the Balaklava Works, where they turn it into all sorts of things."

"And Sir Charles is master of all this?"

"Oh, I wouldn't know that sir. But I do know he owns much of it and is very rich."

"*Very* rich," confirmed the wife.

"Overbearing sort, is he?"

Both the farmer and his wife laughed aloud, "No sir, *no*, Sir Charles is one of the kindest most caring gentleman you could ever wish to meet."

"Looks to his people as though they were his kin," added Betsy Parkin.

"Divorced though," her husband brought an end to the positives.

"Surely, this is unheard of, he must have become a pariah to his peers," the Deacon shook his head.

"Married his housekeeper and she the widow of a collier before that," informed Mrs Parkin further.

"Aye, an' a farm lass even afore that. I remember the Turners well," Mr Parkin dug-deep into his memory.

"Nobody visits him, nor he them, except for the Schillings – but then, Mr Schilling is an American," added the wife.

"Not used to our ways," confirmed the husband.

"Indeed not and, surely, Lady Martin's family have disowned her."

"No, Mr Frank Turner is the right-hand man of Sir Charles," informed Mrs Parkin.

"So he's the baronet's brother-in-law?"

"Aye, that's the case."

"It is all very intriguing, I must add Martindale to my itinerary at once. Are there any clean, reasonable places in which to find a bed there?"

The farmer shook his head as he thought, "The only possibility for a man of quality such as yourself, sir, is the Martin Arms."

"However, if ye're in want of plain accommodation, then ye shall do no better than to contact Mrs Margaret Hardy, in Alexandrina Street, she takes in lodgers."

"Then I shall contact Mrs Hardy as soon as I arrive in Martindale."

"You go there now?"

"No, not just now, for I have several associates who await my arrival, though I shall travel to Martindale as soon as possible thereafter," replied Leakey, sinking back into his seat and closing his eyes to indicate that; as far as he was concerned, their conversation was over.

The Deacon smiled inwardly to himself, for this had been a most interesting and informative chance conversation. He had learnt enough to help him in his search for redress.

*****

Frank Turner saw his wife and daughter into Holy Innocents Church before taking up his role as usher.

At the head of the aisle, Marcus Reno; a pay clerk at the Elysia Colliery, was handing out hymn books.

However, he was in something of a mood for his theatrical ambitions had again been thwarted by Roderick Villiers, who had recently been taken away for unpaid debts.

"You look to be in a fine way with yourself," commented Frank as he came close.

"You're right there, here's me who's wasted time playing the lackey to Roddy and all he ever did was break his solemn promises to me. Were I Miss Fisher I'd count m'sel' lucky he's gone."

"Aye, though now he's away what's going to happen to the theatre?"

Reno puffed out his chest, "I've been invited on to the committee, ye know," he said with a smile, which quickly disappeared when he continued "though the theatre could close."

"I suppose so, though I doubt Mrs Esprey will let *that* happen."

"I hope not, we're due to start rehearsing *Hamlet*."

"It'll be sad if we missed that," Frank shook his head sorrowfully, whilst thinking to himself that; these days, he'd much prefer something to make him laugh.

"I know one thing," put in Reno after a while, "Villiers promised that I'd be Hamlet an' I've carried-out favour after favour for him on the strength of his pledge."

"Aye, you'll make a superb Prince of Denmark, you've got the build for it, lean and tall, like."

"You think so," Marky Reno preened himself, "I've earmarked a fine blond wig an'all."

"Why man, you were made for the role and indeed you're younger than Villiers too - by many a year I'd imagine."

"Indeed," agreed Reno softly smiling, "And do you really think we'll be able to keep the theatre going? I've learned the part and it's the longest in Shakespeare ye know."

"That must have taken some doing," Frank couldn't think of worse drudgery.

"Aye, Mrs Hardy helped me, but I hope it's not all been for nothing."

"The next director couldn't pass you by, surely."

Marcus Reno nodded and began to hand out hymn books with a smile on his face.

Dougie Brass, the butcher and all-round businessman, watched as the church filled up, "Not much heard of Villiers these days," he remarked.

Arabella, his wife hugged tightly his arm, "It's the best Bilious Villiers deserved. He was an awful old lecher," she pronounced.

"People might say that o'me too, me wi' a bride nearly half my age," he looked at his wife, his eyes pleading that she should scatter such fears to the wind.

Arabella, who was the youngest of the Reverend Lander's three daughters, stretched across and pecked him on the cheek, "Then pity help anyone who suggests such a thing to me. There's not even ten years between us, besides which you are handsome and very successful. What more could a girl desire?"

"I could think of lots," he returned glumly.

She smiled impishly and said, "Besides, I love your sausage, it's *so* thick and *so* very long too."

Brass managed to change his laugh into a cough, "Who'd have thought the daughter of a clergyman would enjoy sausage so much?"

Bella tittered quietly and hung on to his arm, her fingers pressing into the flesh of it in a meaningful sort of way.

Two or three rows back from the altar sat a bitter Abigail Turner, and as she gazed around the church her mood became even sourer, for it seemed that she could find nothing to please her these days.

Her eyes alighted fiercely on her husband who was helping one of the older parishioners to her pew. Francis controlled her life completely now, she was his to do with as he liked.

How different the situation had been only a year previously, when the boot had been firmly on the other foot. Then she had been able to lead Francis by the nose in any direction she wished to take him.

She ground her teeth silently, cursing that her dominance over her spouse had ended when; in a fit of temper, she'd spat out the claim that their daughter was the result of an illicit union with Mr Villiers.

Her head dropped and she began to press her long fingernails hard into the heels of her hands, stopping only when she realised that she may ruin her gloves.

Again, her eyes tracked her husband as he returned to his post of duty at the head of the aisle. She sighed deeply, how she hated the beard he'd grown to disguise the injuries he had suffered in the fire at Martin Hall. His hair was sparse and closely cut, but his beard was long, black and curly. She found his whole *ensemble* most distasteful, ugly and completely lacking in gentility.

"Mama, I wants to be with papa."

Abigail was reluctantly pulled away from her thoughts by the voice of her daughter, "Be quiet, Maud, you're in church and grandpapa will gobble you up should he hear you call out."

Maud sniffed and put her head down and wondered why it was that mama never let her do as she wished.

Before Abigail could return to her train-of-thought she was joined by her sister Amelia, who arrived in a flurry of finery.

"Oh, what a rush, such a rush I've had. Caroline insisted I use the carriage, though even so I've had to leave Fred behind," she cried with theatrical breathlessness.

"How I wish *I* could have remained at home," replied Abigail, who nudged her daughter, "Say good-day to your Aunt Amelia," she encouraged.

Amelia patted Maud's head and said, "Fred came back from the ironworks covered, literally *covered*, in red dust. On a *Sunday* too. Can you *believe* that he intended to climb into the carriage just as he was."

"Francis too is easily capable of committing such an outrage."

"How can men be so, *so*...," Amelia was lost for words and merely shrugged her shoulders.

"I presume Fred isn't to join us then?"

"Oh, he's coming all right, once he's bathed and changed, though no doubt he'll miss most of the service."

Abigail smiled bleakly, once she'd been very much the senior of the three sisters, though now the whole order of her world had been turned upside down.

For a full four years she had been the only one of the siblings to have a husband, with the situation looking very bleak for the other two. Then, out of the blue, Miss Caroline Bellerby had returned from America married to a Mr Schilling, whose brother, Fred, had quickly taken a fancy to Amelia. They'd married and were now living at Blanchwell Hall, one of the most important houses in the neighbourhood. As a result of this, Amelia stood upon the top rung of local society.

"*Mmm,*" Abigail muttered to herself gloomily and then she cheered up when she remembered that Arabella's marriage had taken her no higher in the scheme of things than had her own.

It came to Lieutenant-Colonel Jervis Esprey's attention that his wife; Elizabeth, was deaf to the sermon of Mr Lander and was somewhat fidgety in her seat, which was most unusual.

"You're not sickening for something are you, Liza?" He asked quietly.

"Whatever makes you think that?" She replied sharply, her tone daring him to make the same query again.

The colonel sniffed and stared straight ahead.

Mrs Esprey suddenly felt sorry for her sharpness and took his arm and squeezed it. "Sorry, my dear, I was thinking of poor Roddy. I certainly didn't wish to see him driven into an unsuitable partnership, though nor did I want him to be dragged off by bailiffs."

"*Hmm*, I see what you mean. Though, to be honest, I think it's hilarious myself. Serves the rogue right."

"It may seem funny to you, but Roderick Villiers is one of my oldest friends and I know he'd have hated being shackled to Roberta Fisher for the rest of his life."

"She's no catch, I'll give you that, and five minutes with her is much too long," the colonel said.

"Perhaps his creditors did him a greater favour than we know," mused Elizabeth mainly to herself.

"What's to happen to the theatre now that Villiers has gone?" the colonel wondered aloud.

"I can't let it close, it's so important to the community," Liza's response was very swift.

"It's so important to *you*, you mean."

"It is and why shouldn't it be," returned Elizabeth, her irritation making her words sharper than she'd intended.

Recognising that he was treading on dangerous ground, the colonel merely shook his head and grunted.

Elizabeth Esprey's eyes lit up with determination, "The theatre shall *not* close, I'll not have it close."

"Well the Sub-Committee meets to-morrow, doesn't it? Perhaps someone will come up with something."

"I am the only person capable of finding a solution."

"You brought Villiers in, surely you have some other acquaintance who would take on his role."

"Yes," Elizabeth nodded as she spoke before saying thoughtfully, "though I may need to visit the capital to do so."

"If you say so, my dear, but you must take Carew with you."

"I don't need to be nannied, I'll go by myself."

Esprey knew better than to argue but became determined that his wife would not travel to London alone.

A shaft of sunlight evaded the clouds and struck the church full on, bringing alive the colours of its stained glass, and flooding its interior with a rosy warmth.

Venetia Lander exulted in its glow and sighed happily, closing her eyes and imaging herself to be already soaking up the golden sun of Tuscany. She had just finished planning her first visit to Italy. Florence, Sienna, Verona and, finally, to her namesake itself, *La Serenissima Republica.*

This was to be the first proper holiday she'd ever taken; her husband being too poor to go any further than Aunt Charlotte's house in the best part of Harrogate.

However, after receiving a goodly sum from the said Aunt's estate and having suddenly found themselves free of their daughters, a visit to Italy was agreed upon and arranged for the early summer of 1863.

The sun dipped behind the clouds again and the nave became dark and cold once more, then from the mists of her mind there drifted the figure of Aunt Prudence.

"*Prudence?* Whatever are we to do with Prudence once we've gone off?" she asked herself and then groaned.

*****

Thomas Leakey took his ease in the front room of Mrs Margaret Hardy's house and sipped very strong tea.

"Biscuit, reverend?" asked the landlady, "homemade this mornin'."

Leakey took one, his smile beneficent, he nibbled at it and then pointed to a photograph which stood next to him on an occasional table, "Your son? Or perhaps your daughter?"

"I've not had children, Mr Leakey. No, they're friends, but the lass in the picture is like a daughter t'me."

"She appears to be a pleasant and I suspect, a very clever young lady too."

"Aye, she is that. She lodged wi' me for a while, a teacher she was once."

"Really. So pretty, and a teacher you say," he shook his head at the wonderment of it.

"Aye, well she was 'till she took-up wi' Jack Nicholson."

"Oh, so the gentleman with her is a Mister Nicholson?"

"Oh, yes, he's her husband."

"He looks rather out-of-place beside her, she being so attractive and ladylike, whilst he looks so…. Well, so *rough*."

"Aye, he's rough all right. Some say he's the best collier in the district but before he met Miss Jenkins he was also the heaviest drinker an' the fiercest fighter too – though that's nothin' t'be proud of in my eyes."

"Indeed not, I am a man of peace, myself."

"I'd have expected nothin' less, Reverend."

Leakey paused for a while to put on his most reassuring smile, "I wonder if Mrs Nicholson's room is free?"

Mrs Hardy looked more closely at her visitor and there was nothing she could object to in his appearance and demeanour, but there was something not right about him. Something which was *not right* at all.

"You've business in the town?" she asked, seeking time to think.

"Yes, I represent the Christian Workers' Education League. Our aim is to bring learning to the many common folk who yearn to better themselves."

"Plenty of ignorant people 'round here."

Leakey smiled again, "I believe this is just the place to establish ourselves in County Durham."

"Yours must be satisfying work."

"It is, most rewarding, most gratifying. It is the work of the Good Lord above."

Margaret Hardy nodded in agreement at the same time looking at the pale, *pale* blue eyes of her visitor and inwardly she shivered.

"Then you have a room for me?" Leakey smiled ingratiatingly.

"No, reverend, I have not. Mrs Nicholson's room was taken by Mr Reno, a young clerk at the Elysia Colliery pay-office, last month."

"You have no other? This comfortable and God-fearing house would suit me perfectly."

"I'm afraid not," she tried to hide the fact that she was lying by rising from her seat and putting on a brisk smile.

Leaky refused to rise with her and instead continued to sit, just like a long, black spider at the centre of its web. He knew his glance was making her feel uneasy and he wished to enjoy her discomfort for a little longer.

"Well… Well, sir, I've much to do…"

The Deacon delicately continued to sip tea, raising his eyebrows at her from above the rim of the cup.

"Much to do, sir," Margaret Hardy felt ever more certain that she was doing the right thing by denying this man of the church a place under her roof.

Eventually, the Deacon put down his cup, slowly unfolded his body and brought it to an upright position, "Then, for the moment, I'll shall have to make do with the less homely quarters of the Martin Arms.

Chapter Four

Elysia Scott-Wilson, Marchioness of Studland, finished reading the letter she'd just received from her ex-husband, Sir Charles Martin.

"Got what you wanted, I suppose," predicted Jonnie Corsica.

If it's possible to give a straight lipped smile, then Elysia managed it, "I believe so. Charles is such a ninny."

Corsica shook his head in disbelief, "You try to have him killed, you're part of the plot to steal away his children and you're still able to pull the wool firmly across his eyes," his tongue clucked several times.

"As I've said, he's such a ninny."

"So, I suppose that you're just full to the brim with motherly feelings for your children," suggested Corsica, his face breaking into a cynical smile.

"Of course I am, what else should I be," Elysia drew herself up to her full height and tilted her head so that her nose pointed high in the air.

"In truth, you're a vicious creature without a maternal bone or feeling in your body."

"That's most unfair, I love my children."

"If you didn't have a dozen servants to look after them, you'd leave them behind you under a snowy hedgerow, in a blizzard. I know you too well to be so easily fooled."

"You can be so unkind, and it's only because my third child had to be shipped off to Canada. Why, it was more of my father's doing than my own," Elysia put on the face of a badly-done-to little girl.

Corsica leaned back in his chair, his hands reaching behind his head, "Well, come on, tell me, what is it you plan for the little dears? You don't expect me to drown them for you I hope."

Elysia's eyes glittered and narrowed, "I intend to play a patient, waiting game. I will follow Charles' instructions to the letter, but all the while I will undermine him and the common strumpet he now calls Lady Martin."

Corsica shook his head, "My, I can't blame him for ditching you, I only caught a fleeting glimpse of his new lady's petticoats, but, by God she's a stunner if ever I saw one."

Elysia picked up the paperweight which stood on the desk that lay between them and flung it with some force at her general factotum.

Corsica, unconcerned, moved his head slightly to one side, raised a hand and caught the missile neatly, "*Bravo, well caught, sir,*" he cried softly to himself.

The colour drained from the marchioness's face, "Prettier than me is she?"

"'Fraid so, old girl, afraid so, but I expect you'll age far better than her. Besides, you're much, *much* more interesting, especially to a villain such as myself."

"I suppose even one so mean as yourself has his uses," Elysia spoke in her haughtiest tone.

"I have indeed and we need each other, don't we?"

Elysia nodded, "Yes, I suppose so."

"So, what's the agreement with Charlie Martin?"

"He promises to allow the children to visit Winterbourne in the summer for two or three weeks."

"The idiot. I can't believe he's so trusting, especially as he was once your husband and so must know about the little games you play."

"Oh, he thinks he will have me bound up in legal agreements. Next week I've to sign the documents in Hill's presence and in front of witnesses, then everything will proceed. The children will be mine for several weeks this year and they shall have so wonderful a time that they'll be desperate to visit dear mama again as soon as possible."

"And all the while you'll be dripping poison into their ears."

"Yes, very subtly, of course."

You'll turn Albert and Alexandrina against him?"

Elysia considered for a moment, "Yes, but it is more important that Bertie should be the one to become mine in heart-and-soul."

"Then he will be your creature by the time he inherits."

"Yes," confirmed the marchioness before carrying on quickly, "Oh, by the way, you'll need to make yourself scarce when the children visit."

"No need for that, surely. I like it here," Corsica came back quickly.

"They're to be accompanied by their nursemaid, Miss Jackson. You may remember her."

Corsica shook his head, "Her name isn't familiar to me."

"It should be, she's the girl you seduced to get inside Martin Hall. You bound her to a chair instead of doing the sensible thing and, as a result of which I'm sure she'll recognise you immediately."

"Oh her," Corsica shrugged his shoulders in a careless sort of way.

"I've little doubt that you interfered with her once she was helpless, so she won't have forgotten that experience very quickly."

Corsica's expression was pained, "I thought I'd give her a thrill, show her what passion's all about. I had time on my hands while I waited for Charlie's friends to clear off."

"Anyway, she's had sight of you, will add two-and-two together, so it will be best if you've gone before she arrives."

"So be it, before her arrival, I'll go home to Gravesend and enjoy some time in my garden."

"That's unless your crazy mother has burnt the house down or covered your precious garden in quick lime."

"You forget that Miss Kleist is keeping an eye on mama."

Elysia considered carefully for a moment and then ordered, "You may as well send Marta back here, she may be of some use with the children."

Jonnie nodded his agreement and then he suggested, "If I'm to be away, you'll need a proper servicing or two before I go."

"*Servicing*, I'm no prize beast, especially for one so far beneath me in station. In days not long gone by, I would have sent you for a flogging."

"Which ever way you want it, my dear, why don't you go up now and I'll slip along as soon as the servants are at tea."

"You presume too much, Mr Corsica."

"I *know* too much, you mean."

"We both *know* too much," she replied, before she arose and walked towards the doorway, "Am I to leave my corset and stockings on?"

"As usual," he smiled and nodded.

"Make sure you bring the sheath with you, for it is not my intention to be saddled with a fourth child."

*****

George Murphy woke with a start and saw that Mouse was standing over his bed, "*What the*," he cried out in surprise.

"I've wet the bed ag'in," tears began to flood down Mouse's cheeks.

George got his feet from under the blankets and planted them on to the floor, he rubbed his eyes and patted his friend's arm, "Ye haven't done that for weeks."

"I knaw.. I knaw," the tears continued to flow.

"Never mind, it'll be a'right."

"What'll Ma' Annie say?"

Murphy stood up and spoke soothingly, "Never fear, mam, will wash yer sheets and say no more about it."

His friend's words seemed to calm Mouse and he rubbed the tears away from his eyes and cheeks.

"What d'ye suppose brought that on after all these weeks?"

A look of dread passed across Mouse's face, "Nuthin'. It just happened."

"Ben Cook," George rarely used Mouse's new name, but he did so on this occasion to underline the seriousness of his question, "Somethings up. What is it?"

Ben's reply came out in a flood, "I saw the Deacon yesterday."

George shook his head in doubt, "Ye haven't been back to Liverpool in your dreams, have ye?"

"No. *No*, I saw him His hair's short now an' he had a new suit of clothes on, but 'twas him."

"In Martindale?" George Murphy was incredulous, "It can't ha' been him."

"It was, it was I tell you. His eyes were the same, that horrible, staring blue that makes him look blind."

"Well, where was he?"

"On the High Street, not far from Dougie Brass's old place."

"What could he be doin' here?" George's question was rhetorical.

"No, good, George, no good, no good at all," Mouse's expression looked ever more troubled as he spoke.

*****

Elizabeth Esprey was pleased to see that all the members of the Martindale Civic Theatre Sub-Committee were present.

Marcus Reno bobbed his hand up, "May I thank the members for co-opting myself on to their committee, it is a great and unexpected honour," he burbled.

"You are most welcome, Mr Reno," the chairlady favoured the pay-clerk with a smile.

"Perhaps we should move on to the agenda," suggested John Fisher.

"Is an agenda needed?" queried Richard Turner, "For with Mr Villiers unavailable can the theatre continue to function? This is the only question upon which we need to deliberate."

"We've promised the town a *Hamlet*," cried Mr Reno, seemingly stricken to the heart.

"I can't see the point, we've no professionals left," Abigail Turner spoke dully, for without Roddy the Civic Theatre was devoid of interest to her.

"You seem to forget that I too spent many years in the theatre," replied Mrs Esprey, her voice especially chilly.

"Aye, that's true," supported Douglas Brass, whose new bride seemed to have rejuvenated him.

Richard shoved his hands into his pockets and hunched up his shoulders, he'd never wanted to be on this committee in the first place and now it looked as though this meeting would go on for ever, as all the previous ones had.

The colonel's lady allowed the talk of the meeting to flow for a further minute or so and then tapped her pencil against the water glass that stood before her. "Mrs Turner, gentlemen, please, let us proceed."

The room hushed and all eyes were directed at the chairlady.

"We do have performances available for the next six weeks, after which time there is nothing booked. *I* could use the connections that remain to me in an attempt to keep the theatre going for longer than that."

"The colonel approves of such associations?" queried Abigail.

"Colonel Esprey understands that this is merely a temporary measure until such time as Mr Villiers finds himself clear of his current difficulties."

"Have you been in communication with Roderick?" Queried Fisher, thinking that any news he could carry back to Bobbity might prevent her from crying and moaning for five minutes or so.

"I have not, though I am sure it would be Mr Villiers' wish to keep the theatre running for the good of the town," stated the colonel's lady.

"Aye, that's right," put in Mr Brass the butcher, "I propose Mrs Esprey uses her theatrical contacts to find a solution to the present crisis."

Richard's hand was flung into the air, "I'll second that," he said quickly, hoping for an end to the meeting.

"Are there any other proposals?" asked the chair-lady.

No one spoke.

"Then perhaps a vote in favour," Elizabeth looked around the table and was pleased to see that all hands were raised in the affirmative.

"Excellent, then I shall leave for London shortly."

"I expect that I'm still to have the role of the Prince of Denmark, Marcus Reno couldn't keep the eagerness out of his voice.

"I'm afraid not," informed Lizzie Esprey.

"But I've learned *all* the lines," wailed Reno.

"I'm sure they'll come in useful at some other time, but without Mr Villiers, *Hamlet* is an impossibility."

"Thank God for that," muttered Richard who thought the play in question to be a very dreary one.

"Excellent decision," nodded Jacky Fisher in a toadying kind of way.

"What are we going to put on, then?" asked Abigail.

"In the meantime I shall find a play that is easy to produce and one our audiences will be happy with."

All those around the table nodded their agreement, apart from Marcus Reno who looked well put-out.

*****

Frank Turner took his usual seat in the café side of Annie's Pie Shop and was immediately served his favourite dish. He picked up his knife, listlessly cut into the pie before him and watched as the gravy flowed from it and spread across the plate.

"Not hungry the day, Frank," called Annie as she approached his table.

The agent looked up and managed a half-smile, "*No*, I'm hungry enough, just don't seem able to concentrate on eating."

"Why, man, pull yersel' together, ye do realise that it's an insult t' mysel' if you don't start gobbling straight away," said Annie as she sat down opposite him.

Frank nodded, forced a smile on to his lips, took a fork full of pie, swept it into his mouth and began to chew.

"That's better," encouraged Annie.

After a few mouthfuls more, Frank let his cutlery drop before saying, "I can't manage any more to-day, Annie. No insult intended."

"Ye look as though you've more problems than a man drowning in a sea o' black treacle."

Frank nodded, "Life seems to be passing me by these days."

"You're hurtin' from the fire?" Annie asked, compassionately.

"Some, but you made a fine job of putting me back together again – even though I'll never be what I was."

"Why, man ye're the same brave, sensible, friendly Frank Turner ye always were, just a bit the worse for wear. And that beard suits ye, suits ye no end," encouraged Annie.

"I can put up with looking like a freak, but there's others who can't come to terms with it."

"Abigail?" Questioned Annie, knowing at once that this was the case.

Frank shook his head and hunched his shoulders, "I shouldn't say," his voice trailed off.

"No, lad, no, ye shouldn't. But if ye do need to let it out, then I'm always here and what ever ye want to say'll go to the grave wi' me," Annie stretched across the table and patted Frank's hand in reassurance.

The agent looked up and his eyes sought those of his friend, "You've never taken to Abigail, have you?"

"Ye know I'm a straight talker, Frank and I'll not change. The fact is that no one around here is fond of Abigail. I can only hope the Good Lord above cares for her."

The agent nodded slowly, "She can be haughty."

Annie snorted with suppressed laughter, "Aye, ye could say that."

"In the early days, I thought she was good for me, turning me into a gentleman."

"Ye've always *been* a gentleman, Frank, a *proper* gentleman."

"Now I can see it was all flummery. Sir Charles Martin himself has never noticed that my manners leave a lot to be desired and Abigail's refinement of me went only skin deep."

"Charlie Martin has no care about things like that. He takes people as they are."

Frank nodded vigorously in agreement, "Aye, who else would make a friend of a labouring man?"

"And yer brother not t'mention Jack Nicholson," confirmed Annie.

Turner sat quietly for a long minute before saying, "Abigail can't stand me as I am now. She gives no thought to Maud and she'll not lie with me without being pressed."

"Time's a good healer, ye knaw, just give her a bit more of it."

"Aye, I will, Annie."

*****

Lieutenant-Colonel Jervis Esprey came across Corporal Seeton Carew polishing silver in the butler's pantry.

"Ah, Carew, I need a word with you."

"Sir," replied the non-commissioned officer slowly, wondering what complaint his employer could possibly have now.

"I need you to go to London."

"Sir," Carew's eyes widened and he immediately knew that this was something to do with the mistress.

"Yes, Mrs Esprey is determined to visit the capital to catch-up with old friends, she's seeking actors and such like to perform at the theatre."

"Sir," said Carew for the third time, again slowly.

"I want you to accompany her and stick with her. Stick to her like Ganges mud."

"I will, sir."

"Make sure that the *begum* doesn't fall into any, trouble. You understand?"

"Yes, sir." Carew knew the trouble mentioned by the colonel was exactly the same sort of trouble that had so often bothered Colonel Galvin.

"Close eye, Carew, keep a close eye all the time."

"I will, colonel, but I don't like to spy on the mistress," returned Carew solemnly.

"You'll be no spy, but more of a guide, a *hircarra* if you like."

Carew knew that the Hindi word meant to be a spy, guide, messenger or all three, so he could take his pick to salve his conscience.

"She insists she's to stay with friends, but I've booked rooms in a very decent and respectable hotel. Make sure she uses them," continued Esprey.

How am I going to do that if she decides not to? Carew wondered, keeping his face neutral.

Esprey understood the difficulties Carew would have as escort to Liza, but he knew that the corporal would do his best.

"Orders clear enough?"

"Yes, sir. Clear as day, sir," returned Carew with a proper salute.

"Saluting out of uniform and not wearing a hat? Corporal, I'm surprised at you."

"Sorry, sir, it slips my mind sometimes that I'm no longer a soldier."

"Good, well, remember what I've said."

"Yes, sir," returned Carew, though he knew that, clear as his orders were, it didn't make them any easier to carry-out.

As he made his way back to the library for a much-needed cigar, Esprey confounded his own weakness.

Elizabeth had insisted that she travel alone and it was only with some difficulty that he had persuaded her to take Carew along.

"Can't bring myself to say *'no'* to that woman," he muttered aloud, shaking his head as he pushed open the library door.

*****

Richard Turner looked up from writing his next editorial when his wife; waving a letter, swept into the room.

"Look at this," she cried before planting the correspondence before him.

Richard picked it up, saw that was from Roderick Villiers and had been addressed to *Mrs R. Turner*.

"Well, read it," Jane encouraged.

"It's addressed to you."

"Nonetheless, read it."

Richard did as he was asked.

The Marshalsea,
2nd April 1863

My Dear Mrs Turner,

Incarcerated as I am, makes it impossible for me to personally express my sorrow for the wrong I've done to the good people of Martindale. Tears course down my cheeks whenever I recall those friendly, simple folk who so stoutly supported the establishment of a theatre in their community and allowed myself, a complete stranger, a place in their hearts.

Any sorrow I feel is not for <u>myself</u>, but for those I have so sorely let down, not least of whom is my *dearest love, my fiancée, Miss Roberta Fisher. How I yearn for the day when we shall be reunited.*

Alas, this is all done and over for me now!

I have no doubt that you will be wondering why I have written to you. The simple fact is I would deem it a huge favour were you to express; though the organ of your fine journal, my apologies to the people of Martindale and my deepest hope that they can find it in their caring hearts to forgive one who has so let them down.

My present indebtedness began when my poor mother became seriously ill, with; what turned out to be, galloping consumption. I was called away from London; where, at the time, I was playing the lead in 'The Courier of Lyons', to her bedside. Most of the debts I incurred were in order to pay for doctors, medicines and comforts for my dear mama. For how could I ever deny anything to she whose smile had always lit up my heart. Though nothing could save her and she struggled on with life for far longer than my limited finances could bear.

You know the rest of the story, I sought refuge in Martindale at the invitation of; the then, Mrs Galvin and soon found myself to be happier and more content than ever I had been before.

However, the Law always catches up with evil-doers and I now find myself on the wrong side of a prison cell door.

With considerable difficulty I have managed to repay my creditors some of what they are owed and should I be able to cover fully half of my debts, then I believe they would be willing to write-off the rest. I am working to this end and hope that one day, perhaps in three or five years, I may be able to venture north again and even take-up some position, no matter how lowly, in my beloved Martindale Civic Theatre.

*Your Humble and Obedient Servant,
Roderick Villiers*

PS

I have been fortunate in the friendship of Mr Solomon Vasey who; as a fellow thespian, has been of great service to me. It would be much more convenient were you to direct any reply you may care to make into his safe hands at 116, Carters Alley, London.

"Well, I'm blowed," Richard whistled through his teeth.

"Poor man imprisoned by laws that give him no chance to clear his bills. It is iniquitous," Jane thumped the table as she spoke.

"Do you believe him?"

"Why shouldn't I?"

"The Marshalsea closed twenty years ago."

"He may mean another prison."

"It's all a bit convenient, isn't it? His creditors are ready to write-off half his debt," Richard's tone highlighted his doubts.

"I suppose they think half is better than none," replied Jane.

"Then, on top of which, he tries to gull us into believing that he's in love with – of all people – Bobbity Fisher," Richard's tone was scathing and he began to laugh.

He soon stopped, though, when he saw his wife was trying desperately to hold back her tears. Whether they were of sorrow or rage he couldn't be sure.

"You say that you fell in love with me and I'm no pretty watercolour, nor ever have been," cried Jane looking bereft.

Richard took his wife in his arms and kissed her forehead and hair, clucking softly as he did so, "There is no comparison between you and Miss Fisher."

"I don't wish to hear comparisons made between myself and any other woman of your acquaintance," Jane's voice was rising.

"Though no one cares for Roberta Fisher whilst everyone likes you. Besides, no man in his right mind would take her as his wife."

"People say the same about me, I'm sure they do, and you're so handsome," Jane was close to tears once more.

Richard flung back his head laughing, "Why, I'm just ordinary, same as you are, my love."

"We're an ill-matched pair, there's no denying or getting away from it."

"As a couple we work very well. We have children to be proud of and a thriving business. Besides, not only do I love you I *like* you," Richard's words were sincerely spoken.

Jane sniffed and then said, "When we first met you didn't like me at all, you thought that I was far too pushy."

Richard took his wife in his arms and cuddled her warmly, "Well, you *are* pushy, though always in a good cause."

Jane enjoyed being enfolded in her husband's arms and remained there for some time, before duty reasserted itself and she asked, "Well, then, what about Villiers?"

Richard's expression showed that he very much doubted the actor's veracity, "Do you intend to reply to him?"

"Better than that I'm going to spread his story across the pages of the *Chronicle*."

"You believe the town will forgive him?"

"Why ever should it not?"

"Will our readers believe him to be sincere?" Richard smiled cynically.

"I believe him."

"Though will the town?"

"Oh, *Richard*, apart from whether he is an out-and-out rogue or not, just think what the man has done for Martindale. When you were sure that the whole theatre scheme would collapse Villiers made it work."

"Well, I suppose he did. He organised the Gala very well too," Richard conceded.

"We shall need him for the one this year too," added Jane.

"Write it up and we'll put in the day after to-morrow," Richard came to a quick decision.

*****

Virgil Kent, a footman of the Marchioness of Studland, stood waiting beside the desk of his mistress wondering when she was going to acknowledge his presence.

She's a strange one, he thought to himself, sitting there; spectacles perched at the end of her nose, going through papers, signing the odd one with a man-like flourish. Though he had to admit that she was a fine figure of a woman, a bit on the well-rounded side for his taste maybe, but her glittering black eyes could stun a man such as himself at a hundred paces.

There was also talk amongst the staff of her closeness to Mr Corsica, who seemed to have no fixed-duties and was often overly familiar with her.

There's hope for me then, he daydreamed pleasantly.

"*Humph*," the marchioness mumbled, but still did not look-up from her work.

Kent was quite happy to stand admiring the view as her *décolletage* was quite revealing, even though its full glory was masked by a thin layer of a black, semi-transparent material. Besides which, he thought he knew how to play her at her own game.

"Well, Kent," Elysia greeted as she put down her pen at last and removed her glasses.

"My lady."

"I hear you're a man of some ambition."

"Some say so, your ladyship, but only in order to serve you as you would wish."

"Good, I'm pleased to hear it. Suppose I was to say that I'm considering appointing an under-butler. What would you say to that?"

"I'd believe it to be an excellent idea."

"What if I were to propose you as the holder of this position?"

"If that were to be the case, then I'd be very pleased and happy to continue to serve you as I have in the past."

Elysia fixed the footman with a cold-stare which she knew would make him feel uncertain and paused for a long time before she spoke again, "I envisage the post of under-butler to be one which would carry with it many and varied responsibilities, some having little to do with the efficient running of Winterbourne itself."

"It's of no matter t'me, your ladyship, no matter at all."

"Good, then you may do very well for what I have in mind."

Gil Kent's face broke into a smile, for this was a promotion he had expected to be years into the future.

"However, before I do appoint you, perhaps a test? A test to prove that you are truly ready to serve me in any way I desire."

"Anything, my lady, anything at all, you'll not find me wanting," the words gushed from him in his eagerness to secure his future.

Elysia smiled and nodded, "Very well. The children from my first marriage will be visiting early in the summer. They are to be accompanied by a nursemaid; a Miss Cissy Jackson, she is a skinny non-descript sort of girl, but I wish you to befriend her."

Kent nodded, his angular nose appearing to prod the air as if seeking something just out of reach, "Certainly, your ladyship, it shall be as you wish."

"Help Miss Jackson, be there whenever she needs support, make her look upon you as her safe haven. Do you understand?"

"Yes, my lady, she won't be able to wave me goodbye without a tear in her eye."

"Excellent," Elysia paused, "and if you are able to become more to her than a friend… You understand what I mean?"

"Then I shall be the friend she needs, if it furthers the interests of the Marchioness of Studland. You have my word on that."

"Very good," said Elysia again before smiling and waving her footman away.

*****

"Apart from my husband being away at war, I have another deep concern," Caroline informed her friends as she poured them sherry.

"What ever could that be?" Marian asked.

"I often wonder what we can do regarding the early schooling of our children, for we've quite a number between us. I've advertised for a suitable governess for Julia, but have met with no success," explained Caroline.

"I've tried too, but they all seem so grim," put in Marian.

"Or, even worse, they're French," remarked Jane, "though I agree, it is about time we paid some attention to the basic education of our offsprings."

"Stay away from tutors, though, as they very often turn out to be vicious drunkards," mused Elizabeth Esprey, who's knowledge of the world of education was limited to an undergraduate she'd taken a fancy to when she had once played Cordelia at Cambridge.

"*Wait*," cried Jane, a sudden thought striking her, "Why shouldn't we set an example, follow the path of democracy and send them all to the National School in the town?"

Her companions looked at her aghast.

Eventually, Caroline spoke, "This is *much* too democratic for me."

"*What*, send my darlings to Mr Fisher? I can't bear the thought of it," Lady Martin expressed herself forcefully, being well aware of the schoolmaster's reputation as a bully.

Having further considered the problem, Jane nodded and said, "Even so, our children do require a good early grounding, but the idea that they be driven to learning by over-use of the strap does not sit well with me at all."

"It may be useful, you know, to at least send the boys to the National School. It will inure them to the rigours of the public schools they will eventually attend," suggested the colonel's lady.

"Let's not even think about that until we have to," replied Jane, who thought it was about time the great public schools were either closed down or opened up to all.

Marian suddenly stood up, her glass still in her hand, "I've an idea…"

"Come on, then, what is it?" queried Jane.

"Mr John Nicholson's wife, Sarah. She taught at the National School, did she not?"

"She's a very good teacher too, or so I've heard," supported Caroline.

"Couldn't she instruct *all* of our children together? They'd have a proper school to themselves," suggested Marian.

"I'm sure she might," agreed Caroline.

"Wait a moment, though, she does have a daughter of her own," put in Jane.

"Her child could join with ours," suggested Marian brightly.

"Though where could this schoolroom be set up?" asked Jane after a pause.

"Why, Martin Hall of course. It is the most central and we've lots of space for a classroom," offered Lady Marian.

"Martin Hall *is* equidistant from both Byers Green and Blanchwell," calculated Jane.

"What will Charles think of this?" queried Caroline.

"Oh, he'll be all for it I should think," returned Marian.

"In which case, we should invite Mrs Nicholson to the next of our get-togethers," suggested Caroline. "Which of us knows her best?"

"Probably me," said Jane, "I've bumped into her now and again. I'll call to see Sarah when I'm next at the office, I don't know exactly where she lives, though Richard will."

"I say we celebrate this timely solution with another sherry," said Lizzy Esprey, already holding forth her glass.

*****

Fred Schilling, as usual covered in grease and dust, entered Sam Watson's office and found Sir Charles Martin and Frank Turner in deep conversation with the viewer.

"The very man," greeted Charles.

"Aye, he's ready for a challenge," agreed the engineer.

"Ready for what?" Fred asked.

"You've spent a deal of time at the Balaklava works and know them inside out," suggested the landowner.

"I suppose I'm pretty familiar with what goes on there."

"Knows more about it than myself," supported Frank.

"The fact is, Fred, we've just received an offer to tender; from a company in America to supply steel railway lines, fishplates, other fittings as well as locomotive and rolling stock wheels."

"Or as you say over there, *railroad tracks*," Charles was pleased with his grasp of Americanisms.

"*Yes*," Fred spoke slowly, wondering where this was leading.

"It's a big order," informed Frank, nodding.

"A large, *very* large one," added Watson.

"Trans-continental," explained Frank.

"They intend to lay a line from the Missouri river to the shores of the Pacific. They'll need hundreds of thousands, or even millions of rails," informed Charles.

"If we can get the contract to produce even a fraction of these, then the works will have to be expanded," informed the landowner.

Fred grasped the significance of what he was being told immediately, "I gather then, you wish me to find out how viable this company and its scheme is?"

"Of course, for after all, you are an *American*," continued the baronet with considerable enthusiasm, "You speak the language."

"Americans speak English," Fred couldn't quite get the baronet's drift, "and anyway, I'm not an engineer."

"No you're not, but you're as near as dammit to it. In addition to which you are able to survey and can also understand a plan," encouraged Sam Watson.

"Yes, I can do those things, but….."

"You read a plan as well as I can," Frank put in.

"You'll see at once if their scheme is unsound, the work of a trickster or that of a lunatic," added Sir Charles.

Fred still looked doubtful but said nothing.

"Should we win the contract we'll have to invest heavily in order to deliver the goods. So, checking that the scheme is practical is of vital importance," continued the landowner.

"No company is going to begin building a railway sheer across the States with a war raging on," Fred had grave doubts.

"Once the North wins it shan't be long before they *do* make a start, for it's vital to America's national interest," said Charles.

"Aye," supported Frank, "and an early starter could well win the race."

"You forget that, so far, the Union has hardly won a battle and every day sees the Confederacy closer to being recognised as an independent state by most nations."

"My dear boy, it is only a matter of time, for the North *shall* win, they must. However, if we wish to play a part in this great enterprise, then we need to make a beginning now," Charles was absolutely certain of this.

Fred shook his head slowly, "Aren't the Martindale enterprises doing well as it is? Is it wise to take so great a risk?"

Charles spoke up again, his voice softly persuasive, "We are, though we cannot *stand-still* and were we to win the American contract, the jobs of our people would be safe for a dozen years to come."

Fred Schilling had a sudden thought, "Wait, though, what about Colonel Esprey? He has had lots of experience. Why not ask him to go?"

Frank shook his head, "Aye, he has, but campaigning sort of things – setting up camps, as he did for the Gala."

"I do know that he carried out some of the preliminary survey for the projected line from Calcutta to Allahabad, he told me about it," informed Fred.

Charles considered for a moment and then said, "You, know, having the colonel on the Board is not such a bad idea. He has considerable expertise and long experience. Beside which, his wife owns ten percent of the company shares."

Both men nodded and then Frank suggested, "Perhaps we could adopt him as an expert member of the Board."

"Aye, he could be useful at that," added Watson, who was at the age when any help or support was welcome.

Then, all eyes were concentrated once more on the younger Schilling.

Fred, still trying to find a way out said quickly, "What about Amelia? We've just been married."

"She can travel with you. You can show her America – you could count it as a second honeymoon. You've a sister in Pennsylvania, I believe, why not visit her too." Charles pressed his case.

Fred couldn't be sure what his wife would think of this offer, though he was fairly sure that she would welcome it.

"Your expenses will be fully paid," Charles encouraged.

"With all his experience, don't you think Mr Turner would be a better choice than myself for so important a mission?" Fred made his final plea.

Frank forced a laugh, "I'd never find my way there, why, I've been no further than Scarborough in my entire life."

The mine-owner looked seriously at his agent, "Mr Turner can't be done without at the moment."

Then Fred Schilling noticed that every eye remained on him, "Can I have some time to think it over?"

"Of course, my boy, will a week do?"

"More than sufficient time, Sir Charles," Fred replied with a confidence he did not feel

*****

Jack Nicholson had just left Annie's pie-shop when he almost walked into a tall, ecclesiastical figure with very pale-blue eyes.

"What d'ye think yer doin' here?" Challenged Nicholson once he'd got over his surprise.

The Deacon drew himself up to his full height, which was considerably greater than that of the collier, "Do I know you, sir?" He spoke imperiously.

"Aye, ye do. Last I saw of ye was when Joe Dunnett was pummellin' yer backside wi' a birch rod," the collier smiled at the thought.

"I believe it was a rattan-cane," corrected the Deacon, ever pedantic.

"Why, whatever it was, ye well deserved double the strokes you were dealt."

"A grievous and unwarranted assault was made upon my person, which I may say was reported to the proper authorities."

Nicholson spluttered and nearly dropped his parcel of pies, "Ye interfere wi' little boys and have the nerve to complain t'the police."

"This was a completely false allegation. I am Thomas Leakey, a senior, well-respected clergyman of the highest repute and learning. As you have furnished me with the name of my assailant I shall make full use of it."

Jack felt the urge to punch the Deacon but, thanks to being married to Sarah, he restrained himself. "Do what ye will but get out o' town."

Leakey smiled sardonically, "I have the right to travel *to* or remain *within* any quarter of Her Majesty's Realm at my pleasure."

Nicholson' eyes blazed, though he managed to control his temper, but only just.

The clergyman tipped his hat slightly, his milky, dead eyes became hooded and he walked off.

John watched him go and knew that the Deacon's presence in Martindale would lead to trouble.

*****

"Wait outside, Carew," ordered Elizabeth Esprey at the door of her Bond Street dressmaker.

"Colonel said I was to keep with you, ma'am," replied Corporal Carew, his voice in a neutral tone.

Elizabeth sighed patiently and took on the manner of a school ma'am, "It is patently obvious that you *cannot* enter a dressmakers' shop. There will doubtless be other ladies trying on their *ensembles*, who will not appreciate a man; especially one of the soldierly variety, tramping about amongst them."

"But…," began Carew.

"Never mind *buts*, Corporal, just do as you're told."

"*Humph…*"

"I can do without *humphs* too. There is an ale house just across the road – go there for an hour or so then meet me here," as she spoke Mrs Esprey withdrew a few coins from her purse and handed them to Carew before she entered her dressmaker's.

The old soldier watched her go and wondered what she was up to. He was fairly sure that she was up to something. However, he had the choice of standing about in the cold or going for something warming in a local hostelry. The hostelry won and he went off to find it.

Inside, Mrs Esprey discussed purchases with her dressmaker for no longer than ten minutes and then made her way out through the rear-entrance and set off for a nearby street where she expected to find an old friend.

Roderick Villiers heard the door of his room open and looked up to see Lizzie Esprey gazing at him in the discomforting sort of way that she did so well.

"This is very reasonable accommodation for someone who is supposed to be rotting away in the Marshalsea," she observed.

"I can explain all….," began Roderick.

"You did not wish to marry Miss Fisher," cut in Elizabeth, bringing Roddy rapidly to the point.

"Who would?" Returned Villiers quickly and with some force.

"Quite. However, you must have reconsidered, for I see that you've written to Mrs Jane Turner. No doubt in the hope that the good people of Martindale will deliver funds to speed your return to their theatre. Is this not the case?"

Villiers coughed gently, sniffed softly and then replied, "Yes, my dear, it is so. I've nothing here, I find myself forgotten and ignored in Drury Lane. My companion and I owe rent and we are just about on the verge of starvation."

"Your companion?"

"Solly Vasey, you must remember him?"

"Who could forget him. I suppose it was he who arranged for the arrival of the bailiffs in Martindale, just just in time."

Villiers nodded, "I haven't paid him yet either."

"Why am I not surprised, but where is he at the moment?"

"Gone for whatever food he can find, he shouldn't be long," Villiers paused for a short while and then continued,

"Has Miss Fisher got over my departure yet? At least I didn't leave her standing at the altar."

"*No*, she has not got over you, nor forgotten that you are still her fiancé. I hear that she spends much of her time in tears, howling, screaming and, for all I know, pulling her hair out."

Villiers put his head in his hands and began to squeeze tears from his eyes.

"*Stop* at once, Roddy, you're not *that* good an actor and remember, it's Lizzie Harper here and I know you all too well."

Villiers chuckled softly and wiped his tears away, "Always worth a try, my dear."

"Well, then, what's to be done?"

"I would like to return to Martindale, for I *was* a success there. I wish things to be as they were," Villiers' tone of voice showed that, for once, he was not acting.

"Even to marry Miss Fisher?"

"Heavens no, I can't do that. I'd sooner seek shelter in a workhouse."

"If Martindale's your only option, then surely, you must face Roberta Fisher and come to some sort of accommodation with her."

Roddy groaned and shook his head at the thought of who awaited him were he to return to Martindale.

"I'm sure the whole town will welcome you back," began Lizzie Esprey who then paused before continuing, "well, at least the females of the town will."

Roderick Villiers came to a decision, his face lit up as though he were on stage, "May I return with you – a shortage of funds makes independent travel at the moment impossible."

"No, you cannot travel with me, nor will I provide you with funds. Were I to arrive back in Martindale accompanied by yourself, my husband would not take it kindly and, believe me, he is much more dangerous than Miss Fisher."

"Then how…," began the actor.

"Be patient, Roddy, Jane Turner has appealed to the town on your behalf and if I know the people there as well as I think I do, considerable funds will soon be coming your way."

"Mrs Turner published my letter?"

"She published your *story* and passed on your deep regrets and apologies for what happened."

"*Ah*, my dear old mother…," he sniffed, "alas….."

Mrs Esprey cut him short, "Your mother ran away with a juggler when you were fifteen and you haven't seen her since."

Villiers sighed, "Though my version makes a better story, don't you think."

"The true one is the more amusing."

"So, I await a missive from Mrs Turner?"

"It shouldn't be too long in arriving."

"I may be dead of hunger and cold by then," said Villiers gloomily.

Elizabeth Esprey took five shillings from her purse and handed them to the actor, "Here you are, Roddy but don't spend it on drink."

Chapter Five

"I'm sorry, mama, but I really can't take Aunt Prudence in, Caroline would happily sanction it, but I'm off to America with Fred," Amelia shook her head and put on a sad expression.

"I don't mind accommodating her for three or even four weeks, I'm sure Douglas won't mind, he's very fond of her," put in Arabella.

"*Two* ladies sharing a *butcher's* household, why, Mr Brass could never have dreamed that he'd ever become so well connected," Abigail's tone was sarcastic.

Arabella stared at her sister archly, "Well, I'm not the only one to have married beneath me, but the difference is that I'm happy and very content."

Abigail began to steam, for previously she had held effortless power over everyone in her family (with the exception, perhaps, of her mama), but now even her youngest sibling was able to cheek her. "Francis is..," she startled strongly but was interrupted by her mother who gently took her arm.

"*Ladies*, please, you've all done well, *very* well. All married with respectable husbands and able to enjoy lives of comfort and ease which seemed to be impossible only a year or two ago. Stop squabbling this instant and, instead, be grateful and thank the Lord for your good fortune."

"Yes mama," nodded Arabella.

"Of course, mama," added Amelia.

Abigail merely sniffed and looked sharply at her siblings.

"Anyway, I still fear that I *cannot* help," said Amelia.

"I understand your difficulties, my dear," conceded Venetia who then turned to face her youngest girl, "And

I'm grateful, Arabella, that you at least will be able to take Aunt Prudence in for some weeks."

"I will talk to Douglas about it and I'm sure he'll agree."

Venetia paused and looked questioningly at her eldest daughter, "What about you Abigail?"

"Francis won't have her."

"Even though your husband likes Prudence, he's said she's a very pleasant lady. I've heard him say so," Arabella lost no time in contradicting her sister.

"More than once I've heard that from Mr Turner too," Amelia supported her younger sister.

"If you all believe you know my husband better than I myself do, then you may presume he will accept Prudence's presence for a fortnight or so," returned a very irritated Abigail.

"Thank you, girls, wonderful, how wonderful," Venetia clapped her hands lightly now that her route to the Serene Republic was open once again.

*****

"A clerical gentleman to see you, Sir Charles," William Rust finished his sentence with a sucking in of his cheeks.

"The Reverend Lander back already?"

"They're not leaving until next week, Charles," reminded Marian.

"It's a Mister Leakey, sir."

"Do we know him, Rust?" Charles was puzzled, then he looked towards his wife who sat opposite him, "Marian?"

Lady Martin shook her head, "I've no knowledge of a Reverend Leakey."

"Best show him in then," decided the baronet whose curiosity had been aroused.

Shortly afterwards the Deacon entered the room, his hands clasped together in front of him, his face as pleasant as he could make it. "Sir Charles, Lady Martin," he nodded to each of his hosts in turn.

"Please, Mr Leakey, take a seat and perhaps you'll have a glass of sherry," Charles nodded towards the decanter which lay before him.

"I drink nothing other than water, Sir Charles, though I've no objection to others wishing to partake."

"Well, as you do not require refreshment, may I ask what your business is?"

"I represent the Christian Workers' Education League and have been sent here to open our newest outpost. After a short visit, I am quite sure that Martindale is an eminently suitable location for our latest venture."

"I see," put in Charles slowly, wondering how much this charitable undertaking was going to cost him.

"I have already found suitable premises, which a certain Mr Brass is willing to rent out to the League very reasonably."

"That'll be Douglas Brass's old shop, the one by the print works where Richard used to have his office," put in Marian.

"So it is," mused Charles.

"I believe it to be ideal for our purposes," continued the Deacon.

"What exactly are the objectives of your organisation," questioned Charles.

"The British labouring class suffers from a disgraceful lack of education, with most unable to read."

"You'll set up literacy classes then," interrupted Marian Martin, who was becoming interested.

"Yes, we shall do that, though it's often difficult to get working men to take such lessons," the Deacon paused for a moment and then continued, "the League will also provide the beginnings of a small library, to include suitable newspapers and periodicals, as well as our own pamphlets."

"This appears to be a worthwhile scheme," commented the landowner."

"I'm pleased you think so, Sir Charles. However, in addition, there will be debates, guest-speakers and readings from the great works of literature."

"Excellent," declared Charles.

"Indeed so," agreed Lady Martin.

The Deacon smiled and nodded, "I hope so, indeed I do," then his face became serious and he asked, "I come to you, Sir Charles..."

The coal owner held up both hands, palms forward, "A donation? Think nothing of it..."

Leakey interrupted swiftly, "No donations are necessary. Our organisation is very well-funded and an account for this project has already been opened. This is how I've been able to secure premises so swiftly and at such low cost."

"Then, in what other way may I help?"

"It is important to us that Martindale continues to flourish, that it does not go into a decline due to, say, economic troubles or the pull of more prosperous places. I can see that at the moment the town thrives, but I need to believe that this will be the case for some years into the future."

"I quite understand your requirement to begin your project in a town of great vigour."

"Quite right too," added Lady Marian, though there was something about this clergyman which was setting her nerves on edge.

"It is my believe that if anyone knows what the future of the town holds, then it must be yourself, its founder and leading citizen," Leaky smiled ingratiatingly and waited for a reply.

Charles considered for a long thirty seconds before speaking again, for he wasn't sure that he ought to reveal the company's future plans to a stranger, even if he was a clergyman. "We have full order books at the moment and we plan to send an agent to America, who may be able to deliver a contract which will keep our people in work for many years to come."

"In America? With a war on there?" Leakey shook his head morosely, "surely, you do not intend to provide the sinews of war?"

"Heavens no," put in Charles swiftly.

"I am pleased to hear that."

Charles picked up the thread of his tale, "This war between the states cannot go on for ever, after which the Americans *will* be building a trans-continental railway – or several of them even."

"Martindale would provide?"

"*Railroad* tracks mainly," Charles smiled as he used the American idiom, "but other bits and pieces too."

"No doubt this will require further heavy investment?"

"It will indeed."

"Should this contract not be forthcoming, then the town would indeed decline."

Charles thought seriously for a moment, "Yes, it would. Though it's unlikely to happen."

Leakey nodded, smiled again and Marian noticed the clergyman's eyes had a pale though sharp glint in them that had not been there before.

"I thank-you for your time, Sir Charles, Lady Martin, and I'm pleased to say that you've set my mind very much at rest. I'm sure that the League *will* come to Martindale."

"You'll take supper with us, perhaps?" Offered Charles.

"Very kind, sir, though I'd best be about my business," declined the Deacon before he rose to his feet to be escorted to the door by his host.

Marian watched the Reverend Leakey depart and continued to believe that there was something about him that made her very uneasy. She was sure that his arrival in town would lead to….. She didn't know what.

"*Oh*," she sighed to herself, "please, Dear Lord, let's not have trouble here *again*."

*****

Thwack, thwack, thwack.

Young Wallace Denning bit his lower lip until it began to bleed, his four-year old mind determined that he should not shout out.

"Give him some more, Gerald, you're hardly scratching him and he deserves it," encouraged Mrs Denning, looking up briefly from her knitting.

Her husband stopped and wiped a bead of sweat from his brow, "I'm giving him as hard as I've got, but nothing makes the little rogue shout."

Wally closed his eyes and released his teeth from his lip, his tongue tasting his own blood. Has it stopped? He asked himself, before preparing himself to suffer a continuation of the thrashing.

"You've given up on the little swine, you do realise that he spilt all the milk I took this morning. There is none for to-morrow and if the cow's going to be as awkward as Wally is there'll be none the next day as well," Daisy Denning was strident.

"No milk for even a cup o' tea?"

"None, and that means none for Dora either."

An irritated Gerald Denning began to use his belt again in a quick series of blows which struck the thighs, buttocks and back of his adoptive son.

"Little bugger isn't even ours," he called out as his belt struck home.

"Aye, I always knew it was a bad, *bad* contract we undertook."

"Well, it got us here," sighed an exhausted Mr Denning as he flopped into the chair facing his wife's beside the fire.

Mrs Denning's eyes made a slow and very meaningful inspection of their living quarters which was no more than a two roomed log-cabin several miles from the nearest town, "As I've said, a *bad deal*," her voice dripped sarcasm.

So I'm not theirs. Then, if I'm not theirs, whose am I? Wally ran the idea through his immature mind and for some reason felt pleased about it.

"Should I send him to bed without any supper?" Gerald asked his wife.

"Bed's too good for him, put him outside in the cold, Jack Frost may take him off our hands."

Gerald shook his head, "We don't want the money he brings in to dry up, do we? No, we'll have to keep him safe for a few years yet."

"Well, I don't want him anywhere near Dora to-night."

Mr Denning thought for a moment, "I'll put him in the shed, that'll be uncomfortable enough and he'll still be alive in the morning."

*****

Eddy Dobson entered the shop which had been taken over by the Christian Workers' League, though not without some trepidation, for though he was curious at the same time he was wary of anything which was church led or organised.

He looked around and found himself to be disappointed with the place. Shelves had been erected, but he estimated there to be fewer than thirty books on them. There were also half-a-dozen periodicals and three newspapers available, but one of the papers was the Chronicle which most of the town read anyway, "Not much t'satisfy the mind here," he muttered to himself.

"I believe you are Mister Dobson," greeted the Deacon as he slipped quietly in from the back of the shop.

"Aye, that's me. Who wants to knaw?" Asked a startled Eddy Dobson.

"I am the Reverend Thomas Leakey."

"*Reverend* is it. I'm a Christian all right, but I couldn't say I was an attender. Not regular, ye understand," Dobson looked and sounded doubtful, unsure that this was a place he had the right to frequent.

The Deacon clapped the shoulder of the collier in a reassuring sort of way, "We're all God's children, you may never fear for forgiveness nor for the safety of your soul whilst the door of the League remains open to you."

"Aye, that's reassuring," nodded Dobson, who then prepared to leave to seek out some company he was happier with at the Pit Laddie, for there was something about this man of the church that he found disconcerting.

"Perhaps you'd care to share a pot-of-tea with me," suggested the Deacon, at the same time taking hold of Dobson's elbow and leading him to the rear of the premises.

To his surprise, the collier found the room he next entered to be comfortable and well supplied with bottles containing fluids that clergymen should stay away from.

"This is Dougie Brass's old shop, ain't it?"

"It was, but now it is preparing to feed the souls and minds of men rather than their stomachs," replied the Deacon as he brewed the tea.

"Aye," Dobson paused and licked his lips, "Any chance o' a drop of somethin' warming in the tea," he finished boldly.

"My dear fellow, of course," the Deacon's eyes became milky blue and he smiled a humourless smile as he passed down a nearly full bottle of whisky.

Dobson found himself warming to the clergyman as he poured a good shot of the spirit into his tea, "Ye've not much set up for the workin' man out there, have ye," he waved his pot in the general direction of the shop front.

"Give me time, Mr Dobson, Rome was not built in a day and nor were the Cities of the Plain, come to that."

Eddy laughed and took another mouthful of fortified tea, "I canna' see what's in this for you," he said.

"Christianity, Education and the saving of the souls of men," returned the Deacon with evangelical fervour.

"Aye, that's all very well, but m'sel' I'm…"

"A person of radical opinions."

"Who's sez that?" Dobson, once again moved on to the defensive.

"Never fear, Mr Dobson, for I too have a social-conscience. Though change will only come if working men are educated as to whom their friends are and perhaps more importantly, *who their enemies are*."

"Why, that's what I keep tellin' the lads and that lackey of the bosses, Matthew Priestly."

"Then we share the same bench, or perhaps I should say *pew*," the Deacon tittered.

"But you're a clergyman, y'were educated at university no doubt, I don't knaw if yer trying t'make a fool o' me."

"My dear, Dobson, this is patently not the case," the Deacon pretended deep hurt, before taking up the whisky, "here, fortify yourself a little further," he offered.

Dobson held out his pot, received a good measure of spirit and took a greedy swallow. Though he'd taken drink his head was still clear enough and he held the Deacon's eyes in his own, "Well, then, what d'ye want of me?"

"Can you imagine what the country would be like were all working-men both educated and politically aware?"

"Aye, all the bosses, lords and ladies would be gone. There'd be no more bowing and scrapin' t'them. Then we'd all breathe sweet, free air."

"Exactly," agreed the Deacon, "Supposing there were to be formed a new political entity, one which combined the basic tenets of Christianity with the philosophy of Marx?"

"By God, Faith, Hope and Charity joined by all things being held in common," I'd join that party like a shot," Dobson was well fired up with whisky and hot-air.

"There is no such party as yet and perhaps some time will elapse before there is, but we must take steps towards its creation now."

"Otherwise, it'll never happen," said the collier.

"Exactly so."

"Then what can I do? What d'ye want o'me?"

"Nothing from you, but I have information which I believe you should be made aware of."

The miner listened intently.

"You know that a great civil war is being conducted; as we speak, in the United States."

"Aye, I read the papers ye knaw."

"What will happen after that, do you suppose? Considering the wealth of that country after the gold rush of ten years ago?"

Dobson shook his head, "The bosses will do even better – money goes t'money."

Leakey sighed and then explained, "They have the need and the finance to build railway lines right across the North American continent."

Again the miner shook his head, "So what?"

"Currently, they do not have the capacity to supply all the tracks and fittings needed for such a gigantic enterprise."

"Then it canna' be built, or they'll have t'order from abroad."

"Precisely, Dobson, precisely."

Eddy Dobson caught on in a rush, "Ye, mean, some o' the order's coming t'Martindale."

"I know discussions are to take place this summer."

"Why, man that's great news."

"Yes, but it also provides a great opportunity for the working man."

"Aye, there'll be full employment for years."

"Yes, though the political order will remain the same for years too. Unless… "

"Unless what?"

"Unless the situation is used to the advantage of ordinary workers."

"How can we do that when most o' the lads'll be as happy as pigs in shit – beggin' yer pardon."

"The Martindale companies will have to expand in order to fulfil the contract, especially the ironworks and the Balaklava factory. This will cost a huge amount of money, borrowed money probably."

"Aye, that's clear enough."

"Which makes the bosses vulnerable to any actions taken by their working men."

"So, you reckon we should strike?"

"Possibly, though at the right time. It would, perhaps, be better if at first some uneasiness, some uncertainty was spread around the town."

Eddy rubbed his hands together, "Give folk wi' the money a fright, ye mean. Make them more willing to negotiate."

"Exactly so, though we shall have to initiate some point of conflict between the factions. Supposing that the iron-and-steel workers were considered to be key to this railway contract, is it not then likely their pay would outstrip that of the miners?"

"Aye, it could do it. The colliers wouldn't put-up with the idea of it at all," said Dobson.

"In which case, no-coal means no-coke which means no-steel and no contract fulfilled," the Deacon laid it on the line.

"We'd have the bosses where we want them, dancing to our tune for a change."

"You would indeed, Mr Dobson, you would indeed. Now, perhaps we should share a glass of this fine, amber spirit."

"Yes, Mr Leakey, I'm wi' you there."

"Let us work carefully," said the Deacon as he emptied what remained of the bottle into Dobson's pot.

*****

"Why don't you visit Caroline? See if she's had any news of Helmuth," Jane couldn't understand how she'd brought herself to make such a request. It had tumbled from her mouth without rational thought been given to it and she found it hard to prevent herself from trembling.

Richard's throat lumped as he attempted to maintain a neutral expression, "Oh, I don't suppose she'll wish for too many visitors at the moment," he managed to keep his voice steady.

"As you wish, though she may have received some tit-bit from America we could use in the Chronicle," returned Jane, equally calmly, at the same time wondering why she felt the need to test her husband in this way.

Richard said nothing for some long-seconds before he replied, "Perhaps Mrs Schilling would appreciate a visit."

"I'm sure she would," said Jane neutrally.

He knew Caroline took Communion on Sunday mornings though tended not to attend in the afternoon. Dare I visit her? He asked himself.

"Caroline is a neighbour and no doubt is in need of a friendly word," replied Jane, just managing to prevent herself from adding *especially if the visitor were to be her lover.*

"No, it's too early, I don't believe this is the right time," he turned to face his wife directly, "Do you?"

Jane felt her body relax and she could not help a smile of approval to flash across her face, "No, probably not."

Why must she test me like this, Richard asked himself.

Why do I feel the need to test him so frequently, Jane asked herself.

*****

Jack Nicholson entered the back-yard of his house, sat on the doorstep and began to remove his boots. He looked himself up and down and was satisfied that he was remarkably clean, especially as he had spent most of the day at the bottom of the Martindale Pit arguing with Eddy Dobson over what the exact distance was between the shaft-bottom and the coal-face.

"I'm getting' good at this," he muttered to himself, "Sarah an' me ma' will be pleased."

Just then the back door opened and his wife appeared holding the hand of their daughter, Elinore.

"Why, John, you're back early and so, *so* clean too."

"*Daddy*," cried Elinore and flung her arms around him.

Jack raised his daughter high, threw her gently out of his hands and caught her, causing her to squeal with delight.

"Elinore, Grandma has a sweetie for you, if you hurry and find her I'm sure she'll give it to you."

Shrieking her pleasure, Elinor ran off.

Sarah's face drew on a wide-smile, her eyes were filled with the pleasure of seeing her husband return, but they also contained a hint of something else.

The miner's features lit up in the light of his wife's presence, how he loved this woman, he thought.

"Come inside and have some tea, I've something important to discuss with you," Sarah's voice had a serious edge to it.

"Aye, I'll dust me sel' down a bit more while ye pour."

Five minutes later, with Elinore remaining with Nana and a steaming pot of tea in front of him, Nicholson asked, not without some trepidation, "What is so important then?"

"I had a visit to-day from Jane Turner."

"Richard Turner's wife? The firebrand? I expect ye're not plottin' revolution wi' her."

Sarah laughed, "Well, perhaps someday, but to-day was about something much more mundane."

"Aye, well whatever was discussed ye seem pleased about it."

"As well as herself Mrs Turner was representing Mrs Schilling and Lady Martin."

The collier blew up his cheeks and expelled air from them, "Ye don't say."

"They have requested me to run a schoolroom for their children."

"Why, ye're my wife. A married woman canna' leave seein' to her husband," Nicholson was somewhat dismayed.

"My darling man, they say they'd be happy to accommodate Elinore too, so she won't have to attend the National School run by the dreaded Fishers."

"But you're a married woman, you can't teach no more."

"I can't teach in an established school, but this is a purely private-affair and they *want me*, in fact it sounded as though they were desperate to appoint me."

Jack didn't like the sound of this. Sarah was *his*, she belonged to *him*, the highpoint of his day was his return to her enfolding arms. She was the one who had set him on the right path, she was the one who had seen there was more to him than a drunken, fighting hewer.

Jack raised his voice, "Ye canna' do this, Sarah. What about my ma'? She'd have t'go back to seein' to everything. What about me?"

"We can take on one of the washer-women and perhaps someone to help with the cleaning. It will actually take some of the burden from your mother."

"My ma' won't like anyone else interfering in her house…," Nicholson began to further object.

"Your mother's already told me that she knows of a young widow she likes who would be grateful for the money."

"Even wi' my deputy's pay, I doubt we can afford..," Jack was shaking his head sombrely as he spoke.

"I shall receive a salary," put in Sarah.

"They'll pay ye?" Nicholson hadn't considered there'd be a financial side to the offer made by the top ladies of the town.

"Of course, and they'll pay me well."

"There's no schoolroom to be had in Martindale," again, Nicholson shook his head.

"The classes are to be taken at Martin Hall."

"Martin Hall itself, ye say. Does Sir Charles know of this?"

"I doubt Lady Marian would make such an offer behind the back of her husband."

The miner shook his head slowly, "Me ma' won't like it, I'm sure she won't" he found himself rapidly running out of negative responses.

Sarah smiled and took him into her arms, "My dear man, I've spoken to mam and she's all for it."

Nicholson knew that his mother had the highest regard for her daughter-in-law and had doubted that Sarah would ever take up with anyone like himself. Anything Sarah wanted would be all right with his mother.

"Well, I suppose there's no argument I can make ag'in it," he whispered before kissing her deeply, though he worried over what his workmates might say when they heard of it.

*****

"Ye've heard that there may be a big deal with the Americans for railway tracks?" Said Frank Turner as he dropped heavily into his office chair.

"It's the gossip o' the town and Eddy Dobson's trying t'make trouble ower it, ye ken that, don't ye?" Replied Geordie Cook.

"If Dobson's not careful I'll set Jack Nicholson on to him," Frank paused and then continued, "Sir Charles and Mr Watson asked me to go over to America to see about it. They reckon I was well qualified to check on it."

"Well, ye are. Nobody better."

Frank sighed long and loud.

"Though ye didn't want to go?"

"I *refused* to go. It's the first time I've refused Sir Charles anything since I became his agent. It sits heavy on me."

"Sir Charles won't take that ag'in ye, Frank, he's not that sort," supported Geordie.

"Oh, I know that, but then he asked young Fred instead and now I'm worried about this too. War going on over there and he newly wed."

"D'ye reckon he might be bamboozled?"

"Well, he's young."

"Maybe too young, you think?" Suggested Geordie.

Frank considered for a moment before he spoke again, "He's a bright young fellow; very popular wi' the lads, doesn't mind getting' his hands dirty. Aye, an' he is a Yankee, which should help."

"None more popular wi' the lads," agreed Geordie.

"But then there's the people he'll be dealing with, who'll be considerably more experienced than himself. They could be swindlers. There's a lot riding on this deal and if it went wrong, then the whole town could go on to the rubbish heap."

"Why don't you go wi' him? Trip to America, what an adventure that'd be," suggested Geordie.

"If it comes to that, why don't *you* go?"

"*Naw*, what would I do wi' an adventure. It's been adventure enough t'be married to Annie," laughed Geordie.

Frank joined in the mirth, but then his face became serious again, "Still, I don't like the sound of this deal. I'm sure there's something wrong with it."

"Too good t'be true, maybe," said Geordie while he poured himself a glass of milk stout, which Annie had told him would build-up his strength.

"Keep these doubts quiet, Geordie, I don't want any panic starting," the agent requested, his voice very serious.

"Aye, Frank, I'll say nowt."

*****

"Fred, before you leave, I wonder if I may ask a favour of you?" Caroline was finding her request a difficult one to express.

"Of course, Caroline, anything."

"You don't know what it is yet."

"If I can do you favour, I will, you know that."

"Please don't try to carry this out on your own, but, if there's any way you could arrange to have my father's remains returned to Blanchwell...," tears filled her eyes and she shook her head rapidly to drive them off, "*No*, it's too silly of me. Too impossible. I'm sorry I've asked."

"The railroad companies are bound to have surveyors out on the Great Plains, maybe they'll be able to help. There's no harm in asking."

"Please, don't make this a *personal* quest though, but should any opportunity appear, then I'd be grateful."

Fred took both of his sister-in-law's hands in his own and squeezed them gently, "I'll do what I can, I promise," he whispered.

They were interrupted by Amelia who was supervising the removal of the last of her personal baggage from upstairs.

"Thank-you, just pile it with the others," she ordered the sweating footmen.

"I wish I were going too," said Caroline as she looked at the luggage piled high in the entrance hall.

"I wish you were too," replied Amelia Schilling, truly meaning every word.

"Yes, I should say so and how glad Helmuth would be to see you," added Fred.

"If only I could come," Caroline yearned to see her husband and was desperate to tell him to allay his fears that she did not love him.

"Why don't you? The nurse is competent and I'm sure Marian and Sarah Nicholson would look-out for Julia," encouraged Mrs Schilling.

Caroline shook her head, "I can't. Helmuth said I must do as women have done for centuries when their men go off to war, *Look after the home and await their return*."

"I believe Helmuth would retract those words the moment he set his eyes on you," encouraged Fred.

"Your husband truly loves you, you know. I've seen it in his eyes every day I've been here," said Amelia.

Caroline sniffed loudly, but managed to hold back the tears which again were forming in her eyes.

Amelia flung her arms around her sister-in-law, "Oh, my dear Caroline, how I will miss you. You've been so kind to me."

"To us both," put in Fred stoutly.

"Yes, indeed to us both," Amelia continued, "I can't say when I've been happier than when I've lived here with Fred, Helmuth and yourself. It is like living in a wonderland. I can't thank you enough."

"Oh, dear, she's going to start bubbling again," Fred shook his head.

Amelia turned and thumped her husband's shoulder.

"*Ow*," he made the pretence that she had hurt him.

Caroline wrapped her arms around both of them and kissed each on the cheek, "How you two have made this old house ring with laughter, far more laughter than there ever was when I was growing up here. So, all I can beg is that you speed on your way, do what must be done and get back to Blanchwell as quickly as you can."

"We shall, we'll be back before you know it. I may even be able to drag Helmuth with us," cried Fred, he too becoming overcome with emotion.

"Just tell him to keep safe and that I love him and miss him more than he can possibly imagine," this time, Caroline couldn't hold back her tears.

Chapter Six

Captain Helmuth Schilling watched from the river-bank as *J* Company of the 17th Pennsylvania Cavalry charged towards him. He had to admit that they now had the look of a formidable force, holding their line, but keeping the spaces between the various sections intact.

He wondered how splendid they would have looked had their sabres been raised and glinting in the sun.

Then, at exactly the right moment, half of the company wheeled to the right, formed a continuous line and came to a halt in a welter of dust.

The second section, led by Lieutenant Matheson, performed the same manoeuvre to the left, but far less efficiently. His soldiers arriving in disjointed clusters and were finding it difficult; due to the confusion, to hand over their mounts to the horse-holders.

Helmuth was pleased to see how quickly Gibson's troop horses; four to a man, were led thirty or so yards to the rear, whilst at the same time his skirmish line was forming neatly, each man kneeling and directing his carbine to the front.

Helmuth waited until Matheson's section had finally linked up with that of Gibson's before he stepped forward, flung a salute and commented, "Pretty sharp indeed, well done, Lieutenant Gibson. More work required from you, don't you think, Lieutenant Matheson."

"It's the damned horses, they won't…," Matheson began to complain loudly.

"They need leadership, Matheson, *your* leadership, they are your men and you are responsible for *everything* they do," Helmuth spoke quietly but firmly.

Matheson' face turned nearly purple and he was about to make a hot reply until he thought better of it.

Captain Schilling cleared his throat and then said, "Should we allow the men to fire off a round or two, do you think?"

"I'm sure they'd like to," Carter Gibson smiled.

"Then give the command, but better order them to aim at the tree-tops."

Whilst Matheson; still in a silent rage, watched, Gibson raised his voice, "*Company prepare to fire... Aim high, now.*"

There came an expectant silence as the men waited to let-loose with their pieces.

Lieutenant Carter Gibson raised his voice until it began to squeak and shouted. "*Three rounds rapid.... Fire.*"

The skirmish line was immediately enshrouded in smoke which became thicker as further shots were discharged.

The sound of the gunfire was satisfyingly deafening and then, before even the echo of the last shot faded away, a slight breeze came up and wafted away all sight, sound or smell of the fusillade.

"*Whoah....*"

"*Did ya see that...*"

"*Yahoo......*"

The troopers were excited, for they had carried-out this exercise continually for some weeks, though this was the first time it had ended with actual gunfire.

Helmuth smiled, he was generally pleased with what he had seen, so he turned to Matheson and Gibson, "We may as well have coffee, it's a pleasant enough place. Better water the horses too."

"Bring the horses on," commanded Lieutenant Gibson, his voice much more confident now than it had ever been, "Take them down to the river."

The company commander turned to Andy Jackson, "We got enough food for three breakfasts?"

"*Yesirh*, I've nearly enough for the division," replied the ex-slave as he set off to serve the meal.

It wasn't long before the three officers were mopping bacon fat from their tin-plates with fresh, white bread.

"That man of yours is a miracle worker," commented Gibson.

Matheson, still in a huff merely grunted.

"Jackson's desperate to become a trooper, you know, I've often heard him speak of it," put in Carter Gibson.

"Yes, he would give anything to join the company, but it cannot be," said Helmuth.

"How can any black be allowed to dress in our country's uniform?" Matheson spoke in a growl.

Helmuth looked sharply at his junior, "Mister Jackson was born in the United States and since January; when the *Emancipation Bill* came into force, he is a free man with all the responsibilities of a citizen. Amongst which is the right to bear-arms."

"In which case he can have my carbine and I'll go home," Eldred Matheson laughed dismissively.

"It should be obvious, even to you Mr Matheson, the reason why we cannot arm Jackson," Helmuth spoke coldly.

"If he was caught by the Rebs with a gun in his hands, they'd hang him from the nearest tree," said Carter Gibson sombrely.

"So, you wouldn't have any blacks fighting for their own freedom?" Matheson' voice was surly.

"No, quite the reverse, I'd have as many ex-slaves as possible, but properly recruited into the Union Army. They are motivated to the point of obsession and they'd die happy just to see the end of the Confederacy."

"Well, if that's all we're fighting for, I don't know if it's worth it," complained Matheson, "for the South will abandon slavery eventually anyway. My pa' sez so."

"There is another cause which is equally as important," suggested Helmuth.

The two junior officers looked puzzled.

"Bringing the North and South together again. Is that not worth doing? Is that not worth any sacrifice?"

Carter Gibson shook his head, "I don't know about that. I'd hardly heard of the Mason-Dixon Line before the war started."

"Me neither," Matheson shook his head.

Matheson's father was a wealthy lawyer with political ambitions who had insisted that his son take a commission in the Army of the Republic in order to join in the march on Richmond. Eldred had been happy to take a commission as he had been certain that the war would be over in weeks. However, in reality, more than two years had passed and the Rebel capital city was as distant as it ever was.

"Would a split make so much difference?" Queried Gibson.

Helmuth thought for a while before replying, "Lets say the Rebels win and the Union is broken in two, in the decade or so after that, who's to say there wouldn't be a second civil war, or even a third? What if the Confederates invaded Mexico and created a slave holding empire there? Even extending it to Brazil, maybe."

"Why, with Lee and Jackson leading it, the Army of Northern Virginia could do that on its own," Gibson nodded thoughtfully.

"What about Old Pete Longstreet, he'd probably become the Governor-General of Cuba," added Matheson, who then paused before continuing half seriously, "Maybe I've joined the wrong army."

"As well as that," continued Helmuth, "Suppose California and the rest of the West didn't want to join either side, Yankee or Reb? There might then be established a *third* republic on the continent, one that in the future could become vulnerable to threats from the British or French in the Pacific?"

"Or the Russians in Alaska," added Gibson.

"Or the even the *Chinese*." Matheson fell backwards laughing at his thought.

"Indeed, yes," said Helmuth.

"Who knows what would happen," said Gibson.

"One more thing, there'd be no point in building a trans-continental railroad, would there? Where would it be going? Who would be using it?" continued Captain Schilling.

"Why, it'd be like Europe, borders, customs posts, taxes every time you wanted to stretch your legs," commented Carter Gibson.

They all lapsed into silence until Helmuth spoke again, "Well, that's settled that, I think. Gentlemen, let's get the company mounted and moving."

*****

Eddy Dobson, his face livid, burst into the office of Matthew Priestly which was located in an end-terrace house, near the gates of the Martindale Colliery.

Priestly looked up from his seat by the fireplace, "Mornin' Eddy, you seem to be in a bit of a huff with yourself," he greeted mildly.

"Aye, an' I've a right t'be, ye'll knaw all about it I suppose."

"About what?"

"The iron workers."

"We're an association of *colliers*, why would I know about the iron workers," replied Priestly patiently.

Dobson looked as though he were about to blow steam from his nostrils and fire from his mouth, "Aye, our members, that's what I'm bothered about, an' them's who ye should be worried about an'all."

"So what have the foundry workers got to do with the colliers?"

"Ye knaw, dinna' lie t'me man, ye knaw fine well."

"Well, they both play their part in making this town prosperous," suggested the association organiser as he rose to his feet.

Eddy stamped his foot and thrust his chin forward, "The American contract, the Yankee contract for rail-lines. Signed, sealed an' delivered, I've been told. Young Schillin's off t'see to it. Ye knew about that, dinna' deny it."

"No contract has been signed, I do know that for a definite fact."

"It's in the bag man."

Priestly found himself to be puzzled, "Even if it were, what difference would that make to the colliers, apart from securing their labour for years into the future?"

"The ironworkers are t'get a better rate for the job, they'll be makin' more than the hewers even."

"I've not heard that."

"Well, ye wouldn't, would ye. Always toadying t' Watson, Turner an' the rest o' the bosses. Ye'd let them dance over the rights o' your members."

"Aye, you're correct for once, Eddy, I speak to the owners nearly every week, on behalf of our members and that's how I know that there is no American contract yet."

"They've told ye about it, then?"

"In outline, yes."

"They're pullin' the wool over yer eyes, man. It'll end up as I say, wi' our lads missin' out," Dobson just about spat the words.

Priestly's gaze remained serene, "Sir Charles Martin has always been fair with his workers and I doubt that even a huge American contract will change that. Anyway, we'll need to wait to see if Martindale Iron & Coal actually makes a bid. Then we'll have a further wait to see if their bid is successful."

Eddy shook his head violently, "There's nay talkin' t'the likes o' you," he shouted angrily on his way outside.

"Oh, dear, Dobson's on a crusade again," Matthew Priestly sighed to himself as he closed the door which his visitor had left wide-open.

*****

Mr Somers, who was curate of Holy Innocents church, cursed to himself as he saw Mr Hodge, of St. John's at Kirkby coming towards him.

"Ah, Somers," cried Hodge, thrusting forward his hand at the same time.

Somers refused the hand, nodded bleakly and made as though to pass on.

"Roland, are we no longer friends?"

"Roland, *Roland*, sir, you dare to address me so familiarly," his words came out hot and fast.

"Can we still not be friends? Have we not known each other in our cups? Were we not anointed together?" Hodge was almost pleading.

Roland Somers was red in the face, "You, who have denied me my only chance to be noticed where it matters, dare call yourself *friend*. I am amazed, sir, fair 'mazed at your temerity."

"But, Roland, I was offered it, how could I refuse. The same could have happened to me at St. John's."

"I've served this parish since Holy Innocents was built, been at the beck-and-call of Lander – and his girls, if it comes to that – and I'm not to be left in charge while the rector goes prancing around Italy. I call this hard done by, especially when a man I thought of as a friend turns out to be a part of the conspiracy against me."

"It wasn't as you say at all, I knew nought of it 'till the Reverend Marshall told me of Mr Lander's request. Had it gone the other way, would you not have done the same as myself?"

Somers shook his head vigorously, "No, not I," he paused to let some of his spleen dissolve and then his words were cold and hard, "Just stay away from Byers Green, Hodge, stay away, d'ye hear."

"You may be in want of help...," Geoffrey Hodge's words died away as Somers stepped close to his face.

"*Help*, I need no help and you'll get precious little aid or co-operation from me. So, you'll be a busy, a *very busy* man. Good day to you, sir."

The acting Rector of Holy Innocents took out his handkerchief and mopped his brow, "Not a good start," he muttered to himself.

*****

Eddy Dobson downed his pint and ordered another from Joe Heaton, the landlord of the Pit Laddie. He then turned to face three other miners who were clustered around him.

"The American order...," began Dobson, only for his words to be cut off by a burly miner.

"Jack Nicholson says there's nowt in the story of the iron furnace men getting' more money – wi' the big Yankee order, like," the man shrugged his shoulders and pulled a face at the same time.

"Well, he would, wouldn't he," replied Dobson sourly.

"Nicholson's a bosses man now, all for them wi' money," put in a lanky fellow who's eyes had first checked around the room in case Jack was present and had overheard this defamation of his character.

"We're the ones that keep the furnaces goin' wi' out us, there'd be nowt," growled a miner with a very bulbous, blue veined nose.

Joe Heaton interrupted wistfully, "Wish I'd been paid as well as ye lot when I was hewing. Why, y'even get money for tramping t'the coal face. Nowt like that when I was underground."

"Point is but, Joe, it's not right. The ironworkers haven't the skills o' the colliers, so why should they get paid more? The lads will be cheated out o' what they're due," Dobson was in full flow.

"Why, man, cut yer gab, ours must be the only colliers in the county, maybe in the country, what get paid t'walk to the coal-face they're workin'," Joe spoke as one who knew.

"That's not what we're on about, Sir Charles is always claiming how fair he's been, but not this time."

"Have ye actually spoken to Jack Nicholson?" queried the landlord of the Laddie.

"Neither Priestly nor Nicholson can see it," returned Dobson.

"But it hasn't happened yet, has it? This Yankee thing," Heaton pointed out wearily.

"No, but it will," put in Dobson strongly.

"Maybe we should see Matthew Priestly again," suggested the lanky collier.

"*Whaa*, man," Dobson spluttered, "For all that's happened, can ye not see it, Priestly's wi' the owners. Did ye not see him lording it wi' the likes o' Charlie Martin at the Gala last year? Him an' Nicholson are hand-in-hand, leading us down a road that leads to somethin' not much better than slavery."

"Matthew Priestly's no use t'either man nor beast," agreed the squat miner.

"Aye," supported the blue veined nose.

"What we need; an' we need it now, is direct action," Dobson's voice rose to a shout as he spoke, "Revolution's what we need, turn everything upside-down, get rid o' those who trample us into the mud."

"Now hey, hold on," Joe Heaton called, "I'll ha' nowt like that said in my pub."

"Well, I suppose it's a'right that *ye* can make your opinions well enough known," replied a disgruntled but quieter Eddy Dobson.

"Aye," supported the bulbous nosed miner.

"That's right," agreed the lanky collier.

Joe Heaton raised himself to his maximum height, his face took on a craggy, belligerent look, "Aye, well, I can, 'cos this is my pub."

"Ye're only the landlord of it," corrected the squat pitman.

"That's as maybe, but it's still my rules that stand in here, an' if yer don't like 'em, gann an' drink elsewhere."

*****

Caroline Schilling found herself at a loose end, Fred and Amelia had gone, Elizabeth was in London and Marian was very much involved in the schoolroom they'd set up together at Martin Hall.

"Perhaps I should visit Jane," she thought to herself and then wondered if such a visit would bring her into contact with Richard.

She had managed to stop thinking about him, after a period of reliving his embraces, his kisses and the touch of his fingers. The more she thought about this doomed love affair the further distant it seemed. It was as though their passionate; but brief, encounters had happened in the plot of a romantic novel, which somehow she had transferred into her own life.

"*How silly of me,*" she whispered to herself.

She still wanted Richard, though once her friendship with Jane developed; seeing his children and the depth to which he was engaged in a successful and growing business, she had managed to avoid contact with him.

Next into her consciousness swam Helmuth. He had been so *very good* to her, providing everything she had dreamed of and had wanted nothing in return except her love. She had denied him this, intimated to him that though she was very fond of him, she did not love him.

"*Is this still the case?*" She questioned herself aloud.

Fred had been instructed to pass on to his brother word of her deep love for him. *Had she meant that?* She asked herself this question three times rapidly. As she did so, the figure of Richard faded further into her memory whilst that of Helmuth sharpened and came into ever clearer focus.

"Do I truly love Helmuth, or am I just concerned because he is in mortal danger and I owe him a very deep debt of gratitude?"

"Or do I *really* love Richard, but will not admit to it because of my friendship with Jane and my loyalty to Helmuth?" She spoke aloud to herself.

These were difficult questions and she could find no immediate answers to them.

She stamped her foot in annoyance, "All I want that Helmuth should come home safe and in one piece."

Then an idea struck her which she thought would help her through the ordeal of knowing that her husband was in daily peril. Her publisher had been quite insistent that she write a follow up to *My Life On The Plains* and there had even been talk of a lecture tour.

"I will begin to-morrow… *No*, I shall pick up my pen this afternoon," she commanded herself, "And my next book will be about a raw, new town; spawned by coal, without the support of a husband who's away at war."

*****

"*Shush*, I can see them through the window," whispered Eddy Dobson over his shoulder to his band of followers, mainly young, inexperienced miners."

"Ye're sure they're all puddlers in there?" questioned a young putter.

"Why aye, man, who else are they gan'a be, chorus girls maybe?"

"We divn't want to be hurtin' other miners, do we," replied the putter.

"*Look*, this pub is one *always* used by the iron-workers, there'll be none o' our lads who'd care t'drink in there."

A bookish looking stove minder spoke up, "Eddy, I canna see how breaking a few inn windows is going…"

Dobson didn't let him finish, "The Revolution has t'start somewhere."

"Why, but, this is no Bastille, man," complained the bookish one.

"It's a start, if workin' men took this action all ower the country it would make them above us think. We'd make the bosses nervous and our folk would rally t'the cause in their tens of thousands."

A tall, well-built hewer pushed his way to the front hefting a sizeable rock he had picked up on the way, "Are we doin' this, or what?"

Before Eddy or any other of the group could speak further the missile was flung at a window of the saloon bar of the Crown.

The shattering of glass galvanised the rest of the raiding party into action and a volley of missiles were flung towards the public house, breaking more windows and causing shouts of anger and surprise as well as curses to filter into the night.

"Who's oot there..."

"Whaaa.... 'Ave yer seen my head..."

"Ah'm bleedin'...."

"Look out, there might be more...."

"Come on, lads, lets out an' get them."

A huddle of iron-workers charged out into the street only to find it deserted.

"Shy buggers have run off," said one puddler stating what the others were thinking.

Just then an old miner appeared around the corner, making his way home from the Voltigeur, he looked up, saw the ironworkers and didn't like the way they were approaching him.

"Bloody hewers," cried a puddler.

"Look at my heid," shouted a wounded trolley man.

"Let's get him, lads," yelled a cradle-man.

The aged collier ran but was not fast enough to escape. Soon he fell to the ground under a welter of punches and kicks and was left there bleeding.

*****

Sarah Nicholson looked around her school-room and found everything was to her satisfaction. There being a wide range of books and instead of the ubiquitous slates-and-chalk there was a plentiful supply of paper, pencils, paints and crayons.

"I want mama...," screeched Julia Schilling, who; at only three years, was the youngest of the group.

"Oh, do shut up, Julia," cried Guido Turner as he looked up from the picture of an elephant he was attempting to copy.

"Hush, now children, and Guido, be kind to the little ones," Sarah patted him gently on the head and dropped her voice to a conspiratorial whisper, "I'm relying on you to be my *special* helper."

Guido beamed, went across to Julia and began to comfort her.

Mrs Nicholson then saw to it that all of her charges had something to keep them usefully occupied.

The door opened and Cissy Jackson slipped into the schoolroom, Albert, Alexandrina and Robert immediately jumped from their seats to greet her.

"*Cissy*," cried Drina rushing to her nurse holding wide her arms.

"Oh, Nanny," called Albert, "We're having so much fun. Are you to join us. We *should* be very pleased were you to."

Sarah stepped forward and took both of the nursemaid's hands in her own, "Cissy, how nice to see you."

"Thank-you, ma'am."

The teacher noticed how the scar on the nurse's cheek was still livid and how conscious of it the nanny was.

"Lady Martin says you're to take lunch with her, while I see t'the class," informed Cissy, managing to hug all three of the Martin children at the same time.

"How very kind of her, though I'd better make sure these ruffians get some work done well before then."

"I'm not a ruffian," proclaimed Bertie, "I'm a baronet."

"No you're *not*, papa's a baronet and you're a *nobody*," Drina rarely let her brother get away with much.

"Anyway," put in Guido from the other side of the room, "You'll not become a baronet until your papa passes on and I'm sure you wouldn't wish for that to happen."

Robert Martin on hearing this burst into tears, he wasn't sure what *passes on* meant, but it didn't sound too good to him.

Maud Turner, who was still smaller than she should have been, sat silently, assessing all that was going on around her and neatly filing it away in her mind.

Jonathan Turnbull, who was the son of the tenant of Home Farm, felt completely out of place, sitting here in the Big House, when he should have been mucking-out or seeing to the beasts in the top meadow.

"I'm so pleased you've been able to join us," the teacher gave Turnbull a comforting pat, "I suppose you'd rather be out in the open air though?"

"I would that, Mrs Nicholson," his face took on a wistful look.

"Well, there's more to life than fields and woods, Jonathan and I hope you shall soon discover this whilst you are here."

"I got let out o' the National School last harvest time and planned not t'go back. Ma's *made* me come here, pa's not bothered – sez he's a pair of hands short."

"I'm sure your father will soon see the correctness of your mother's insistence with the passage of time."

"He always does what ma' says, *eventually*," put in Jonathan dourly.

Sarah next stopped at the desk of Martin Cowley who was the only child of Doctor Cowley, "You seem very busy and I can see that your cursive has improved enormously."

Young Cowley hardly looked up from his penmanship, though nodded and replied, "Thank-you Mrs Nicholson."

He then went red in the face, for it was common knowledge amongst the other class members that already he was in love with his teacher.

Cissy joined Sarah, "There's a lot more children here than I ever thought there'd be," she said.

"I know, though I'm glad of it, very glad. How democratic it is of Sir Charles and Lady Martin to allow it. I intend to do my very best to ensure that this school is a great success."

Cissy smiled widely, "I'm sure ye will be that Mrs Nicholson, never been more sure of anythin' in me life."

They were interrupted as several children began to lose concentration. Sarah Nicholson took immediate charge and brought them back to their duty before going off for luncheon.

"How nice to see you, Mrs Nicholson, or may I call you Sarah?" Asked Marian Martin as the teacher arrived in the dining room.

"Of course, Lady Martin, I much prefer informality."

"Then you must call me Marian."

Sarah looked doubtful and shook her head slightly, "Oh, I don't know about that...," she began.

Marian Martin took her guest's arm, "Remember, I'm not so fine a lady as many hereabouts. Not long ago I was plain Molly Jones, a collier's widow and before that a farm lass who was not used to having *any* airs and graces."

"I too am the wife of a collier and there's not a man in the world I admire more than he," Sarah began to feel comfortable with the lady of the manor.

Marian smiled broadly and took both of Sarah's hands in hers, "Love is so wonderful, is it not? It can even make a lady out of a simple farm lass."

"And, perhaps, a plain collier into a great man too," agreed the schoolteacher.

Both women laughed and Marian began to serve soup, "I tend to dine informally when I can," she said.

"This certainly suits me," replied Sarah.

Marian's tone became more serious, "How has Mr Nicholson settled to the idea of his wife returning to her profession. I must say that I feared he would forbid it."

"I don't believe he was too pleased with the idea at first, but his mother persuaded him. Mrs Peggy Nicholson has always been a friend and supporter of myself, she often says that she can't see what I ever saw in Jack."

"Though she's secretly proud of you both?" Guessed Marian.

Sarah laughed, "Yes, I believe so."

Marian passed a basket of freshly baked bread rolls, "And how do you feel our little school is progressing?"

"Very well," informed Sarah, "though the number of pupils is much smaller than I'm used to and there is a much wider range of ages – however, I'm sure I'll be able to cope."

"The children behave well?"

Sarah smiled reassuringly, "I have *a way* with children, Marian, you need not fear on that score. They will learn but will hardly realise it."

"Good, very good, it is so comforting to have you with us. All the ladies were delighted when they heard that our little scheme was not to be still-born."

"You must pass on my thanks for giving me the opportunity to take up my vocation once again, especially as I believed it to be lost for ever."

Lady Marian took a sip of her soup and, as a sudden thought struck her, said, "Why don't you come to our next get-together and tell them all personally how our project is developing?"

"I should be delighted to, more than pleased."

"Then that's settled," replied Marian before dipping into her soup.

*****

"I'm not sure about comin' up here on a Saturday night, these days," remarked Geordie, his eyes never still as he spoke.

Jack Nicholson looked around and noticing the streets were teeming with groups of ironworkers and colliers, said, "Aye, ye're right there, Geordie lad, I can sniff trouble in the air."

They continued on their way to the Pit Laddie, passing the Crown which still had its broken windows boarded up.

Here and there were groups of miners and ironworkers glaring at each other from across the streets.

"Maybe we should go home," suggested Geordie.

"What an' miss my Saturday night half-pint," replied Jack, "Anyway, these buggers is just makin' their mouths go and not much else. They'll have t'have a few pints more in them 'afore they'll summon up the nerve for a set-to."

"Aye, maybe we'll be finished an' gone before the scrapping breaks out," replied Geordie as he opened the saloon bar door of the Laddie."

"What's it like out?" Queried Joe Heaton as he pulled a pint for Geordie and a half for Jack.

"There's goin' t'be bother," informed Geordie.

"What d'ye think, Jack? Do I need t'put me shutters up?"

Jack Nicholson took a swallow of his beer before replying, "Who, knaws, Joe, but the police are no where t'be seen."

"What's set it all off? The miners and the others have got on well for years, so how come they're at each others throats now?"

Matthew Priestly joined them from the other end of the bar, "I'll tell you that in one – *Eddy Dobson.*"

Jack and Joe groaned while Geordie shook his head.

"He's not expecting t'start his revolution by breakin' a few windows, is he?" Asked Jack.

"Stupid bugger," put in Joe, "I think I'll ban him from here."

"Dobson seriously believes that revolution is sure to come and he wants to make certain that he has a leading part in it," informed Priestly.

"Aye, Ah can see that," began Jack Nicholson, "Though what has he used t'turn the lads ag'in each other?"

"It's this American contract, expansion of steel production, increase in the size of the Balaklava works," informed Priestly.

"Why man, surely that's good news, keeps every man-jack in work," Joe couldn't believe what he was hearing.

"Dobson's spreading the word that the ironworkers will be offered a big pay rise, which'll make them better off than the colliers," continued the leader of the Association.

"Who says so?" Asked the landlord.

Priestly shook his head, "Dobson wouldn't tell me, but he seems certain of his source. Says it came straight from Martin Hall."

"That canna' be," Geordie discounted this story immediately.

Just then, with a clashing of doors, a group of five young colliers came in, full of beer and bravado.

"Any fuckin' iron men in 'ere," their leader shouted.

"Divn't use that language in my pub," called Heaton, "I'll not have it."

"We was just askin' a question," put in a tall, thin interloper.

"Aye, so giz a pint each an' we'll say no more of it," ordered a squat, aggressive one.

Jack Nicholson continued to sip his beer.

The leader of the bunch looked Nicholson up and down, "Why, lads, here's a girl drinkin' halves," he burst into laughter in which he fully expected he would be joined by the rest of his mates.

The others of his party recognised who the half-pint drinker was and stepped a little away from their leader.

"I'm not frightened of his reputation, not that he has one now. Bosses man, he is," the leader pushed his luck even further.

"You lot, get out, before I chuck ye out," ordered Joe Heaton who was becoming worried about his fixtures-and-fittings.

Jack continued to take delicate sips of ale.

The leader of the gang patted Nicholson's shoulder, "Come outside," he challenged.

"No, I don't think I will," replied Jack before returning to his half-pint.

"See, lads, see what ye're all afright of, he's turned soft – yellow soft."

Jack left his pint, stood to his full height, which was some inches less than that of his tormenter, his eyes blazed but his voice was calm, "Ye've had too much t'drink, son, it'd be best if ye'd go home and sleep it off."

Geordie Cook spoke up, "Ye don't know how lucky ye are, been given the chance to bugger off before ye get hurt."

"Go home lads, do the sensible thing," encouraged Matthew Priestly.

"Aye, get out, before I calls a polis," ordered Joe Heaton.

The leader sensed rather than saw his party were edging towards the door and after a second or two he joined them, though not before threatening "I'll see ye outside Nicholson, for I'm not frightened of ye, not now 'cos ye're livin' on yer reputation."

"We could slip out o' the back door as there's five of them," suggested Geordie Cook.

"No, if he's waiting on me, I'll deal wi' him and then the pair of us will go home in peace."

*****

From the upstairs window of the Christian Workers' Education League, the Deacon rubbed his hands together as he watched ever more workers come into the centre of the town for their Saturday night out.

Even from where he was he could still sense the tension in the air and was sure that Martindale's troubles were being well stoked by Dobson and his riff-raff.

As he watched he saw a group of colliers facing up to a similar number of men from the steelworks. Though he couldn't make out definite words, he could see that they weren't friendly ones.

Eddy Dobson had done exactly as he expected, the Martindale workers were at each others' throats and soon a riot would break out.

There would soon be broken bones and smashed heads and ill- feeling would spread until it affected every household in the town.

"Then, it shall be the turn of Dunnett, Nicholson and the ever so high and mighty Charles Martin," he muttered to himself.

Just then his eyes were caught by the sight of Jack Nicholson coming along the street, with a small fellow who he believed was Geordie Cook, the surrogate father of his Nemesis, George Murphy. Following them were a group of five young miners who were obviously shouting insults, but these were seeming to have no effect on Mr Nicholson.

*****

"See lads, he'

s runnin' away home to 'is posh teacher woman," crowed the leader of the gang.

"Bet she's nice between the sheets. Naked and ready, like," the squat one shouted.

All five ground rapidly to a halt as Jack Nicholson turned abruptly to face them.

"Now, lads, ye can say what ye like about me, but you two," Nicholson pointed to the leader and his squat friend, "ye've talked of my *wife* in a manner no husband'll put up wi'."

The leader of the pack turned to face his gang, "Ha'way, then, lets sort him."

However, the gang stood stolidly where they were, looking around for some way of carrying out a face-saving withdrawal.

Seeing his leader motionless, the squat one launched himself forward expecting that his weight and low centre-of-gravity would carry Nicholson off his feet and into the dust.

Because of his slight size most of Jack's opponents had underestimated his speed and the strength of his punch. Unless; of course, they had seen the fire-burning behind his eyes.

The squat one was surprised when he found he had made no contact with his opponent but instead had been sent tumbling by a trip.

Seeing that Nicholson's attention was otherwise engaged the leader stepped forward, half-closed his eyes in concentration and launched a haymaker which was directed towards the side of his head.

The second of Nicholson's assailants was also surprised when his punch hit nothing, and then he felt an excruciating pain as he was thumped in rapid succession on the chin, the side of his head and stomach. A fraction of a second later and struggling for breath, he joined his compatriot in the dust of the High Street.

Nicholson gazed for a second or two at his assailants before turning to their friends, "Bugger off before I start on you. I'm just warmin' up."

The other three beat a hasty retreat.

The leader and the squat-one struggled to their feet, but the fight had gone out of them and they slunk off to lick their wounds.

"They were hardly worth the bother," said Geordie.

"I'm not dusty, am I?" Asked a worried Jack Nicholson.

"Naw, ye'll do fine."

"Divn't tell Sarah I had a bit of a fight."

"Yer secret's safe wi' me."

Chapter Seven
3rd *May 1863*

"Oh, no, we're not halting *again*," muttered Lieutenant Carter Gibson as he began to dismount.

"Afraid so," replied Captain Schilling, as he too swung out of the saddle.

As they quietened their horses, in the distance they began to hear the rumble of artillery pieces and the less measured, staccato rattle of small-arms fire.

Helmuth Schilling handed the reins of his mount to Andy Jackson and walked forward to see if he could see anything of the battle which was being fought all around them.

After half-a-minute he had seen nothing of the action as it was hidden from sight by one tree covered hill after another.

"It seems as though we've mounted and dismounted every fifteen minutes since breakfast," complained Gibson.

"Tiresome, isn't it," replied Helmuth lightly. He was pleased that the regiment had been kept away from the action, for he was certain that his men; though much improved, were not yet ready to face the South's finest.

They'd done better at Kelly's Ford than on the Occoquan, but not much better.

Sergeant Crittenden rode up, "Any chance of a battle or at least a bite to eat, Cap'n, the boys are becoming restless."

Helmuth shook his head, "The moment we light our cooking- fires we'd be ordered to move on again."

"That's the army for you," agreed Crittenden.

"Pass the word to the men that they're to chew on their hardtack and take a swallow or two of water and I'll let them brew coffee as soon as I'm sure we're not going to have to gallop off somewhere else."

"Yes, sir," the sergeant made as if to turn his horse, but Captain Schilling took hold of its bridle.

"You dealing with things, all right? With Lieutenant Matheson not being with us?"

"Never been happier, sir," the sergeant smiled, mounted and rode off.

"Matheson must have some fine connections to be appointed an aide-de-camp," mused Gibson.

"It's only temporary and, apparently Matheson is an aide to his uncle, a mere colonel on Hooker's staff."

"I'd much prefer Crittenden alongside me if it came to a fight," Gibson spoke sincerely.

Helmuth fully agreed, though he said nothing. However, he became determined to push Colonel Kellogg into putting the sergeant up for a commission.

Gibson sniffed the air and gazed around, "Quiet as the grave in these parts. If it weren't for us galloping like demented fiends, here, there and everywhere, you wouldn't believe that nearby men are fighting for their lives."

"God, I hope something does happen – *anything*."

"Well, I doubt we'll see action to-day. Battlefields are like that, in one part all hell is breaking loose whilst a mile or two away another group of soldiers believe it to be just another boring day."

Gibson was silently thoughtful for a while and then asked, "Captain, back at Occoquan, when we all ran for it, you'd have stood if the rest of us had, wouldn't you."

Helmuth considered for a short while before he said, "I'd like to think so, but who knows what will happen when bullets begin to whiz close by."

"I'm scared. I'm scared at this minute, I'm scared every time we come anywhere near Jonnie Reb," the lieutenant's voice dropped to a whisper as he made his confession.

Helmuth patted his junior-officer's shoulder, "Hell, Gibson, my heart finds its way into my mouth every time we face the enemy."

"Really? It don't look that way."

"Maybe not, but it's true just the same. Sometimes, when I'm about to shout an order, my throat blocks-solid and I feel sure fear has made me incapable of speech."

Gibson shook his head and laughed gently, "Though you keep going, your orders are always clearly delivered."

"No good *being* yellow and *looking* yellow," Helmuth snorted.

"Rider comin' in, cap'n," Helmuth looked up to see Crittenden pointing back along the road."

"Looks like a despatch rider," said Gibson, straining his eyes.

"It could be. He's alone and coming on at a lick."

A minute or so later the messenger reined his mount to a stop in a flurry of dust and small stones. "From the colonel, sir," he said, saluting.

Helmuth returned the salute, read his orders quickly and sent the despatch rider on his way.

"Are we off to Richmond at last?" Gibson spoke more in hope than expectation.

"*Dammit* no, Lee's done it again, he's sending us packing," Helmuth just managed to hold back a string of oaths.

"We're in retreat?"

"Yes, Jackson's troops have struck at our flank, just down by Dowdall's Tavern and sent XI Corps reeling. It appears that Howard's men will be of no further use today. The line is broken so we're to withdraw *again*."

"So Joe Hooker hasn't done the business with the Rebs either," observed Carter Gibson, "I had high hopes of him, as at least he *sounded* confident."

"If Lincoln doesn't find us a general soon…," in his disappointment Schilling couldn't finish his sentence, he shook his head sadly and then ordered, "Saddle the men up, we're on the move. We have the honour and pleasure of guarding the regiment's rear."

"A wonderful end to a wonderful day," commented the lieutenant before he pulled his horse around to carry out his orders.

*****

"An excellent sermon, Mr Hodge, most impressive," congratulated Sir Charles Martin as he was leaving Holy Innocents Church.

"Indeed it was, I always find *positive* messages of love and beauty so re-assuring," Lady Martin backed up her husband.

"I much prefer it to a continuous diet of fire-and-brimstone," added the landowner.

"Why, thank you My Lady, Sir Charles," Hodge smiled his pleasure.

"Short too," added the baronet.

"Not too short, I trust," the Reverend Hodge was now a little concerned. It was important that he was successful at Holy Innocents which he hoped would set him up nicely for the living of St. John's at Kirkby once the current incumbent had passed on… One way or another.

Charles Martin took the clergyman's hand and pumped it vigorously, "No, you may rest easy, sir, I've never enjoyed a sermon so much for some time."

"Truly, Mr Hodge," again Marian backed up her husband and favoured the clergyman with the sort of smile few women can successfully pull off.

Geoffrey Hodge basked in the warmth of her smile and twinkling eyes for as long as he could and then returned to attend to the rest of his congregation who were now streaming from the porch.

*****

As Charles turned away to proceed down the churchyard path, he saw his agent was walking a short way ahead of him, "Frank," he called.

The agent pulled his hat closer over his head and turned to face his sister and brother-in-law, "Charles, Marian," he smiled.

"Abigail not with you, Frank?" Queried Marian.

"Hurried home to be sure the servants have set-out the tea things properly," Frank winked and grinned as best he could, for he knew that his wife no longer liked to be seen out with him.

"Frank, I'm becoming worried over the unrest that is afflicting the whole town at the moment. What's it all about?"

"There've been broken bones and broken heads, or so Cissy has told me," put in Marian.

"I can't make it out," Frank shook his head negatively, "It seems to have come out of nowhere. Some of the hot-heads among the colliers are saying they are to receive lower pay-rate than the ironworkers once the American contract comes through."

"Well, how on earth have they come to that conclusion? We've only discussed it amongst ourselves, though young Fred disappearing from the works may have set tongues wagging."

"Matthew Priestly is sure that Eddy Dobson is behind it. That fool believes he and his rabble can bring about a revolution," informed Frank.

"Though where did his information come from?" Charles' tone betrayed the depth of his puzzlement.

"There was that strange clergyman who called about the Workers' Education League," remembered Marian Martin.

"Surely not. A clergyman behind this sort of trouble," said Charles.

"Well, the more I saw of him the less I liked and trusted him," Marian nodded emphatically as she spoke.

"Jack Nicholson was lately on about seeing that villainous *Deacon* fellow in town, him from the New Church Asylum, you remember, where young George Murphy was imprisoned. I never saw the man myself, but I wonder if Leakey could be him," considered Charles slowly.

"Should it turn out that Leakey *is* the *Deacon*, I'll go around and see to him," offered Frank grimly.

"No, we can't do that. He *is* a man of the cloth and by all accounts a gentleman, even if he is a twisted one."

"We don't know how genuine his claim to being a member of the clergy is, though, do we?" Suggested Marian thoughtfully, who then continued, "We must look him up in *Crockford's*."

"Indeed we must."

"Dunnett and Nicholson dealt with him in Liverpool, perhaps they should make a friendly call to suggest he returns to wherever he came from," said Frank.

"Leakey would go to Law were anyone to assault him. Both Dunnett and Nicholson could end up in goal," Charles patted Frank's shoulder, "Can't have that, can we?"

"Something must be done, or the town will be in an uproar every weekend," replied the agent.

"I've always found that reasonable men, faced with their problems, will tend to act sensibly," said Charles.

"What about those who are not reasonable?" queried the ever- practical Lady Martin.

Charles smiled and thought for a long moment before he spoke again, "Let's see if we can get together representatives from both the collieries, the ironworks and the Balaklava works. I'm sure that Matthew Priestly would be happy to function as convener."

*****

The Reverend Mr Hodge continued to greet each of his parishioners as they left the church and then was about to depart himself, when he felt his arm gently tapped.

He turned to find a lady looking up at him. She was very much smaller than he and had such a wonderful, sunny-smile that his day immediately brightened.

"A very impressive first sermon, Mr Hodge," she congratulated, her voice having the velvety softness of honey on a summer day.

"Why thank-you, thank-you very kindly," returned Hodge.

"Far better than my nephew ever manages," she whispered conspiratorially.

The clergyman was at a loss and then it struck him, "You are the Reverend Lander's aunt?"

"I am Prudence Urquhart and though Mr Lander is my nephew, he is in fact, some years older than myself."

Hodge did the sums and concluded that the woman before him was in her early forties, though she didn't look a day over thirty, with perfect skin and eyes which had true depth, "Really?" was all he could find to say.

"In the absence of my nephew and dear Venetia, I am staying with Arabella and Mr Brass."

"Really."

"Yes, however, I wonder if I may ask a favour of you?"

"Of course, dear lady, anything I can do for you."

"I dabble in painting, being something of a water-colourist. However, I've left my sketch pad and some of the paints I require at the rectory. I wonder if I could call at some convenient time to collect them," she finished the sentence with a further smile and violet eyes that brooked no refusal.

"Of course, Miss Urquhart, would to-morrow morning suit?"

"I'm not an early riser, Mr Hodge, perhaps late afternoon?"

Hodge's face fell, for he'd planned to visit a few of his congregation who were old, infirm or sick. Then he glanced down at the face smiling up at him and his heart skipped a beat, "Of course, would four suit?"

"Perfectly, Mr Hodge."

*****

I saw the Deacon again yesterday, he put his eyes square on me. He's goin' t'hurt me, I know he is. He's plannin' t'hurt me bad," Mouse was just about to break into tears.

George Murphy gripped his friend by the shoulders, "Don't worry so much. You're safe here, with us," he comforted.

"They're letting him stay to set-up the shop he's got, they believe him and they don't believe us."

"That's because it's only *our* word against *his* and they think he's a real deacon," George shook his head at the unfairness of it all.

"One dark night he'll get me, I knaw he will," Mouse really was crying now.

"Then it looks like we'll have t'sort him out ourselves," determined Murphy.

"How are we going to do that? We're only lads.... Only lads," Mouse struggled to speak through his tears.

*****

A worried looking Mr Hodge opened the front door of the rectory to Miss Prudence Urquhart and was about to speak, but before he could she had slipped past him and into the hallway.

"Good afternoon, Mr Hodge, I'm so pleased you were able to accommodate me," her voice sang the words.

"I'm sorry, Miss Urquhart, but I…," he began.

"Oh, call me Prudence, please," she interrupted.

"I'm sorry, Prudence, the thing is…," he tried once more.

"May I presume to call you Geoffrey?" she cut him off yet again.

Mr Hodge looked as though he'd stuffed a cream cake into his mouth and was trying to speak through it.

Prudence put her head to one side and opened her eyes very wide, "Your name is *not* Geoffrey?"

The curate swallowed and nodded quickly, "Oh, yes, oh, dear me, yes it is. Only…"

Again his words were cut short, "My watercolours have been stolen away in the night perhaps?"

"Oh, no, I'm sure you'll find them wherever it is you left them," he speeded up his words, determined not to be interrupted again, "The fact is, there are no servants here. Mrs Lander dismissed them for the time she'll be away. I have no need of them, you see."

"Silly man, what difference does it make if we are alone here? I'll take a sherry if you're unable to brew a pot-of-tea."

"No, no, Prudence, it's the correctness of the thing. What will people say about a bachelor entertaining a single-lady without a chaperone? Especially as we have not been formally introduced."

"Are we not adults? Surely, I'm too old to require an escort, especially to the home of a clergyman," Hodge could see that Miss Urquhart was becoming irritated.

"Well.. Perhaps on this occasion... Please come into the drawing-room," he said before turning to open the relevant door.

As his back was turned, Prudence quietly and swiftly pushed the front door bolt into place before following him.

"Perhaps I should collect my sketch book whilst you pour the sherry?" She suggested.

"I'll make some tea," he replied, not willing to trust himself with both the heady-effects of alcohol *and* an attractive woman.

A few minutes later they sat opposite each other sipping tea and nibbling biscuits, Mr Hodge feeling very uncomfortable under the searching, gaze of Miss Urquhart's divine eyes.

"You seem ill at ease, Geoffrey." She commented.

"I must admit that rarely have I been left alone with a woman, apart from close relatives," he replied, his eyes checking for the nineteenth time that no other visitor was approaching the rectory.

Her voice dropped to a soft hush, "We are two adults sharing a pot-of-tea, how can anyone find fault with that?"

"Of course they *shouldn't*," Hodge forced himself to agree.

"How are you enjoying being in charge of Holy Innocents?" Prudence decided to change the subject.

Hodge's eyes lit up, "It suits me very well and I have hopes of finding a living of my own very soon."

"Is not the Reverend Mr Marshall very old?"

"Being vicar of Kirkby had taken up most of his life and he is loathe to leave it, but after all, he is eighty-nine next birthday."

"You believe the living will be yours when the inevitable happens?"

"I think so, for I'm on good terms with the Cathedral and I know Mr Marshall has often spoken well of me to the people who matter there."

They sat in silence for a while and then Prudence crossed the short space between them and placed her portfolio on his knees, "Perhaps you'd care to see my pictures. I'm sure a clergyman could do no other than give me a truly honest opinion of them."

"Yes, my pleasure," he replied before beginning to leaf through the watercolours.

Prudence sank gracefully to her knees beside him, her crinoline puffing out all around her and forming a frame for her perfect, heart-shaped face.

Hodge's pulse rate increased exponentially.

Prudence watched as he leafed through her paintings and commented on each picture as he came to it.

"Oh, this one is very, *very* fine," he cried.

She reached across and pointed to the head of a swan she had painted, "Do you see the way I have captured its gaze," she asked leaving her hand resting on his thigh.

The curate noticed how an extreme warmth was spreading from his thigh to his loins. He wondered if she would take it badly if he were to remove her hand, however, instead of taking any such action, he turned over another page.

"Oh, I do like this one. Of all of them it is my favourite," Prudence called, her hand tightening its grip.

"Yes… *Yes*….," he croaked, his voice had become very husky and he wondered if he was developing a cold.

As they worked their way through her sketches and pictures, Miss Urquhart boldly began to move her hand inch by inch towards his crotch.

Mr Hodge couldn't make up his mind what to do next. He knew that she should be sent packing, but he was feeling an urgent need that he couldn't, indeed had no wish to be rid of.

Then she began to run her fingers gently across the length of his penis which had grown to an unheard-of size, far too large for the tightness of his trousers.

"*Prudence*," he sighed, "*I can't…*"

"*Shh… my dear, Shush…,*" she soothed him.

"*But someone may call.*"

"I bolted the door, we're alone and I have you all to myself," her voice became sharply determined as she began to unfasten his britches.

"I've never," he tried to begin, but stopped as his cock was brought from its hiding place and found itself pulsating in the daylight.

"Close your eyes, my dear and think pleasant-thoughts," cooed Prudence.

Hodge did as he was told, the caressing of his member went on and on, his head began to toss from side to side and his voice wouldn't be still, coming out with sounds it had never made before.

"I think we're ready now, Geoffrey," he heard her say.

"*Oh, yes*, Prudence, I'm ready for *anything*."

Then, amazingly, his penis became even warmer as though it had been plunged into a pool of warm, half-set jelly and he could feel it being caressed by… *Was it her tongue?*

He glanced sharply downwards and couldn't believe that a lady such as Prudence most definitely was, *had* taken his member into her mouth and was appearing to enjoy doing so.

"Oh, Prudence, *Prudence...*," he finished with a succession of low-moans of a type he'd never previously emitted.

Then, as suddenly as it had begun, it stopped. His cock was aching for it to be completed, but Prudence had stood up and was looking at him her head to one side.

"Geoffrey, I believe it to be my turn now. I shall go to my room and undress. I shall be completely naked and waiting for you. Give me ten minutes.

He was about to speak, but before he could she had left the room and he could hear her dainty footfalls on the stairs.

Ten minutes later, Mr Hodge, his trousers pulled back into place and after checking that none of his parishioners were coming up the rectory-drive, climbed the stairs too.

The sight that met his eyes was one that he'd never seen before, nor had ever been able to properly imagine. Prudence lay stretched out on her bed, her hands folded behind her head, her breasts and pubic area in full view.

"Do you like what you see, Geoffrey?" She asked.

"Oh, yes. *Oh, yes.*"

"Then strip quickly and come and lie with me."

Throwing caution and his creed to the wind he did as he was asked and soon lay beside her, unsure of what to do next.

"I'm not a rag doll, Geoffrey, I'm a living, breathing woman who has needs that only a man can satisfy. You may touch me," she invited.

"*Oh, I..*," he stuttered then her hand took his and led it to the cleft at the bottom of her stomach.

"*Ohh....*"

"You may use your mouth on my breasts," she instructed further.

He set to with a will and found great joy in his ability to bring forth juiciness from her vagina, whilst her nipples became hard to his touch.

"Now is the time, I think, Geoffrey," she said softly.

Within a few seconds his very erect member had penetrated her and he found himself to be no longer a virgin.

Ten minutes later they lay quietly, with Prudence wondering if she could get him to perform again before she'd have to return to the Brass household.

Geoffrey Hodge felt happier and more relaxed than he ever had before and was sure that he was in love. Not the cold, abstract sort that he often preached about, but the hot, delicious human sort which until now had been a mystery to him.

"So, you believe it likely that you will soon be vicar of Kirkby?" asked Miss Urquhart.

"Yes," he replied huskily, his fingers still stroking the warm, unbelievably soft smoothness of her inner thighs.

"I suppose you have someone in mind for a wife?"

"Oh, no, there is no one."

"Do you not suppose that your candidature will suffer were you *not* to have a wife?" She asked.

Mr Hodge had often worried about his bachelorhood and the effect it might have on his ambitions, "I suppose it might be taken into consideration."

"I, myself, would very much like to be mistress of Kirkby Vicarage," she spoke boldly.

"A wife, I don't know that I could afford..," he began.

She cut him off, "I bring with me three hundred and fifty-six pounds a year," she said.

Hodge's eyes widened, "As much as that? And it goes with you should you marry?"

"It increases to five hundred and ten pounds per annum."

"Is this really so?"

"And were I to have a child, even at this late stage in my life, it would go up even further. Such a birth would also see the arrival of a lump sum of several hundred pounds."

"Good Heavens!" Hodge exclaimed softly, "Really?"

"Yes, really. You could read the first of our banns on Sunday coming."

"Yes, I could, but what would the Reverend Mr Lander have to say about that?"

"We're both old enough not to need his permission, don't you think?"

"I agree," Geoffrey Hodge nodded furiously.

"Anyway," said Prudence airily, "In God's eyes we're all ready man-and-wife."

"Yes, indeed we are," he said before kissing her and pushing his fingers into her sex opening.

Oh, good, Prudence thought to herself, he is able to rise again.

*****

George Murphy peeped around the corner towards the premises of the Christian Workers' Education League and saw the Deacon carefully lock the door before setting off towards the Martin Arms.

"He's goin' back t'the Arms ag'in," George couldn't keep the disappointment out of his voice.

"It's all he ever does," grumbled Mouse.

"We've watched him for a week an' he's never gone anywhere else," observed George.

"Are we goin' home? I'm tired and sick o' this."

"Hold on, Mouse, remember we *knaw* him and he'll be up to something, I've no doubt o' that," considered young Murphy slowly.

*****

Frank Turner turned to his wife, "The Reverend Hodge has delivered yet another intriguing sermon and see how full the church is."

Abigail bristled, "He has not the learning of my father and Hodge's degree is far inferior, you know."

Frank, who thought his father-in-law's sermons were often tediously long and unfathomable, replied, "Though, Hodge talks of love, friendship and caring, exactly as states the Christian message."

"*Love*," dismissed Abigail darkly, "there is no more to it than a will-o'-the-wisp."

They were interrupted by the Reverend Geoffrey Hodge who began to read the banns for that week.

"Miss Alice Turnbull, spinster of this parish, to Mr James Donald, bachelor of Tudhoe Colliery. This is the third time of reading."

"She's already five months gone," whispered Roberta Fisher to her brother.

Fisher's eyes widened, it seemed that no chance of fornication ever came his way, but he merely replied, "There is sin all around us in this godless town."

The curate coughed and then continued, *"Mrs Edwina Hutchinson, widow of this parish, to Mr David Deering, bachelor of Ferryhill. This is the second time of reading."*

"I'm pleased Mrs Hutchinson's found another husband," commented Lady Martin to her spouse.

"Yes, it's awful to be alone," Sir Charles Martin took the hand of his wife.

"Indeed, it is," whispered Caroline Schilling, who sat alongside them.

Charles placed his free hand over that of Caroline and squeezed it, "Not for ever, my dear. Without Helmuth we are all much lonelier."

"And his brother too," Marian supported her husband and her friend.

"Blanchwell is much less lively without Amelia," added Caroline.

There then followed a long, *long* silence and eventually the eyes of every member of the congregation became focused curiously on the curate, for he seemed to be choking and finding it a struggle to continue.

"Is he ill, d'ye suppose?" questioned Colonel Esprey.

"Looks like he's about to take a fit, he's gone very red in the face," returned Elizabeth Esprey.

Then Hodge coughed again and the church became expectantly silent, "Finally…," his eyes took on a far away look as though the congregation weren't there, "Finally, the marriage of Miss Prudence Urquhart, spinster of this parish to…. *To the Reverend Mr Geoffrey Hodge,* bachelor of Kirkby. This being the first time of reading."

"He can't marry Prudence, she's a ward of my father," Abigail was aghast and very loud.

"Prudence is old enough to do as she wishes, I like her; come to think of it, everyone likes her and I wish her much happiness. I couldn't be more pleased," Frank Turner took a solid, positive stand which brooked no disagreement.

"You *would* say that, Francis, you know so little of her past," replied Abigail in venomous tones, "Anyway, I shall soon put a stop to this little farce."

Frank took a powerful grip on his wife's arm, "*No you won't*, you'll do no such thing."

"Father must know… I'll…., Abigail squirmed.

Frank tightened his grip even further, his voice dropped to a threatening whisper, "Hear me well, you'll do *nothing.*"

"*You're hurting me,* had I known you'd become such a brute…."

"I'm less of a brute than you are a snob and come to think of it, who else would have put up with you for so long."

Colonel Esprey clapped his hands gently, "Excellent, I hate to see a bachelor vicar, makes them seem even less human than they are."

"It doesn't look or sound as though Abigail's very happy about it," nodded Eliza Esprey towards the Turner pew.

"Abigail's rarely happy about anything," observed the colonel.

The organ struck up as Hodge ended Sunday worship and began to climb down from the pulpit. He was pleased this test was over and all he had to do now was wait for the wrath of the Reverend Lander to descend upon him.

Then he gave thought to the dainty, sweet, *wanton* Prudence and found he didn't give a fig for the approbation of the Rector of Holy Innocent's.

Chapter Eight

"I'm concerned over how our rail-tracks are to be transported to the railhead, especially as there is a war going on," said Fred Schilling, shaking his head.

Thompson D. Widmark flung up his hands in exasperation, "Why, sir, it ain't as if you're expected to deliver the tracks t'morrow, is it?"

"No, but my brother is with the Union Army and he can see no end in sight, especially after Chancellorsville."

"These set-backs will come and go though numbers always triumph in the end, and we northerners got the numbers in barrel loads. Besides, look t'the west, why General Grant's doin' great things, making his way down the Mississippi like rolling thunder," Widmark tried to swing his guest back to the positive.

"That may be, but..," began Fred.

"We got 'Orleans," interrupted Widmark.

"As well as the war, I have other concerns. So far, I've only received vague reports and seen no plans or figures to speak of," Fred Schilling's tone expressed his doubts.

"Why, Mr Schilling, how many times must I say it? We *ain't* a railroad company and have never claimed t'be. We're a company of entrepreneurs, men of vision who will be ready to sell to the *actual* builders of the railroads everything they'll need and at very competitive prices too."

"Though who *are* these men of vision, I've yet to meet one?"

"There are many, you couldn't hope to meet them all."

"Exactly, I haven't met *any*."

"They spend their time, which is *valuable*, making investments or further developing their trading position.

One or two are men of great wealth, but in common they are all quick to recognise a good thing when they see it."

"So, they've put money in already? Enough to prepare for and secure the contracts from the railroad companies, if and when they come in?" Fred continued with his questions.

"Yes, of course, this company already holds millions of dollars in reserve."

"I haven't seen the company's books."

"Then you shall, I'll take you round to our accountants, a major city firm with a reputation which is beyond reproach. Why, sir, you ask around about *Everett, Willmott & Dougal*."

Fred nodded, feeling that if the accounts showed the *Great Western Supply Company* was solvent he would feel much happier."

"Mr Schilling, this whole scheme is a winner, let me remind you, once Martindale is supplying the goods, they'll be shipped up the Mississippi and Missouri rivers to Omaha. Where, by then, we'll have established a depot. From there the railroad builders will be able to draw what ever they need to link the continent from Atlantic to Pacific. It'll be cash and carry and besides which, what an engineering feat it will be."

"Is there to be a depot on the Pacific coast too?"

"Sacramento has been chosen for that and we'll have a base there. As soon as this damned war ends, we'll be in business."

"*Hmm*," thought Fred, before he asked slowly, "There is another thing on my mind."

"Whatever that may be, I'm sure I can set your mind at rest."

"How did you hear of the Martindale Iron & Coal Company in the first place? We're not exactly a huge concern, there are many much larger."

Widmark smiled broadly, "Why, that's easy to answer, we heard o' you from our London agents. They were tasked with providing us with a list of suitable companies – yours was one of 'em."

"Very well, if I am satisfied with your accounts and if the numbers add up, then I'll return to England with a positive outlook."

"Good, very good. When shall that be?"

"You aren't in any hurry, are you?"

"Heavens no, sir. Spend as much time as you wish, as you say the war isn't going to end much before next year and that's a fact."

"Amelia wishes to remain in New York for a little longer. Then we're to visit my sister and hopefully by brother, in Gettysburg, before sailing."

"Gettysburg?"

"It's a small town in Pennsylvania, nothing much ever happens there."

"Well you stay on at the Metropolitan Hotel at our expense for as long as you like and we'll open an account for Mrs Schilling at Bloomingdales. You ought to keep so a pretty lady happy, you know, it's what we husbands do."

Fred smiled broadly for he knew that his wife would very much like the idea of this.

"Theatre tickets too, leave those t'me, you'll see the best shows sitting in the best-seats."

Fred's grin became even broader, for he so liked to please Amelia.

"Oh, by the way, that request of yours for the remains of your sister-in-law's father, we may be able to help."

"I thought you had no survey parties out?"

"We don't, but we've got fellas working on the Omaha depot who could send somebody up along the Missouri to see what they can find. Then it'd be a simple job to ship the poor gentleman's remains back down to St. Louis and across to New York for the journey home. It's a Mr Moses Clapp that needs contacting, is it not?"

Fred smiled brightly, "Thank-you, sir, my sister-in-law, Caroline, will be delighted to have her father's remains returned to his ancestral home."

Widmark nodded gravely, "It'll be an honour, sir."

"Well then, perhaps we can go to the accountants at once?"

Widmark threw back his head as he laughed, "Why, what's the hurry, I'll need to let them know you're coming so they'll have the figures ready for you. Besides, you'll wish to speak to a senior accountant to talk you through the numbers. How about to-morrow afternoon – you can spend the morning shopping with that pretty little wife of yours."

"Yes, should I meet you here, at say one o'clock?"

"Tell you what Mr Schilling, I'll meet you and your lovely lady for lunch at the Metropolitan at Noon and we'll go on from there." Replied Widmark as he led Fred across the room and saw him out into the corridor.

Once his visitor had gone, Widmark leaned heavily against the door-frame, brushed a hand across his forehead and felt relieved.

At the opposite side of the office a further door opened and Sir James Hannibal Wright passed through it, "You managed him quite well, though he was rather more astute than I believed he could be."

"Fell for it hook, line and sinker, I'd say."

Wright shook his head, "I think there's a little more work to do before we can reel him in."

Widmark's face took on a puzzled look, "I still can't see why you're so set on ruining this Martindale, a town of no account as far as I can see. Seems a lot o' trouble to me."

"It's personal, to do with my daughter's ex-husband, who has crossed me too often. His town will be destroyed and that will be much harder for him to bear than his own ruination."

"That's as maybe, but it's a grudge that's cost you about five thousand dollars so far and there's the money gone into the dud company account – it ain't makin' a cent of interest."

"That shall be withdrawn once the deal is done."

Thompson Widmark had a sudden thought, "At least there's no need to send out lookin' for dead-man's bones."

Wright spoke sardonically, "Think it through, once the remains of poor Bellerby reach Blanchwell how far will that go to legitimising the Great Western Supply Company?"

"They'll believe it to be the genuine article," Widmark caught on at once.

"They shall indeed, the pathetic remains of a hopeless man will ensure the bait slips down so much the easier. Anyway, it's the least I can do for poor old Bellerby."

*****

Venetia Lander leaned back in her chair and gently closed her eyes, "*Ahh*," she breathed softly to herself. Here she was in *Firenze* with the Arno the throw of a stone away and surrounded by the gently rolling hills of Tuscany.

Venetia decided that life had never been better, as the warm sun caressed her features and seemed to make them come alive.

She had just enjoyed a further small but very strong Italian coffee, served to her by a handsome and attentive *cameriere* who addressed her as *Bella Signora*. She allowed the atmosphere to wash over her and sighed deeply and with great contentedness.

"Venetia, *Venetia*," she heard her husband calling and by the tone of his voice she knew that he was in some distress. She opened her eyes to see him crossing the square, his face red, his chest heaving heavily and waving what looked like a telegram.

"Oh, Venetia, disaster, *disaster* has overtaken us. We must pack for home."

"Sit down, Edwin and have a refreshing lemonade," said Venetia calmly.

"Oh, I can't sit, come, *come on*, we must pack immediately."

"The girls are well, I presume," a little edge of concern crept into Venetia's tone.

"How would I know," Edwin Lander shook his head violently, "It's nothing to do with the girls."

Venetia took her husband's arm and said, "If that's the case, then I'm not moving from here for any other reason."

"It's Prudence. We've been betrayed by Hodge, he's turned out to be a viper, a serpent of the lowest kind."

"He's murdered Prudence?" Venetia spoke lightly.

"No, *far* worse than that. Come, *come* back to the *pensione*, we must away."

"What could be worse than he killing her?" Venetia asked.

"Far worse, far worse, the villain plans to *marry* her!"

Venetia relaxed back into her chair and waved the waiter over and ordered a further coffee and a lemonade.

She silently thanked the Good Lord, for her world was now perfect, as someone else was willing to take responsibility for Aunt Prudence.

"I don't want lemonade, I want to go home," argued the Reverend Lander as he unwillingly took a seat beside his wife.

"We are *not* giving up our first ever holiday for the sake of preventing a marriage which we would be unable to prevent anyway. Presuming that both Prudence and Geoffrey are of age, which we know they are," Venetia's tone mirrored her determination.

Lander thought for a while, "Though what will people say?"

"Why should they say anything? What is there to say? The pair will be merely another couple entering into a state of matrimony – hardly news. Surely, no one can object or would wish to gossip about that."

"But Venetia...," he paused as he thought and then continued, "What about her three hundred a year?"

"It turned out that she controls this herself and though she has been very liberal, we will hardly miss it, especially as we still have Aunt Charlotte's Bounty."

"Oh, yes, I see," his eyes narrowed, "We haven't spent much of it, have we."

"Be calm Edwin, see across the square to the Basilica of Santa Croce, look at its fine architecture and once inside wonder at the marvellous frescos by Giotto. Sip your lemonade when it arrives, enjoy the sunshine and be delighted by what you see."

Edwin turned his eyes towards the church, "Very fine, mainly neo-Gothic, but Papist I'm afraid," he said, though now in much gentler tones.

Venetia shook her head, "Well, my dear, once all of us were of the Mother Church."

*****

"Oh, *do come* to bed," Amelia's tone was alluringly husky.

Fred Schilling turned from the letter he had just written and blew her a kiss, "Just a moment or two longer, my sweet," he promised.

"Do hurry, or you may find me deeply asleep and *impossible* to revive," his wife threatened.

Mr Schilling nodded and began to read quickly through the letter he had just written to Sir Charles Martin.

Metropolitan Hotel,
New York City,
25th May 1863

Sir Charles,

I have inspected the books of the Western Supply Company at the office of their accountant and it appears they have five million dollars lodged there.

The accountants themselves look solid, having extensive premises on Wall Street. The office was busy with many clerks at work, giving the impression it was not something set-up in order to fool a country boy such as myself.

On the face of it, the seeming solidity of the Western Supply Company inspires confidence, but I wonder how difficult it would be to close down their office, retrieve their funds and disappear?

I have been shown plans of depots which are currently under construction at Omaha and Sacramento. However, they have not proposed that I should travel to the Missouri to inspect the Omaha site. On paper, everything appears feasible and set to begin as soon as the current war is over.

However, I do wonder how the Western Supply Company is able to offer a contract to Martindale Iron & Coal when it hasn't yet won any contracts from the railway builders. Unless they are working hand-in-glove with the construction companies, which is not beyond the bounds of possibility.

Before Amelia and I move on, it is my intention to see what I can find out about the <u>actual</u> railroad builders.

President Lincoln brought two companies into Law last year, these being the Union Pacific and the Central Pacific Railroads. The first is to strike out west from Omaha, Nebraska, whilst the CPRR is to build east from Sacramento, California.

Do you suppose that either of these companies have ever even heard of the Western Supply Company? If they have not, I would suggest you do not proceed with any investment which relies on a contract from them.

If the Western Supply Company <u>is</u> fraudulent, what can they hope to gain by duping us? We shan't be handing any cash over to them, so on the face of it they can gain nothing. It's a puzzle, and one which doesn't reduce my suspicion of them an iota.

Amelia and I have been treated royally by our hosts and I can't decide whether this is just good old American hospitality or perhaps has a more sinister intention?

I intend to move on to Gettysburg, where hopefully we'll be able to meet up with Helmuth.

However, Amelia is determined to remain in New York (she so likes it here!) for another week or so first.

I will write again as soon as I have further information of any use.

Your Servant,

Fred Schilling.

PS

Mr Thompson Widmark has promised that connections of his will send a party out from Omaha in the hope of finding and recovering the remains of Mr Bellerby.

Whether this occurs or not may throw some light on the genuineness of the Western Supply Company.

Should you tell Caroline of this, then it would be best not to raise her hopes too high.

Fred yawned, cleaned the nib of his pen and put it aside, then his attention was drawn to his wife who was climbing from her bed.

"Oh, Fred, it's so *humid*," she whispered languidly.

Fred nodded, his eyes lighting up at the sight of Amelia raising her arms high above her head and stretching. Even though her nightgown was of a heavy linen material, her movements made it mobile and intriguing.

"Yes, yes, it is hot," he managed to stutter.

"Far *too hot* for this heavy nightwear, I think I'll have it *off*."

Fred's eyes widened.

"You don't mind do you?" Her eyes took on a coquettish look.

"No, not at all – I may do the same," he spoke rapidly and then began unfastening his shirt, but not taking his eyes from the figure of his wife at the same time.

Amelia raised the hem of her nightdress until it reached mid thigh and then she said innocently, "Are you *sure* you have finished with your correspondence?"

Fred's throat became very dry but he managed to squeak out, "Yes…"

"Oh, good, then I shall continue," smiled Amelia.

*****

"I'd much rather have reached Martindale in the dead of night, for, *As a dog returneth to his vomit, so a fool returneth to his folly,"* Roderick Villiers recited dolefully.

Solomon Vasey clapped his hands mockingly, "Thought *you* said that your welcome would be that of a returning hero and I'd get my money."

"You shall, dear boy, you shall. Though I'm finding this like the first-night of an indifferent play, you know how it is, stage fright. I'll be sparking again once the curtain goes up in the morning."

"Suppose the crowd turns nasty?" Asked Vasey.

"If there *is* a crowd," Villiers replied.

"Suppose there *is* and they start throwing things? I'm telling you now, I'm not getting out of this carriage until we're met either by cheers or complete silence."

Just then they came to a halt beside the well-lit main doors of the Martindale Civic Theatre.

Villiers took a cautious peep through the window and wasn't sure whether to be pleased or disappointed, for there wasn't a single-soul in sight.

"Why, not a man, woman, child or mangy dog to be seen. I thought you said you were popular," scoffed Vasey.

"It *is* quite late, anyway, let's go inside, I've a bottle stashed away which I hope is still where I left it."

Soon the thespians passed by the ticket office and were making their way into the auditorium where they were amazed to be met by a solid wall of cheering.

The two actors looked around in surprise, for the theatre was packed to overflowing and they were surrounded by a moving, rollicking sea of smiling faces where every hand was being used to clap a welcome.

"Well, you *are* popular after all. I'd never have believed it," Solly scratched his head.

Before Villiers could make a reply two burly colliers came from behind, took him in their arms and hoisted him on to their shoulders.

Immediately getting into the swing of things, Villiers raised both arms above his head in a triumphal salute to all those who had assembled to welcome him back.

A rip-roaring chorus of *For He's A Jolly Good Fellow* was sung as Roderick Villiers was returned in triumph to the stage of the Martindale Civic Theatre.

The singing continued for quite a while; the eyes of the actor glittering with teardrops, with him seemingly overcome by emotion.

Eventually, the cheering and singing eased away, the miners deposited the actor centre-stage and he opened his eyes to see Jane Turner ushering forward two young ladies who looked vaguely familiar to him.

"Mr Villiers, may I present two of the town's fairest maidens, who are great supporters of you and our theatre," introduced Jane.

"Why," began Villiers, his actor's memory coming to his rescue at the last second, "If my eyes do not deceive me, it is Miss Violet and Miss Milly."

The crowd roared with pleasure that he had recognised two of their own.

The girls swooned and nearly required the application of smelling salts, whilst, at the same time, the uproar continued.

"*Eee, 'ee's remembered them la*sses…"

"*Aye, and wi' all his troubles too*…."

"*God bless him for a gentleman*…"

"*I'm pleased he's back, it's not been the same here wi' him away*…."

These and many other positive comments caressed the ears of Villiers who's heart was pumping with both adrenalin and pleasure.

Abigail Turner sitting in the front row twisted her mouth at the sight of Villiers with the two pretty girls and wondered how she could reawaken his interest in *her*.

Mrs Jane Turner crossed the stage and brought Violet and Milly to stand one on either side of the actor.

"These girls have given up many hours of their time to support the public subscription, raised to clear your difficulties," she announced.

She was then interrupted by a storm of cheering.

Once this had passed, Jane continued, "so I feel it is only right that they should be the ones to present you with a draft, made out in your name, for two hundred and forty-four pounds, sixteen shillings and five pence farthing."

"Which miserable bugger put the farthing in?" Queried a collier from the back.

Again the house roared but became still again as the presentation was made.

Violet bobbed her head, "We're so pleased you've come back to us," she said.

"So, *so*, pleased," supported Milly as she joined with her companion to hand over the envelope which contained the draft.

Villiers took the proffered envelope, put it carefully into his pocket and then he elegantly kissed the hand of each of the Martindale maidens.

The girls blushed-red with pleasure and then rushed from the stage, giggling into their hands.

Jane Turner followed them once she had shaken hands with the actor.

"Good, I should get my money now and about time," muttered Solomon Vasey to himself.

Marcus Reno clapped heartily along with the rest, but in his heart he knew that whatever chance he'd had of playing the Prince of Denmark or any other leading part had now gone.

Jane Turner re-occupied her seat in the front row beside Elizabeth Esprey, she turned to her companion and said, "Well, this worked according to plan."

Elizabeth nodded, "It did indeed."

"Tell me, was Villiers really taken by bailiffs, or was he just avoiding Bobbity Fisher?" Jane asked.

"That would be telling," returned the colonel's lady with an enigmatic smile.

Roderick Villiers moved to the front of the stage and raised his arms high into the air, the theatre became silent and it was obvious to those watching that he could not prevent a flood of tears coursing down his cheeks.

Those teardrops look genuine even to me and I know him, thought Vasey to himself.

"He really is crying, you know," commented a surprised Elizabeth Esprey.

"Not acting then?" replied Jane Turner.

"Not this time."

Villiers sniffed loudly, blew his nose, wiped a final tear from his eyes and began to speak.

"Good folk of Martindale, as an actor of many years experience, I have been called upon to play parts too numerous to mention. On stage I can display any emotion, from high-temper to icy- contempt. On stage I am able to leap in a flash from a fiend in the foulest of moods to a loving and caring angel. In other words, when I am standing here; on stage, I am able to portray *any* character and *any* human emotion."

The actor paused, coughed and waited a long time before he began to speak again, though this time with a break in his voice, "However, to-night, every emotion I have expressed has been a *real* one, each springing from the very depths-of-my-heart. For now you no longer see an actor standing before you, but a mere human, with human frailties."

The crowd roared their pleasure and began to clap and chant.

"Who do we want?"
"Roddy!"
"Who do we really want?"
"Roddy.... Roddy.... Roddy."
"Who do really, really want?"
"OUR RODDY....."

Villiers again raised his hands, a wide smile creasing his classical features and tears running down his face.

The clapping and chanting slowly decreased until there was silence and every eye was focused on the lone figure on the stage.

"My mind has been fully occupied trying to put together words adequate enough to express my delight at what you have done for me," the actor began to speak quietly, but even so his words reached to the very rear of the auditorium.

Then his voice rose higher, "Releasing me from debtors prison as well as from the debt itself. However, this evening, I realised what I had planned to say was mere flummery, *flummery* suitable for a play, perhaps, but not for this, a golden moment in my life. I have realised all that is needed is to offer everyone of you my deepest and most heartfelt THANKS."

Pandemonium broke out again, the two colliers lifted the actor on to their shoulders again and insisted that he come with them to drink his health in every public house in the town.

*****

Fred and Amelia Schilling paused on their way to the Broadway entrance of the *Metropolitan Hotel* to visit the reception desk.

"Sir?" asked the clerk there.

"Please arrange to have this posted to-morrow, take care with it, for it's very important."

The clerk smiled, took the proffered envelope and read out the address; "*Sir Charles Martin, Bt, Martin Hall, Martindale, County Durham, England,*" he looked impressed, "a proper *Sir,* though what's the *Bt* for? Is it a medal?"

"No," explained Amelia, "it stands for *Baronet.* Meaning that Sir Charles is a member of the lowest-order of the English peerage."

"So, he's a lord?"

"No, not quite that, but if he continues to be a good boy, then no doubt his fairy-godmother will make him one at Christmas."

The clerk looked puzzled but placed the envelope in a bag which stood under his desk.

"It'll go to-morrow, sir, have no fear of that."

Fred nodded, "Thank-you," took his wife's arm and they proceeded on their way to the theatre.

Once they'd gone, the clerk surreptitiously removed the letter from the post bag and placed it in his inside-pocket. He was certain this was the letter that Mr Widmark was willing to pay twenty dollars for.

*****

Jacky Fisher looked up from his copy of the Chronicle as he heard a knock at the door.

Roberta half rose to her feet in anticipation, "Oh, I do hope it's Roddy. Do you suppose it is him?" Her voice was filled with a heady-mixture of hope, anxiety, joy and fear.

"It could be," replied her brother, doubtfully.

A short period of silence ensued before their housemaid entered, "Mister Villiers is here, sir."

"Show him in," ordered the schoolmaster.

Bobbity's ears strained to hear the tread of footsteps along the passageway which would be harbinger of; at last, the return of her fiancée.

Villiers entered the room and bowed his head, his face a moving tableau of expressions, he took Roberta's hand and kissed it.

When he spoke his voice was sonorous and full of feeling, "*My* love, *my* dearest, how can I express the sadness I feel for so long a parting. For many nights I lay awake in my place-of-confinement and wept… Yes, *wept* until I had not a single tear left"

Roberta couldn't restrain herself, she flung her arms around the actor's neck and pulled him into her not inconsiderable bosom, "Oh, my love, I always knew you would return to me."

Eventually, Villiers managed to release himself from her octopus like embrace, and held her at arms length, "My special one, how much weight you've lost," he observed.

"Oh, she has," agreed Fisher, "She has indeed."

"How perfect is your complexion, so smooth and pink," continued Fisher.

"Oh, her complexion glows," Fisher agreed again, "It's probably due to the amount of water which has flooded down her cheeks since your departure."

Roddy's eyes caught those of Roberta, "Then you have shed tears for me?"

"Yes, dear Roderick, I have, every day," sniffed Miss Fisher.

"Yes, she has, she cried and cried and *cried*. Some days I thought she'd never stop," informed the schoolmaster.

The actor heaved a deep sigh of compassion, "And to think, I was the source of such unbearable sadness."

Again, the tentacles of Bobbity's love reached out, took Villiers by the neck and pulled him close, "Though now you're home again and we're soon to be married."

"*Hurrah*, for that," cried an enthusiastic John Fisher, "I expect; as your brother-in-law, I shall be given decent parts to play in all your future productions. No more the second rat-catcher as I was in *The Coal Miner's Daughter*."

Villiers stifled a groan at the thought of marriage to Roberta *and* at the same time having her brother creating mayhem on his stage. It was to be impossible to bear.

Miss Fisher beamed, "Yes, we shall be so happy together."

"Roberta has become reconciled to living life in the theatre. Have you not, Bobbity?"

Again the arms of his fiancée encircled Villiers' neck and he felt wet kisses arrive on his cheek.

"Name the day of our wedding, sweetheart," Roberta positively crooned.

Villiers swallowed hard and managed to retrieve his upper body from the grip of his fiancée, "Oh, if only we could be together soon, my love...," he began and then found himself to be the subject of the most horrific stare he'd ever witnessed, he felt sure he was about to be turned into a slab of rock-salt.

"Why can we not be MARRIED NOW?" Roberta's voice reached its highest pitch and her words seemed to rebound from the ceiling and then reverberate around the room in a continuously rolling wave.

Villiers took an uneasy step backwards, his hands came together in supplication, "My love, our wedding would be to-morrow if I could have it so..."

Roberta's eyes narrowed suspiciously as she waited for an explanation, like a ravenous hunting tabby waiting beside a mouse-hole.

"The fact is, my love, I am still in debt. I cannot; in all conscience, take a bride until I am clear of it."

"Though you have money, the whole town raised more than enough," Miss Fisher's voice was seeking another crescendo.

Roderick Villiers stepped forward took his fiancée's hands in his and then kissed her on the lips as a sure way of preventing any further racket.

"*Oh, Roddy,* that's the first kiss you've given me," the Siren's voice became as soft as she'd ever been able to make it.

"Yes, my love, the first of many more to come. However, even though I do have the money, I have not yet cleared what I owe. Our married life must begin with a tally-sheet of virgin white," Villiers spoke quickly.

"This is reasonable enough, Bobbity," John Fisher supported the thespian, his mind full of the theatrical glory he might once more enjoy.

Roberta nodded slowly and then asked, her voice full of determination, "Very well, though you must set a date. Set a date NOW."

Villiers couldn't stop his head nodding, "Yes, yes, yes.... Let me see now... Sept..."

"Far too distant," Roberta stopped her fiancé in mid-speech, her voice full of steel.

"Mid July, I'll have the banns read," promised the actor, his mind full of turmoil.

"*Early* July," Bobbity would brook no delay.

"Yes, my dear, it will be as you say," Roderick Villiers knew when he was beaten.

"Perhaps a sherry, I have a drain somewhere," offered Jacky Fisher who was light-headed with relief, for his sister would soon be off his hands and as a married woman would no longer be able to teach at his school.

"Can you make it a large one," begged an almost delirious Villiers.

*****

"Need any clothes pegs or washin' done, sir?"

Frank was brought back from deeply unpleasant thoughts of his future life with Abigail, when he believed he recognised the voice. He looked around to see a thin figure of a woman huddled against a wall, her head downcast and her hands full of crudely made wooden pegs.

"*Rosemary Spence.* Rosemary, is it you?"

"Aye, it's me," she seemed to have difficulty focusing her eyes and then she said; not without a touch of warmness, "Why, it's Frank Turner... Sorry, sir, I meant, *Mister* Turner."

Frank was shocked, the Rosemary he remembered was a plump, clear-skinned girl who often giggled the day away. In fact, he'd once planned to marry her, but this was when he still had a farm to work.

"Will ye take a peg or two? Or I do good washing, my washing's as clean as a good scrubbing can make it," she pleaded.

Frank took both her hands and removed the pegs from them, "I'll buy them all, happily, I'll take them all. But what's happened to you? Are you not still at Cherry Tree?"

Rosemary shook her head, "It' all gone, Frank. Wright sold our farm after the Bellerbys left and the new owner had a tenant of his own in mind for it."

Wright again, thought Frank to himself before he asked, "What of your father and mother?"

"Both dead, eighteen months since, died within a week of each other."

"So where are you living?"

"Queen Anne Street, down near the gasworks, I share a room there."

Frank's face looked grim, the street in question was one of the first built by Wright's contractors. These houses had been thrown up in a hurry and later developed into the least salubrious part of town. He could only imagine the conditions his old neighbour and friend lived in.

"I'm all right there....," she began and then her voice betrayed her desperation, "Frank, can I have money for the pegs. I've got t'pay my share o' the rent the day."

"Aye, Rosie, I'll give you money for your pegs, as much as you need," he said slowly before continuing, "though first you must eat. Come on, we're away to Annie's Pie Shop and you shall have a good feed, which I can see you sorely need."

Rosie began to demur, but Frank would have none of it, taking her by the arm he led her to the High Street and a hot-meal.

"You did not marry?" Enquired Frank as he watched Rosemary devour the last crumbs of her pie.

"No, Frank, I turned one or two away, though. It weren't the same wi' them, and then, when we lost the farm nobody was interested."

Frank nodded slowly and his heart became full of sadness as he remembered the rosy cheeked, plump and happy girl of his youth.

"Everything went wrong at the same time," continued Rosemary as she sipped from a pot of tea, "what, wi' both parents gone, only a little money to hand and nowhere t'live."

"So, how do you manage, then?"

"I've done all I can do, sewin', mending, washin' an' sellin' pegs – which ye haven't paid me for yet."

Frank looked up sharply, "*Oh*," he began and then he saw the old, the familiar, Rosemary Spence grinning at him.

Frank closed his eyes as everything came back to him in a flood, warm summer days walking the ridge after church, Christmas visits to Cherry Tree Farm and the odd tumble in the hay. His hand reached across the table and took hers.

"Oh, Frank, ye may not be as handsome as y'were, but ye're still a fine, gentle man," tears came into her eyes.

"Abigail wouldn't say so," replied Frank, laughing gently.

"Then she doesn't recognise true-gold when she has it."

Frank laughed again, "Now that *is* far fetched."

Rosemary smiled, sat up straight and freed her hand from his, "Well, Ah must be away," she said.

"Must you?"

"Aye, I must, there's still some washin' t'be done, and I'll need to be finished before five- o'-clock."

"What happens then?" Asked Frank.

"If I canna' pay the rent I'll be locked out wi' nothin' t'my name."

"Then what will you do?" The answer which he knew was coming saddened him.

"There's only the workhouse at Oakland left," she spoke unemotionally but her eyes betrayed her desperation.

Frank took his friend's hands in his and looked around, catching the eye of Annie Cook.

"This is an old friend of mine, Rosemary Spence," he introduced as Annie approached.

"Nice t'meet ye. If you're a friend o' Frank's ye're a friend o' mine."

Rosemary nodded and smiled shyly.

"I've a favour to ask," began the agent.

Annie eased her bulk on to the form to sit beside Rosemary, "Aye, if I can help, I will, ye knaw that."

"There's nobody in the room upstairs, since the Keoghs left, is there?" Frank pointed a finger at the ceiling as he spoke.

"That's right."

"Can Rosemary have it?"

"Aye, but there's no proper bed an' there's a lot of stores up there now."

"Though Rosemary could squeeze in, you think? If not it's the workhouse for her," Frank's voice was as serious as he could make it.

"I hate t'see anyone forced t'take that particular road."

"Upstairs would be all right for a week or two, though, d'ye think?"

"Aye, maybe a bit longer if she can stand the crush."

"Oh, I couldn't. It's too much to ask," interrupted Rosemary Spence, her face turning pink.

"Why yes you can, why ever should you not," said Frank.

"No, I can't stay, I've only coppers for rent," Rosie shook her head vehemently and began to rise to her feet.

"I'll pay the rent," put in Frank quickly.

Rosemary's face became determined, "I'll not be a kept woman, Frank Turner, I'll not allow m'self to sink to them depths."

Annie took Rosie's arm and brought her back on to her seat, "No need t'be so proud, 'cos I could do wi' a tenant, at least for a week or two."

Rosemary settled herself down and waited for Annie to continue.

"Frank's a partner here, wi my husband; Geordie an' my son," she couldn't help pausing and smiling as she spoke of George, "So what we say here goes."

"And what do you say?" Enquired Frank.

"I say that Miss Spence helps me out in the bakery an' the shop."

"So I won't have t'pay rent?"

"No, yer work will cover the rent and some left over, but it can only be for a few weeks. We need the space, y'see."

"Hold on Annie..," began Frank strongly.

"Calm yersel' Frank," Rosemary interceded, "That's the best offer I've had since you asked for my hand all those years ago."

Frank moved his gaze to that of his long-lost sweetheart, "Will this really suit you, Rosie?"

"Suit me, Oh aye, it'll suit me fine," she almost cried, "But I don't know if I'll be able to get my belongings back from the landlord."

"Oh yes you will, I'll come with you and my size as well as the grim state of my face works wonders when I go seeking anything," Frank spoke knowingly.

"Aye, an' what his face can't accomplish, my own right arm can," added Annie.

"I'm quite lookin' forward to this meeting now," laughed Rosemary.

*****

Thomas Leakey ate alone every evening in the small-dining room at the *Martin Arms*, where he was usually the only diner. This suited him as he did not wish to become too well-known in the town.

It appeared to him his plan was running to schedule and it wouldn't be long before Dunnett learned what it was to cross the Deacon.

Leakey shivered and closed his eyes as he remembered how he had been pressed hard across warden's desk by the gamekeeper. How he had been humiliated in front of those dregs of society, Mitchin and Cruikshank. Then he recalled the solid strokes coming down on his vulnerable posterior.

"*One... Two... Three*," Leakey counted in a hoarse whisper.

"You all right, sir," enquired his waiter, surprised by the strange tone of his only customer's voice and puzzled by the expression of sublime pleasure crossing his face.

Leakey shook himself and pulled himself upright, "Yes, yes of course I am. Why shouldn't I be?"

"Sorry, sir, I thought you were takin' a turn."

"A turn? A man counts to himself and he is believed to be taking a *turn*."

The waiter nodded, "Sorry, sir," he apologised before shuffling off to the kitchen no longer expecting a tip.

The fact was, as Leakey knew too well, that he *had* taken a turn. He had been whisked back to Doctor MacGregor's school-room where the slightest mistake was punished with several strokes of the birch.

He was sure it was there that he become fascinated by the receipt and application of corporal punishment. He had to admit that; over the years, it had become such an addiction that he rarely thought of anything else.

Of course, it had been so easy for someone of his ilk and calling to indulge in his passion. Every parent was ready to believe it did their children good to be thrashed on a regular basis, and he had never minded delivering what was required of him.

Enjoyable thoughts of the past continued to run through his mind for several minutes and then he snapped out of his reverie.

"Best check on Dunnett," he said to himself as he looked at his pocket watch.

He got up from his table and made his way half-way down the stairs, from where a good view of the bar area was available and as he expected, Dunnett had been exactly on time.

"A man with a timetable," mused Leakey, "how useful is that."

*****

"Ma'am, I fear there's a mouse in the Master's dressing-room," from the tone of her voice it was obvious that the housemaid had a mortal fear of small rodents.

"Oh really, then set a trap," Abigail brushed away her servant's concerns airily and continued to read *Framley Parsonage*.

"But, Mrs Turner, there's papers."

Abigail stifled a yawn, "What can papers possibly have to do with a mouse? Surely, it's not reading them," she smiled to herself.

"We moved the wardrobe t'see if there was a hole in the skirtin' an' a big envelope dropped out."

"Of the closet?" Abigail was becoming interested.

"No, ma'am, it was stuck *behind* it."

"Bring the envelope. Set traps for the mouse. Put the furniture back in its proper place," ordered Abigail rapidly, before she returned to the concern Lady Lufton had for her errant son.

Five minutes later, Abigail was about to jump from her chair to go and complain about the banging-and-bumping sounds coming from above her head when the maid re-entered the room. She was carrying a large, oilskin covered package tied with sealing-waxed knots.

"Good heavens," she muttered before biting her tongue as she had intended to show no surprise at all.

"Here it is, ma'am."

"Just put it beside me, on the table," Mrs Turner struggled to keep her tone one of indifference.

"Yes, ma'am," said the maid, doing as she had been instructed.

"Do *not* mention this to the master," ordered Abigail coldly before she sent the serving-girl on her way.

Once the room was clear and she was certain the door had been securely shut, she turned the package over several times to find there was no address on the cover and indeed, there was no writing on it at all.

"To whom could this belong?" She asked herself as she weighed the package in her hands. "It must have something to do with, Francis," again, she pondered to herself. "Though why has he hidden it away?"

Her hand reached out for her sewing basket and brought out the scissors there.

"Dare I open it?" She asked herself as her fingers beat a rapid tattoo on its lid.

Abigail found herself in something a quandary, for were she to cut the seals it was unlikely she'd able to disguise it.

"If I *do* open it and it contains nothing of interest, I should find myself very awkwardly placed," she thought for a second and continued, "Perhaps I could I blame the maid.*"*

Then she was overcome by so strong a wave of curiosity that the sensible, sane side of her was thrust aside and she withdrew the scissors from the basket.

"This *must* be an important package to Francis and so, as his wife, I've a perfect right to know what is it he needs to hide."

It was the work of a few moments for the scissors to open the envelope and twenty minutes later Abigail's jaw-dropped.

*****

"What happened next, Mrs Nicholson?" Asked Drina Martin.

"The Queen arrived at Tilbury mounted on a white horse and wearing armour."

"Armour!" exclaimed Guido Turner, "but she can't have been, *girls* don't wear armour."

"A woman she may have been, but nonetheless, she wore a breastplate and then made an amazing speech," continued the teacher.

Bertie Martin half-closed his eyes, for he wasn't too keen on speeches.

"The Queen's voice rang clear and confident, cutting through the noise and confusion of her army's camp."

"What did she say," asked Adele Turner eagerly.

Sarah Nicholson took a deep breath and began to recite, *"I know I have the body of a weak and feeble woman, but I have the heart and stomach of a king, and of a King of England too; and think foul scorn that Parma or Spain or any prince of Europe, should dare to invade the borders of my Realm."*

"*Huraah*," cried Robert Martin, who wasn't too sure whether he was doing the right thing or not.

"I've an idea," put in the teacher once the class had settled down again, "Perhaps we could devise a *tableaux*."

"What's a *tableaux*?" asked Bertie Martin.

"It depicts a scene from history, or from a famous work of art or literature."

"I shall be Queen Elizabeth," proclaimed Drina, looking around daring anyone to deny her the principle-role.

"You'd make a fine queen, my dear, but we must choose someone who is able to sound positively regal and very self-assured," Sarah looked around the class, wondering who could fulfil such a demanding role.

"I know I have the body of a weak and feeble woman, but I have the heart and stomach of a king, and of a King of England too..."

It was as though Good Queen Bess herself had returned to the Martindale Hall school room and had already won the hearts and minds of her assembled army.

Who had spoken those words so perfectly? Sarah was amazed, she couldn't make it out. She scanned the faces before her and realised that they were all looking at Maud Turner.

"Was that you, Maud?"

"Yes, Mrs Nicholson," the child's voice was as soft, subdued and shy as ever and there was no sign of Elizabeth the Great to found in it.

"Are you sure it was you? Mrs Nicholson looked sharply at the other faces, "Are you all playing a trick on me?"

"No, Mrs Nicholson, it was Maud," confirmed Jonathan Turnbull.

"Yes, she's good at voices," put in Martin Cowley.

"Maud often makes us laugh when she mimics *yours*," giggled Drina before slapping her hand across her own mouth.

"She's sounds exactly like you," added Guido Turner.

Sarah laughed with the children, for she was delighted that the shyest, most withdrawn child among her charges had handed her teacher the key to unlocking her talent. She clapped her hands in delight, "Excellent, a *tableaux* we shall have and Maud Turner will be transformed into the *Faerie Queene* herself."

*****

"Well, Mitchin, I see you managed to reach Durham without difficulty."

"Yes, Deacon, we came on the train."

"I'm amazed you didn't try to walk here."

"Aye, I am too," put in Losser who wished he was at the asylum, rubbish though he now understood it was.

"The others will arrive next week, as arranged?"

"Yes, sir, Wednesday, we're to meet them at the station."

"Good, then Dunnett shall be dealt with first."

"He's a big lad, mind, an' then there's the other one, the little one wi' the big punch," Grubby Mitchin rubbed his chin and sounded doubtful.

"I never saw them, but I hear they're hard men," put in Losser uneasily.

"*Pah*, what have you to fear? There will be at least four of you," the Deacon's tone was scathing.

"Aye, but he'll be armed – he's a gamekeeper isn't he?" Again Mitchin's tone expressed his doubts.

"I have observed his arrival on a dozen occasions and he sometimes arrives at the *Martin Arms* unarmed, especially on Saturdays."

"Aye, but, *that* night he might….," began Losser.

Leakey forced his voice into a tone of sweet-reasonableness, "It will be *easy*, I've kept my eyes open and know that Dunnett stays at home most nights, though he *always* visits the Martin Arms on Saturdays. He leaves the saloon bar there; often unsteady on his feet and returns to his cottage in the woods. So, on Saturday next you shall be waiting for him. You shall have formed an ambuscade, seize and thoroughly beat him."

"I'm not killin' no one, mind" put in Losser who was still far from sure.

"Me neither, I've been wi' you a long time but….," Mitchin began his explanation.

"I'm not asking that you murder him, I just want a few of his bones breaking so that he'll never forget who it is he has crossed," Leakey spoke in a threatening whisper.

The Deacon's companions nodded slowly in time with each other, "Well it all sounds simple enough," said Mitchin.

"Aye, I suppose I don't mind doin' that," agreed Losser, though he was determined to take to his heels if anything went even slightly wrong.

"Good, shall we say Saturday coming then?"

*****

"Am I to be paid or not, Villiers? Come on, out with it," Vasey was tired of his companion's evasiveness.

"My dear boy, of course you shall."

"Well where is the money? I know you have it, you've hundreds now, so come on, stump up."

Villiers sighed, "You may remember that I wasn't handed notes or even coinage, I was given a draft, a bankers-draft. I can't tear a part of that off and pass it to you, can I?"

"Cash the blessed thing and pay me what you owe."

Villiers sighed deeply before he began to explain the simple facts of financial life to his companion, "I'd have visit Durham, and even then hard cash wouldn't immediately be forthcoming. I would be persuaded to open an account and to do that references would be required."

"Who'd be daft enough to sign for you?"

"*Exactly* dear boy, you hit the nail directly on the head."

"So, you've money but can't access it."

"Eventually, in a week or three I'll be able to pay you what I owe."

Vasey groaned, "The quicker I'm able to disappear back to London the better I'll be pleased."

"Oh, Solly, you're so short sighted I despair of you."

"Short sighted?"

"Yes, can you not see the golden opportunity which has opened before your very eyes?"

"Golden opportunity," repeated a perplexed Solomon Vasey.

"Martindale, the theatre of which I am the director. Thousands of workers and their families seeking entertainment…"

"Martindale's a dump, there's nothing here but noise, smoke, stink and *very* rough people."

"During my incarceration….," began Villiers.

"You were *never* actually incarcerated," Vasey pointed out.

Villiers sighed deeply, "All right, whilst I was away I read Mr Dumas' most interesting novel *The Corsican*

Brothers and came to the conclusion that it would make a fine play."

"Starring you, of course."

"You miss the point, *Brothers*, my dear Solly the story concerns *brothers*. Can you not see it, *two* leading roles, each equal, one brother good the other evil."

"Won't Monsieur Dumas be annoyed should you steal his story?"

"How will he ever hear of it? Anyway, I shall move the setting from Corsica to the Scottish Borderlands – a far more dangerous place, from what I hear."

Vasey began to nod slowly, indicating to Villiers that his companion was just about hooked.

"I even have a title, it'll be called *The Riever Brothers*."

"So," began Solly, "we play the brothers?"

"Precisely,"

"You promise equal billing?"

Roddy clapped his colleague's shoulder, "Of course and we'll have Lizzie playing a duchess or some such and there's a young chap, Marcus Reno, who I'll have to find a suitable part for, as I promised him he'd be our Hamlet."

Solomon laughed loudly, "He didn't fall for that old chestnut, surely. If you're in charge no one else is going to have so much as a sniff at the greatest part in all of Shakespeare."

"With the possible exception of Lear," Roddy mused.

"Or perhaps the Moor of Venice," added Vasey.

"Yes, but then the Bard could conjure up great characters in the winking of an eye," sighed Villiers.

"So, then, you wish me to stay on here?" Queried Vasey after a short silence in remembrance of the Swan of Avon.

"Absolutely."

"Do I still get my money?"

"Certainly."

"Though, when, Roddy, when?"

"As soon as I have some hard cash, my dear boy. You have my word of honour on that."

Vasey shrugged his shoulders, "And I wonder what that's worth in pounds, shillings and pence."

*****

"I'm really looking forward to this," said Marian Martin to her husband.

"Mrs Nicholson has certainly worked wonders with the children, fancy, some of them as young as three years, taking part in a tableaux," he replied.

"She had them make their own costumes, you know."

"Really."

"Made their own costumes too."

Charles was both surprised and delighted.

"They had so much fun, Drina even managed to make a ruff!"

"A ruff!" Exclaimed the baronet, "this gets better and better."

"Bertie's playing King Philip II of Spain."

"That's strange, Philip only met the Virgin Queen once and this was when she was the young Princess Elizabeth," even Charles Martin could be pedantic at times.

"I believe Bertie's role is to sit at a desk in a corner scribbling away and appearing to be in a huge huff."

"Oh, I understand now."

Then they were interrupted by the beating of a drum and the sounding of a tinny trumpet.

"I cannot see why Mrs Nicholson; the wife of a collier, should have been offered so important a post," Abigail Turner was put out.

"*Hmm*," Frank ignored his wife, his eyes being firmly fixed on the temporary curtain which was posing awkward questions to those who were trying to raise it.

"I suppose not much else can be expected from *Lady* Martin who was once the wife of a common miner," Abigail carried on, the strength of her hostility making her forget the lady in question was the sister of her husband.

"You'll say no more, Abigail, not another word."

Abigail seethed though kept her tongue still. However, she thought she had found a way to regain her position of power over her husband, and *then* she'd no longer be so easily silenced.

Doctor Cowley was very pleased that he had been spared the expense of sending his son to a day-school and from what he'd seen and heard great progress had been made and at little cost to himself.

"They're starting, please pay attention, dear," whispered Mrs Cowley, "Martin will question us endlessly once the performance is over."

"I'm so nervous for Adele I can hardly breathe," admitted Richard, who's eyes had never left the stage.

"Sir Francis Drake will look after her, never fear," replied Jane.

"I'd entrust Adele to Drake, but I'm not so sure about Guido."

Jane laughed before saying, "Sarah Nicholson has also found a place for young Julia Schilling and the child can just about walk and talk, she is indeed a gem of a teacher."

The room became hushed as the children came on to the stage in their home-made Sixteenth Century finery and took up their positions.

A further fanfare from the shrill trumpet sounded and the drums began to roll again.

From the wings a wooden horse; upon which was mounted Her Majesty Queen Elizabeth the First of England, appeared.

Her soldiers roared their approval (joined by the audience) whilst Philip II jumped to his feet, threw down his pen, upset his inkwell and roared *"Pah, My armada will grind her into the dust."*

"Boo, Boo, and Boo," howled the assembled tableaux (joined by the audience).

Then the clear, strong-voice of Maud Turner cut through the hub-bub and stilled it. She visibly drew breath and launched into the famous Tilbury speech of August, 1588.

Frank Turner could feel tears coming into his eyes, for he was sure that he'd never heard anything so pure, clean and beautiful, especially from, his *own* daughter, a little girl who'd always seemed to pathetically shy.

Abigail gazed stonily at the stage, her mind full of Roderick Villiers.

"Even you must be pleased with our daughter," Frank suggested to his wife.

Abigail sniffed, "And what good will play-acting ever do for her," she commented.

"It's done all right for Villiers," replied Frank pointedly.

Abigail felt it would be wiser to say no more.

"I see that Bertie merely played himself," Charles Martin laughed.

"Yes, he did, didn't he," returned Marian, "though he's very good in that role."

"Drina looked in a huff," commented the baronet.

"She didn't feel the role of a lady-in-waiting suited her."

"She's right about that, I should think."

The tableaux came to an end, the children cleared the stage with huge applause and many cheers from the audience. Then, after a struggle, the curtain was forced to come back down.

"Sir Charles, ladies and gentlemen," announced Martin Cowley, refreshments have been set-out in the dining room, and for the members of the cast there is jelly and custard in the nursery."

Sarah Nicholson was very pleased with the children in her care and carefully sought each one out to congratulate them.

Chapter Nine

Thomas Leakey, hearing a muffled knock at the door of the Christian Workers' League, looked to see if his visitor; Eddy Dobson, was both asleep and so befuddled with whisky that he was aware of nothing. This done he went to let in his visitors.

"Deacon," greeted Mitchin as he entered, followed by Peter Twiss, Losser, Cutter and Carver.

"Who's that in the back," asked Losser nervously, glancing through into the rear-parlour.

"No one of any interest to you."

"What if he wakes up an' sees us? He'd be a witness," Mitchin was worried.

"He's had much more drink than he is capable of taking, forget him, he knows nothing and shall remember nothing."

"There's so much as can go wrong," Losser wished he had no part in this conspiracy. Dunnett had never done him any harm and he didn't like the idea of risking his neck over some scheme of revenge initiated by the Deacon, who he was sure was more than half-deranged.

Leakey was about to answer hotly, then decided that coolness was required, "Your job is a simple one, it's to be carried-out quickly and then you may flee back to Durham to enjoy a drink or two and await my further instructions."

"I'm, lookin' forward t'some action," Twiss spoke, he being the only member of the party exhibiting any eagerness, "I haven't used my fists or boots in an age."

"Aye, sir," replied Mitchin, though with no willingness.

"Yes," put in Cutter and Carver as #one.

"I suppose so," muttered Losser.

"Good, then let us run over the plan once more."

*****

Frank Turner left the track that led to the ford and entered the drive of the Old Hall at Byers Green. He could see that his brother's home was still well-lit, so he dismounted and approached the front door.

A minute or two later he was led into the drawing-room and had refreshments set before him a short time after that.

"Nice to see you, Frank, our paths haven't crossed for a week or two," said Richard.

"How is Abigail, well I trust," Jane brought herself to ask after the woman she liked least in all of Martindale, if not in the whole of County Durham.

Frank nodded, "She's as well as she ever is."

Jane noted the lack of enthusiasm in her brother-in-law's tone and wasn't surprised, for she was sure that Abigail would have tried the patience of Job.

Frank coughed and his face took on a tinge of pinkness, "I've come to ask a favour of you, Richard."

"Anything, Frank, you know that."

"Do you remember Rosemary Spence?"

Richard thought for a while and then said, "Why, yes, Rosie from Cherry Tree Farm. Nice lass, always was, she taught me how to milk a cow."

"That's her," put in Frank quickly before a flood reminiscences could begin, "She's fallen on hard times."

Jane pricked up her ears, she always ready to hear of the misfortunes of the less well-off in society.

"Oh, I'm sorry to hear that. Then, I presume you've come here on her behalf."

"Aye, it turns out that when Wright took Blanchwell from Mr Bellerby, he sold off Cherry Tree. The buyer wanted his own man in and so the Spences were thrown out."

"Disgraceful," cried Jane, "I suppose the Spence family had been tenants of the Bellerbys for years, too."

"They had that, farmers there for decades if not centuries," informed Richard.

"Same as the Turners, but without the luck," added Frank, who shook his head sadly and then continued, "Anyway, both Mister and Mrs Spence died a year and a half ago, leaving Rosemary with nothing. She's on the streets, selling clothe-pegs, taking in washing and doing any cleaning and mending jobs she can get."

"I'm very sorry to hear this," put in Richard.

"Worse still, Rosie can't afford a decent place to live, so she shares a room in Queen Anne Street, but can't even earn enough to pay her rent there."

"She's to be evicted, I suppose," snorted Jane, annoyed at the very thought of it.

"Indeed so, if nothing can be done it'll be the workhouse for her."

Jane jumped to her feet and called for her hat and coat to be brought, "I'll visit Miss Spence and pay her rent for the rest of the year."

"No, *no*, Jane, Rosie is in a place of safety at the moment."

Jane slumped back into her chair, "Oh, this is such a relief."

"Where is she?" asked Richard.

"She's helping Annie Cook out at the pie shop, living in the upstairs storeroom."

"Why that'll not be a lot better than Queen Anne Street," said Jane who looked just about ready to leap to the rescue again.

"The room will only be available for a week or two more, anyway," Frank told it as it was.

"Then she must have money to see her through until she can find a position which suits her," said Jane.

"She won't take charity. I've tried," informed Frank.

"I see," said Jane slowly, her admiration for the troubled Miss Spence growing.

"So, the favour you've asked for has to do with Rosie?" Queried Richard, hoping to get to the point of the tale.

"Yes," Frank stopped short, he wasn't sure how to go on, but eventually he did, "Do you think Mrs Schilling would be willing to find Rosemary somewhere to live on the Blanchwell estate?"

"Why don't you ask her yourself?" Asked Richard immediately, he being aware of the emotional ramifications of visiting Caroline.

"You should visit Caroline, Richard," said Jane through pursed lips.

Frank observed clearly the body language on display and realised that he had inflamed an unhealed wound.

"It would be better if Jane were to go, Caroline's one of the Coven," returned Richard quickly.

"Look, it was never my intention to cause trouble and no doubt I'll find something for Rosemary myself in a day or two," Frank reached for his hat.

"The only person in trouble is Miss Spence and if Richard can help, he will do so. Won't you Richard," Jane's voice brooked no argument.

Frank breathed a sigh of relief, "Mrs Schilling may need a milkmaid, Rosie was always good at that."

Richard smiled, "Yes, she could get quarts more out of a cow than anyone else I know."

Frank smiled and looked at his brother and sister-in-law in turn, "Then one of you will see what can be done?"

"Yes, Richard will go to Blanchwell tomorrow," said Jane with determination.

"But," began Richard and then realised that this was yet another test he had to be seen to pass, "All right, I'll call at Blanchwell in the morning."

*****

Roddy Villiers and Solly Vasey made their way unwillingly to the residence of Mr John Fisher.

"Is it really necessary that I accompany you?" Queried Vasey.

"*Sweet Vasey, moving through his clouded heaven With the moon's beauty and the moon's soft pace, I call him Brother, Englishman, and Friend,*" misquoted Villiers in reply.

Before Solly could reply the front door opened and Jacky Fisher appeared, "*Ah*, brother-in-law," he greeted.

"Bring them straight into the dining-room, John, for I see they are some five minutes late," Bobbity much preferred her guests to be punctual.

Fisher bundled his visitors inside as quickly as he could and opened the door to the dining room for them.

"Not so much as a sherry to greet us," muttered Vasey to his companion.

"Don't expect any wine, either," warned Villiers.

"No wine?"

"Be thankful for that. Any wine Fisher may pour will be execrable," whispered the actor-manager.

"I've onion soup to begin," informed Roberta once they'd sat down.

"*Ah,* French onion soup, now that would set anyone up," Vasey was enthusiastic at the thought, especially were crusty French bread to be served with it.

"*French* onion soup! The very idea, sir, the very idea of it. I'll have nothing *French* in my house," Bobbity was strident.

"We only have English onion soup here," smiled Fisher.

The meal was eaten with very little to be said about it, on top of which the portions were small.

"As this is a special moment in our relationship," Roberta smiled at her brother, "John has purchased port-wine for us and I have decided to break with convention and take a glass with you gentlemen."

Both actors groaned inwardly.

The port was passed from hand to hand, though it soon became evident that it had not been decanted.

"*Ah*, an excellent vintage, do you not think?" John Fisher enjoyed one of the few alcoholic drinks he'd had since the arrival of his sister.

Villiers felt that the back of his throat was on fire, nodded and replied hoarsely, "I can't say I've ever tasted *anything* like it."

"Yes," agreed, Vasey thinking that the port reminded him of a cough-linctus his mother had forced down his throat many years previously.

"Will you not miss teaching?" Enquired Vasey of Miss Fisher, he filling a long silence as the port made its fiery way down his gullet.

"Yes, surely all the girls will be distraught at your leaving," added Villiers, who then winked knowingly at his fellow actor.

"Heavens, yes," Bobbity paused for a moment, "I thought I'd found my true vocation at the National School."

"Yes, she did, indeed so," supported Fisher, smiling to himself in a self-satisfied way.

"Will you not miss teaching, when you marry?" Queried Vasey, following the plan they had hatched on their way to the Fishers.

Miss Fisher's face became very seriously set, "I suppose so," she turned to her brother, "you will find it hard to cope without me to support you."

Jacky Fisher nearly choked on his port, for the last thing he wanted was his sister assisting him for years to come, "*Yes... No....,*" he spluttered.

"*Yes! No!* What ever can you mean?" Roberta voice hardened.

"Oh, *yes*, my dear, definitely *yes*."

"To think, what your pupils will miss once you have deserted them," Vasey's head shook from side to side sadly.

"*Indeed yes*," Bobbity's voice was as close to a whisper as she'd ever managed before.

"But, Roberta, think of your new life, your *married* life with your true-love, Mr Roderick Villiers," the teacher raised his glass in salute.

All eyes were now on the actor-manager, "I cannot feel other than shame that I am to be instrumental in removing, my darling, my first and only love, from her vocation and *duty*."

"Yes, *duty* must come before pleasure and romance," put in Vasey, sagely.

Bobbity's eyes narrowed, she looked hard at each of the men in turn, "Roderick, are you trying to wriggle away from your promise to me?"

"Heavens, no," replied Villiers quickly.

"He thinks of nothing other than marriage and a happy home life," supported Vasey, for the woman who sat opposite him appeared to be a dangerous sort.

"School will have to manage without you," said a relieved Jacky Fisher, as he poured more port.

"To the happy couple," Vasey proposed a toast.

"To Miss Roberta Fisher," Roddy offered another libation.

This port's not too bad once a glass or two of it has been drunk, thought *Vasey, in other words it's the complete opposite of the blushing bride to be.*

*****

Richard Turner entered Blanchwell feeling extremely nervous. He was no stranger to the house having visited several times accompanied by Jane. However, he doubted he could complete his mission regarding Rosemary Spence without his blood- overheating at sight of Caroline.

"The mistress will see you now, sir. She's in the drawing room," the butler spoke politely.

"I know the way, thank-you," Richard dismissed the servant and then soon found himself standing next to Mrs Schilling.

"Richard, how nice to see you," Caroline greeted him warmly though her eyes remained cool.

"And you too, Caroline."

"Have you come on *Chronicle* business or is this a social call?"

"Mission of mercy, really," replied Richard.

"Oh, then please speak of it."

"I'm sure you remember the Spences of Cherry Tree Farm."

"Of course I do. I was very sad to hear that Wright had sold their farm off."

"Aye," considered Dick, "Did you know that the Spences were evicted and both Mister Spence and his wife died eighteen months ago?"

Both of Caroline's hands went to her cheeks, "Oh, dear me, no. They were such a nice family and excellent tenants too. Though what of their daughter… Rosemary? How does she fare."

"Badly, I'm afraid."

"This is shocking news, my father would have been distraught had he been alive to hear it."

"He would that, for he always kept his tenants at the forefront of his mind," mused Richard.

Then Caroline remembered her manners, "Oh, how remiss of me, please, Richard, sit down and I'll have tea brought. Are you hungry, would you care for lunch?"

Richard was already forming the word *no* in his throat when he changed his mind, "Yes, that would be very welcome."

They ate in the conservatory and had enjoyed asparagus soup followed by boiled ham with a crisp salad when Caroline asked, "Now, apart from Rosemary Spence, why have you come?"

"Honestly, I came only about Rosemary, Frank asked me to and Jane insisted that I should be the one to visit you."

"Really, why didn't she come herself?"

Richard shrugged his shoulders, "I've no idea," he lied and then continued, "Frank is able to help Rosemary for a short while, but she will soon need another place to live."

"Yes, I can see that."

"Well, you probably don't know it, but in the old days Frank was quite soft on Rosie, he was going to marry her until we lost our farm."

"Really."

"Aye, well, he still feels for her and wants her settled."

"Somewhere on the Blanchwell estate?" Caroline caught on quickly.

"Yes, he thought Rosemary might help out with milking when needed, but he's willing to pay any rent you may care to set."

"The gatehouse that stands on the Croxdale road might do, but it is rather cramped."

"She's by herself so size doesn't matter and it's bound to be better than any room available on Queen Anne Street."

"The cottage I have in mind will be filthy and possibly damp, it not having been occupied for a year or two," Caroline mused chiefly to herself.

"I can't think of anyone more capable of making it sparkle than Rosemary Spence," said Richard.

"I'll pay her for odd-jobs around Home Farm and in the kitchens here when we've guests," offered Caroline, after only a moment's thought.

"This would be splendid, but don't mention the rent is being paid by Frank, for Rosie's won't like the idea of being a kept woman."

"What decent woman would," commented Caroline.

They were enjoying coffee when Richard looked across the table straight into the eyes of the Mistress of Blanchwell and discovered once again their depth and warmth. Was this directed towards him or just the effect of a good lunch on a summer day? He asked himself.

Caroline's eyes held his gaze firmly and she favoured him with a sweet, sunny smile.

"Do you ever think of us? The way we were?" Queried Richard, her smile and warmness encouraging him.

"Sometimes," she replied honestly.

"If I'd had more courage, do you wonder how different our lives would have been?"

"When I was in America, you mean?"

"Yes, but even before then."

"If you had been braver, you would then have cast-off much of your honour," Caroline formed her words carefully.

"Do you still love me?" There, thought Richard, I've let the genie out of the flask. What a damn fool I am.

Caroline breathed deeply and Richard thought that she was about to order him from the house.

"I'm sorry," he apologised, "I should never have asked that."

"*No*, you shouldn't, you are attempting to gain access to an area of my heart which should be best left alone."

"I'm sorry," he repeated himself.

Caroline got up from the table and began pacing the length of the conservatory, her fingers brushing various hot-house plants as she passed by them.

Richard didn't know what to do, at first he thought to leave, but then the devil in him made him get up and follow in Caroline's footsteps.

She abruptly turned to face him, her expression uncertain and troubled.

He couldn't help taking her in his arms and kissing her hard, passionately and for a long time.

Caroline was taken by surprise and for a brief second she thought of pulling away, but then her heart won out and she returned his kisses one-for-one.

Once their lips had broken free, Caroline slumped into a nearby chair and held her head in her hands.

Richard cursed himself roundly for taking; once again, this forbidden, though well-worn, path.

"Sorry... Caroline, I'm sorry... This doesn't make it easier for either of us," Richard felt miserable.

"I'm as much at fault as yourself, I should never have invited you to take lunch."

"What now, Caroline perhaps...," his words trailed off.

"Yes, Richard, indeed here we are again. Yourself with two children and Jane at home and myself with a husband *away at war*."

"I'd best go," his words came out flatly.

"Perhaps you should."

"Will it always be like this between us?" Caroline asked.

Richard thought for a while, "I suppose so, it may be different once we each have reached ninety or so years."

She laughed, "As bad as that?"

"'Fraid so."

*****

"Did you see Caroline?" Asked Jane Turner as her husband entered the *Chronicle* office.

"Yes," said Richard shortly.

Jane immediately knew that her worse fears had been realised. Her husband, the father of her children had succumbed to the charm and beauty of Mrs Schilling. However, she managed to keep her voice steady, "Had she accommodation for Miss Spence?"

"Yes, there's a gate-keeper's cottage she can have."

"Good," replied Jane before she buried herself deep into her accounts.

Richard knew that his expression, tone of voice and overall demeanour had announced to his wife that he had not been faithful to her."

"There's really nothing between Caroline and myself now, you know," he spoke softly.

"Though I am sure there *is*," Jane looked up briefly from her work.

"We're just friends, close-friends who became closer when she faced difficulties she was so ill prepared for."

"So, I've nothing to fear? My children have nothing to fear?" Jane's voice rose and almost cracked as she completed her sentences.

"No, nothing. I would *never* leave you and Caroline would *never* desert her husband."

"Suppose Helmuth does not return from war? What then?"

Richard found himself to be at loss for words.

Jane struggled with herself for a moment before she stood up, threw down her pen and cried, "I'm going out."

"I'll come with you," Richard was desperate to put things right, though had no idea how he might manage it.

She shook her head negatively, "No. Leave me be."

"But..," he began and then her expression silenced him.

"I don't *need* you, I've never *needed* you," Jane spoke as harshly as she could, though knew that her words held no truth in them.

*****

When Richard had left Blanchwell, Caroline cursed herself roundly. Why had she allowed him to kiss her? Why had she returned his kisses so easily? Why had she allowed herself to *enjoy* his kisses?

Pacing the length of the conservatory, she stopped to pull off the head of a fuchsia in temper and frustration.

She had only just made up her mind that Helmuth really *was* her true love and had relegated Richard to be the object of a distant, unfulfilled romance.

Though yet, it had taken the briefest of moments for her to end-up in his arms.

"This is too complicated, too annoying," she muttered harshly to herself, "I may as well have allowed Richard to carry me off to bed, to get it over and done with, for I couldn't have done much more damage had I succumbed to my desires."

Then she remembered the tingling of every nerve in her body when Richard had held her close and kissed her.

"How on earth am I going to resolve this," she cried, "Indeed, can it be resolved?" This was something over which she had grave doubts.

*****

Richard tried hard to work but could not concentrate and then he decided to go looking for his wife.

Just then the office door opened and Jane appeared.

He rushed to her and held her close, "Oh, Jane, I can't tell you how sorry I am."

At first she resisted him, but eventually succumbed to the comfort of his arms and relaxed.

"Where have you been for so long?" He asked.

"Just walking and thinking."

"You have no need to fear, my love. Though Caroline and I have had a close relationship in many ways, I have never…," Richard gulped.

"Taken her to bed," his wife finished for him.

"No, I swear that we've never been intimate in that way."

Jane looked into his eyes and saw he was telling the truth, "I believe you."

Richard began to breathe more easily, "I've hurt you."

"Yes, because you're not completely mine, nor ever have been."

"Men are often foolish."

"They are indeed, even when they've so much to lose," said Jane.

"You wish me to go? I would understand if you did."

Jane smiled, she knew Richard held their relationship dear and if that were the case she was happy to let it continue in the hope that his desire for Caroline would dwindle with the passing of time.

"Of course, what should I do without you," she replied

Again, Richard held his wife close and kissed her tenderly.

Jane basked in his affection though begged Lady Fortune to allow Helmuth Schilling to return home in one piece.

*****

George Murphy peeped around the corner of the passageway which led to the rear premises of the Christian Workers' League and saw that its lamps were still lit. "They're still in there," he informed his companion.

"Is Michin and Losser wi' him," Mouse's voice quivered with fear.

"Grubby's there, and about another three, though there's no sign o' Losser."

"He'll be in there, he's sure t'be," Mouse shivered at the thought.

"What can they be up to?" Wondered Murphy, more or less to himself.

"Nothin' good. Let's get away afore they see us," begged Mouse.

George thought for a moment, "If we could only hear what they're sayin'."

"Well, we cannot so let's go."

"I'm goin t'see if I can get into the back-yard, you know from the court opposite where the print works used to be, I might get to hear somethin' from there," Murphy came to a risky decision.

"*No!*" exclaimed a shocked and frightened Mouse, "*No*, Oh please, George, don't go."

"Calm yersel' bonnie lad," you keep watch from here and if anythin' goes wrong, get Geordie, or better still, Geordie *and* Jack Nicholson."

Mouse was about to argue further but found his friend had slipped away,

Then he caught sight of his friend climbing the wall at the rear of Dougie Brass's old shop.

Breathing heavily, George let himself down into the pitch blackness of the yard. He felt his way forward until he came to the back door, the sneck of which he tried but found it to be locked and bolted.

Pushing his ear to the window he could make out voices, though only just.

"You understand your instructions?" it was the distinctive voice of the Deacon.

George heard a number of mumbled assents.

"As usual, Dunnett is drinking at the Martin Arms and by the time he leaves for his cottage, you shall be waiting for him. You know what you're to do then?"

Again, the question was answered in the affirmative by a number of voices.

Having gleaned as much information as his shredded nerves could bear, George climbed back on to the wall as quietly as he could, his mind full of how best to counter the Deacon's scheme against the game-keeper.

After a quick glance to check that he hadn't been spotted, he dropped back into the lane and ran to rejoin Mouse.

However, his friend was nowhere to be seen.

George began a search of the nearby streets, though of Mouse there was no sign and so he eventually decided that the youn lad's nerve had broken.

Murphy was about to return home himself and raise the alarm, but then he considered again, for Joe Dunnett had to be warned of the danger he faced. By the time he went for help the gamekeeper could have been set-upon by four or five of the Deacon's bullies.

"I'd best warn him," he muttered before going off at a run.

*****

"Look what I've found," gloated Peter Twiss, dragging Mouse in by the scruff of the neck, "spying on us, he was."

"Well, *well*, young Mouse back into the bosom of your family I see. You must be pleased to see all your old-friends are here," the Deacon smiled.

"*Ye're not my friends, ye never were…,*" his words trailed off as he saw the expression of menace appear on the Deacon's face.

"An ungrateful, wretch, is he not, gentlemen?"

Mitchen and the rest nodded their assent.

Mouse trembled, "I've done nothin'. Let me go, just leave me alone."

"*Leave you alone?* The very idea is abhorrent. Why should you be allowed to desert your place-of-safety? The institution which cared for you, brought you up."

"Ye never even bothered to name me," Mouse broke into the Deacon's diatribe.

"He's been fed too well," Grubby Mitchin put in his opinion.

"Indeed, too many tasty pies have come his way," agreed Twiss.

"Aye," Cutter and Carver spoke in tandem.

Thomas Leakey reached forward and pinched Mouse's flesh in several places, "Yes, I can see you've put on quite some weight, you are very well rounded now. I must say I like what I see."

Peter Twiss stuck his face close into Mouse's and poked him in the stomach, "I remember you, you're a little squealer, you squeak like a pig, come on then, *oink, oink.*"

"Don't touch me, *please*. Please, let me go, I've done no harm," begged Mouse who didn't like the glint in Twiss's eyes.

"*Let you go?* Why, my dear boy, we would be remiss in our duty were we to allow you to leave," said the Deacon.

Twiss joined in the general laughter that followed and in doing so Mouse felt a slackening of the grip on his neck.

He kicked backwards and caught his tormentor on the shin, then lunging forward he broke-free and made for the door.

However, this was a forlorn hope as there were too many bodies blocking his way, and in a short while still; kicking and screaming, Mouse was flung to the floor where he was pummelled and booted for what seemed like hours.

"Silence, all of you, SILENCE," Leakey's command was instantly obeyed.

Every member of the gang looked towards Eddy Dobson who; they were relieved to see, continued to slumber peacefully.

"Should we gi' him a bit more, Deacon?" Asked Cutter in a whisper.

"No, you have other business to-night, so get about it."

Twiss nudged the sobbing Mouse with the toe of his boot, "What about him?"

The Deacon considered for a second and then ordered, "Bring him to me, upstairs. What a charming trio we shall make."

"We'll be a man down now," complained Losser.

"Twiss will trail Dunnett from the Martin Arms," the Deacon consulted his pocket watch, "so he will be only half an hour behind you."

A gloomy quartet shuffled towards the front-door, none of them happy with the task they'd been set.

Leakey held back Twiss as he dragged Mouse towards the staircase, "Afterwards you're to see to this boy in the woods," the Deacon nodded knowingly as he spoke.

"Yes, sir, I understand what's in your mind."

*****

A breathless George Murphy arrived at the Martin Arms and rushed inside, looking frantically around for the gamekeeper. "Joe Dunnett... Is Joe here?" He shouted at the barkeep.

"Gone fifteen-minutes ago, " the barman shook his head in a puzzled kind of way, "He only had the one pint the night. Not like him, not like him at all."

"Aye, he was in his best stuff too," Marcus Reno looked up from his game of dominoes.

"Didn't have his gun neither, I always put it behind the bar for him," mused the barkeep to no one in particular.

"Where's he gone?" Asked George.

"How would I knaw," replied the bar tender who then added, "Ye wouldn't have a pie on ye, I suppose."

"The shop sold the last of them at five o'clock," George shook his head and made for the exit.

Once outside he couldn't make up his mind what to do. Should he try to catch up with Dunnett and warn him of the danger he was in? Or would it be wiser to go home and get help? After a few seconds thought he decided on the first option.

*****

"Well, Susan, I'd best be off before we start tongues wagging," Joe Dunnett smiled warmly at the widowed Mrs Russell.

"Why, Joe, ye've just come and, anyway, who's goin' t'see you down here in the woods?"

He kissed her and pulled her close.

Susan Russell let out a gasp of pleasure once her lips had been released, "By you're so gentle for a big man, you make me feel so warm and..., I don't know, ...*wanted*."

"You're special t'me, Susan an' I believe it's time we enjoyed somethin' more permanent. D'ye not think?"

Susan flung her arms around his neck and was sure that she'd never been so happy since young Billy was killed.

"I reckon that's a *yes*."

"Yes. Oh, aye."

"Then I'll visit Sir Charles to-morrow to see if he approves."

A look of doubt crossed her face, "Will he not think it's too soon. Ye know, after…," tears tried to form in the corners of her eyes.

Again he comforted her, "No, it's the right-time and Sir Charles will have nothin' but congratulations for us."

"I'm a chapel-goer, mind."

"Makes no difference t'me," smiled Joe as he prepared to leave the cottage.

"Don't forget yer shotgun," she took the weapon from the corner where it stood and handed it to him.

Joe shook his head, "I never go out in these woods wi' out it, especially at night," he smiled as he hefted the weapon beneath his left arm.

*****

"He's not comin' I tell ye, we've missed him," Losser just wished to be clear of the dreadful, dark wood he found himself in.

"What'll we tell the Deacon," moaned a worried Carver.

"That we've missed him, what else can we say," put in Cutter.

"Can we even find our own way out of here?" Queried a doubtful Mitchin.

"You shy buggers, I don't how the Deacon puts up with you," condemned Peter Twiss.

"It's a'right for you…," began Losser and then he didn't like the way Twiss was moving towards him and decided to shut-up.

"What a set of frightened old women I've to put up with. I've told you, Dunnett's coming, he's just stopped off to see his lady love," informed Twiss, before continuing, "No doubt he'll give her a good humping and then he'll be along."

Mouse, who had a hood pulled over his head, hoped that the confusion his captors were in might lead to a chance of escape for him.

"If only he'd come an' we could get it over with," said Cutter.

"Aye, if only he'd come," parroted Carver.

"I just want away out o' these woods," moaned Losser.

Peter Twiss, leaned easily back against a tree and nodded at their captive, "Don't forget, he's still to be seen to."

"That's your job, nowt t'do wi' me," replied Losser quickly.

"Aye, I want nowt t'do wi' that little bugger either," grumped Mitchin.

Just then the gang heard a cheery whistling, seemingly quite close, and so took the opportunity to slip into the undergrowth beside the path, thus setting their ambush.

Twiss sat heavily on Mouse, knocking the breath from him, "Keep quiet if you know what's good for you," he growled.

*****

George Murphy entered the Martin Estate following the path through the woods which he knew led to Joe Dunnett's cottage. The night was quiet with not a breath of wind and the wood was as black as a cloudy night could make it.

Better take my time, thought Murphy as he struggled along a route he hardly knew.

However, he found it difficult to keep to the narrow path and often blundered off it and into quagmires or thick undergrowth. After this he became disorientated and it took him some time to find his way.

In addition, the wood was far from quiet, with rustling and scurrying going on all around him.

At one point he jumped nervously and stood stock when something large blundered through a nearby thicket. Every nerve in body remained stretched close to breaking-point until he realised that he'd merely had an encounter with a wild creature of the night.

Then, from not too far away, George heard voices and began to creep cautiously forward, a short step at a time, his eyes straining into the darkness.

At any moment he was expecting to hear his enemies approaching and glanced continually from side to side preparing to take any cover which was close to hand.

Then the voices became shouts and screams which, in their turn, were drowned out by the long, reverberating boom of a shotgun going off.

"I hope Joe's got the lot," cried Murphy as he dived to the ground and scrambled his way under a bush, his face and hands receiving multiple scratches and scrapes as he went.

Then there was silence. Such a complete silence that George thought it to be the worst period of all, for in his mind's eye, his enemies were creeping up on him from all sides and were about to pounce.

However, little by little the wood recovered from its shock and the nocturnal birds and creatures emerged to continue their natural business.

Feeling braver; though only just, Murphy crept from beneath his sheltering hawthorn and began to feel his way along the path one footstep at a time.

After about twenty yards he felt, rather than saw that he was in a small clearing.

He got to his feet and while looking about him, he tripped and fell over a, soft object which lay directly in his way.

After landing on the ground he rolled over-and-over again until he lay on his back looking towards the tree-tops.

Breathing heavily, he lay still, but found that he could not stop his teeth from chattering.

Then, through the branches above him, he saw the clouds were thinning and the light of the moon was making a long, thin, puddle in them.

George realised he couldn't remain where he was forever and clambered on to his hands and knees and crawled his way back towards whatever it was which had tripped him up.

"Please, God, let it *not* be a body," he prayed to himself.

This appeal to his Maker failed, for it soon became obvious that a body lay before him. He forced himself to come nearer to the shape, which he was sure was lifeless.

George knelt beside the dim form and allowed his hands to tentatively begin an exploration. The fingers of his right hand soon became very wet and sticky and he knew it was because of the blood which covered them.

His stomach revolted, he retched and spewed bile. Coughed and then retched and spewed again.

"Whose blood could it be?" Murphy asked himself once his stomach had settled again.

Just then the moon broke completely through the clouds and a beam of its light lit up the small clearing. As his eyes focused to accommodate the increased illumination, he was able recognise the body as being that of young Mouse.

George flung his head back and howled. Then he howled some more, he couldn't stop howling. He no longer cared, nor was he afraid of Losser, Mitchin, the Deacon or any of them. They could come and kill him ten times over if they wished, for his life was worthless to him now.

"*IT's ALL MY FAULT,*" he screamed, repeating the phrase several times.

Eventually, exhausted he slumped down and rested his back against a tree-trunk, unstoppable tears coursing down his cheeks.

Then he heard a series of groans nearby.

"*Ohh..., Gh..., Awh...*"

George got to his feet and only a few yards on he came upon Joseph Dunnett, who'd pulled himself into a sitting position and was holding his head in his hands.

"Joe is that you, Joe," asked Murphy.

"Aye, 'tis me."

"What's happened t'ye?"

"I was goin' home when summat hit me, knocked me senseless," the gamekeeper brought a hand to his temple and rubbed it gently.

"Did you know that Mouse...," George's voice broke, "Mouse," he tried again, "Is lying *dead*, just down the path there."

Despite the knock he'd taken to his head and the soreness he felt in his ribs, Dunnett got to his feet and went to check for himself.

George came up behind the gamekeeper, "I tripped ower him," he sobbed.

"Aye, well ye would in the dark," said the gamekeeper pulling a box of matches from his pocket and lighting one, bringing the flame close to the body of young Mouse.

"Looks like a gunshot wound," began Joe Dunnett and then the import of this fact hit him and he continued quickly, "Where's me gun?"

They both looked around and George eventually came across the 'keeper's shotgun lying under a bush.

"Oh, hell, *Oh, hell*" the desperate words of Dunnett were repeated again and again until they became a mantra.

"You didn't do it, Joe. Ye couldn't have."

"I don't knaw what I did nor what I didn't do," the gamekeeper shook his head violently as he spoke.

George took his companion's arm, "Take my word, there's no blame in this for you. *All* of it is mine to bear for the rest o' my life."

*****

An uncertain looking Losser was awaiting the train which would take him back to the familiar surroundings of the New Church Asylum. His face was ashen and drawn, whilst those of his companions; apart from that of Twiss, looked to be in no better shape.

"Pleased t'be away from here," said Cutter almost in a whisper.

"Aye, I've seen things I'd rather not have seen," Carver's comments were barely audible.

"Shut up, both of you," ordered Peter Twiss, his voice low and vicious, "do you want us to be taken? Remember, you're all in this as deeply as me."

"Why, I wasn't expecting what happened," Mitchin spoke with desperation in his voice.

"Aye, me neither," Cutter backed his companion up, "And I'm takin' no blame for Mouse, mind."

"It was Twiss," said Carver, looking for agreement from the others, "he used the gun."

"Yes, and I'll use it again on any of you who's planning to play the Judas," Twiss's tone was threatening.

"I don' know that we should go back t'the Asylum," Losser mumbled more to himself than to the others.

"Aye, ye're right there, but where'd we go, we've nowhere," said Carver morosely.

"Why don't we get a train to Sunderland instead an' see if we can get to sea," suggested Cutter.

"That'd be as bad as goin' back t'the asylum," put in Losser.

"I'm too old for the sea," added Mitchin, who began to massage his aching knee-caps.

"Just as well, because you're *all* coming back with me," Twiss made it plain that it would be unwise to disobey him.

In the distance they heard the whistle of a locomotive and as one they shuffled to the edge of the platform, each of them looking along the track to the north.

As the train chuffed closer, Losser's mind became full of the murder of Mouse. The screams of the little boy mixed in with the thunder of the approaching train to create a symphony which he had no desire to listen to.

The train stopped and they began to board. Losser watched them all into a carriage before he shouted, "I'm *not* goin' back."

Mitchin called loudly, "Why, what else could ye do, at least there's a bed and food back where we come from."

As the train picked up speed, Twiss thrust his head out of the window, "Keep yer mouth shut. Or else I'll...," he shouted, though his words were soon lost in the noise and slipstream of the train

Losser shook his head violently and shouted, "I'm away t'be free," before he ran back down the platform and mingled with the crowd waiting to pass by the ticket collector.

*****

Virgil Kent, unasked, took Cissy Jackson's chest and led her up to the servants' quarters.

"Her ladyship's seem nice children," he commented.

"Oh, they are."

"They've both got the look of their mother, d'ye not think?"

"I suppose they do."

"Mind, her ladyship is something of a tartar, I wouldn't like to cross her," continued the footman.

Cissy made a non-committal noise and became determined to say nothing that could be carried back to the Marchioness of Studland.

They arrived at what was to be the nursemaid's room, Kent opened the door and placed her luggage at the bottom of the single bed.

Though the room was small, it had a window which let in the afternoon sun, giving it a warm glow.

"This is nice," commented Miss Jackson.

"I saw to that," said Kent, "the butler was going to put you in a pokey attic-room, but I told him you were more of an honoured guest than a servant."

"That was good of ye," commented Cissy, warming a little towards the tall footman.

"Aye, well that's what the marchioness ordered."

"Really, she said that about me," Cissy was very surprised.

"Yes, and ye'll be eating with the governess."

"Fancy that," Cissy was amazed at this rise in her status, especially in so large and impressive a house which swarmed with servants.

"Yes, and if you need anything and I mean *anything*," just ask for me, Gil Kent."

*****

"Had you heard that Mr. Dunnett's been arrested for the murder of that unfortunate child the Cooks took in?" Asked Jane Turner of her husband.

Richard shook his head in disbelief, "Joe would never murder anyone, he's as straight as they come, I should know, I came up against him once."

"Well, he was found next to the body and with his shotgun nearby, which had been recently discharged."

"It *must* have been an accident, Joe Dunnett wouldn't kill a child."

Jane thought for a while, pursing her lips, before she said, "Perhaps not, but the best he can expect is the charge of murder being reduced to manslaughter."

"George Murphy is sure that it has something to do with that Leakey fellow, who has been behind the unrest in the town lately."

Jane considered for a moment and then laughed, "I must say I don't like the look of him and if he's a true Christian then I'm a rabid reactionary."

"And that you're certainly not," returned Richard.

"I suggest we make it our business to look into the career of the Reverend Thomas Leakey," suggested Jane.

"A sound idea, my dear," agreed Richard, "especially if such an investigation were to clear Joe Dunnett of any crime."

Chapter Ten

"*Ah*, Cissy," smiled the Marchioness of Studland as the nanny entered the drawing room.

Cissy bobbed and inclined her head, "Your ladyship," her voice was little more than a whisper.

Elysia came closer and her expression showed deep concern, "Why, what has happened to your cheek? You have such a nasty scar."

"It was a knife as did it, m'lady," Cissy's chin fell to her chest and her words were virtually inaudible.

"A knife, at Martin Hall, surely not. Was there a disagreement with the cook or one of the other servants?"

"No, your ladyship, it was a man who I'd let in t'the house..," Cissy couldn't stop herself from sobbing, "he did this t'me, but worse. Much worse, he stabbed Joe Dunnett and killed young Billy Russell."

Elysia placed a comforting arm around the nursemaid's shoulders, "There, there, my dear. All wounds heal eventually, do not take on so, I'm sure none of it was your fault."

"But it was," blurted Cissy.

The marchioness led the nursemaid to a chair and had her sit down, "Be calm, have a good cry, then blow your nose and wipe away your tears. This is what I do when I'm upset."

The nanny couldn't quite grasp this, for the Elysia Martin she had known had never spoke pleasantly to *any* of the servants, nor had she asked after them nor cared about them in anyway whatsoever.

"I know how unhappy you must be, for I have been unhappy myself. When I resided at Martin Hall, I was very young, inexperienced and immature. I did not know how a great house should be run and how important it is that the servants *see* the mistress as someone who cares for them and watches over them," Elysia thought she knew what was going through the nanny's mind and her words dripped compassion.

"Thank-you, my lady," Cissy couldn't believe that this was her old mistress, the *Tartar of Martin Hall.*

"Are the servants here kind to you?" Continued Elysia, gently brushing an unruly lock of hair away from Cissy's forehead.

"They are, my lady, Mr Kent is most helpful."

"Oh, Kent, yes he's a good man. I suggest you rely on him at all times."

"I will your ladyship."

"He's a handsome young fellow-my-lad too, is he not," Elysia spoke lightly.

Cissy smiled, nodded and then hung her head.

"Good, then I shall allow you to accompany him and the children this afternoon when they go riding."

"Riding? Sir Charles don't allow them anyways near a horse," Cissy became rather disconcerted.

"This is only because he frequently falls out of the saddle himself. Don't worry, though, Bertie and Drina won't be allowed to tumble from their mounts, Kent will see to that."

Though Cissy felt uneasy about allowing the children in her care to go riding, there didn't appear to be any way to prevent it, so she nodded and dipped into a curtsey before leaving the room.

*****

Annie Cook gently shook the shoulder of her surrogate son, George Murphy, "Haway, lad, have somethin' to eat, ye've had next t'nowt for days so ye must be hungry," she spoke softly.

George pulled his pillows over his head and buried his face deep within them, "I'm not, I'll never eat again," not even the muffled sound of his words could reduce the amount of pain in them.

Annie pulled the bed covers from him and spoke with greater authority, "Come on, George, you knaw ye don't mean that."

Murphy groaned and flung himself upwards until the top half of his body was stiffly erect, his eyes were blood-red, contrasting vividly with the ashen shade of his complexion, *"IT WAS ALL MY FAULT,"* he shouted, seemingly in agony.

"*Shush*, boy, *shush*, ye can't take the blame for poor Mouse," Annie comforted as best she could, throwing her arms around his shoulders.

"But 'tis, all my fault. I should never have left him. He was hopeless by himself. *Hopeless.*"

"Though you weren't t'know what would happen."

"He told me not leave him, begged me not to, but I ignored him, an' went anyway," George's head dropped to his chest and his tears began again, streams of them coursing down his cheeks.

"Aye, all of that's true and it's somethin' ye'll never forget. But were ye the one what pulled the trigger?"

George didn't answer.

Annie took his shoulders, "Come on, I asked a question," she pressed him.

He rapidly shook his head and attempted to dive back under his blankets, but she wouldn't let him.

"Son, Mouse is *dead*. He canna' come back an' there's nowt we can do about that. But ye're still *alive* for which I thank the Good Lord every day."

"I shouldn't be... I should be dead, like Mouse, stone dead," cried George's whilst the tears continued to flow.

Annie gripped the shoulders of her surrogate son tighter, "Ye're alive, be thankful for that, as thankful as Geordie an' me are."

"Oh, I would if I could," the tears continued.

Annie held him closer, "There, *there*, ye'll see this through, ye will, ye will," she whispered before finishing strongly, "I'll see t'that."

*****

Elysia Scott-Wilson led Albert and Alexandrina Martin to the door of the playroom, "Now, children, close your eyes and don't open them until I say so."

Alexandrina screwed her eyes tight shut.

Bertie Martin left his half-open.

"Albert, tightly shut, I said," ordered Elysia, after which she flung open the double-doors and called out, "You may open up now, my dears."

"*Ohh*, look at that!" Exclaimed Drina, there's a rocking horse nearly the size of a real horse."

"*Oh,* goodness, there are regiments – *whole* regiments of lead soldiers here," Bertie was ecstatic, "And a huge fort, a fort with...," he counted quickly, "ten cannon."

Both children ran into the room, closely followed by Cissy who was also amazed by the number and quality of the toys on display.

"Good, I knew you'd love our playroom, stay here as long as you like and I shall have tea sent up to you in an hour or so," said Elysia as she left the room.

"This is so much better than the nursery at Martin Hall, don't you think, Cissy?" Asked Drina as she jumped from the rocking horse and began winding up a musical box.

"It is, Miss Drina, but I much prefer the Hall back home, m'sel'."

"Oh, ignore her, Cissy, ordered Bertie, "come and play soldiers with me. You can be the Russians and I'll be the British Army."

Cissy got down on to her knees and took command of the grey clad Tsarist infantry. She still couldn't work out why Elysia was being so kind and accommodating. The marchioness had never so far uttered a cross word and seemed very much at ease with her children.

Just then the doors were opened wide and a small boy of about four rushed in as though he'd been propelled by a whirlwind. He was followed by the Mistress of Winterbourne and Fraulein von Kleist.

"Hello, you two," began the child, "I'm Warren Scott-Wilson, the Sixth Marquis of Studland."

"Hello," greeted Bertie and Drina as one.

"You may call me Warren," the Marquis's tone was somewhat haughty but at the same time uncertain.

"*Hmm*," Bertie could think of nothing to say.

"A *warren* is where rabbits live," informed Drina.

"Yes, and otters live in a *holt*" Bertie joined in.

"Hares make a *form* their home," put in Drina rapidly.

"You only know that because Mrs Nicholson told you," accused Bertie, who then put his tongue out at his sister.

"Yes she did, but she is forced to spend much more of her time with *you*, for you are by far the dimmer," Drina pulled no punches.

Warren stood perplexed by these exchanges.

Drina noticed her bewildered half-brother, smiled nicely, considered for a moment and then said, "I'm going to call you *Bunny*."

Warren thought seriously for a while, his head on one side, then he laughed uproariously until tears came into his eyes. "*Bunny*, I like that, I like it a lot."

"You're the Marquis of Studland, you cannot be called *Bunny*," said Martha Kleist.

"Indeed not," supported Cissy, "It's not proper."

"Well, I'm *Bunny* from now on, whether you like it or not," said the marquis firmly.

At this all three children huddled together and rolled around the floor screaming with laughter.

Once everything in the nursery had quietened down, Elysia drew Drina to one side, "Who is this Mrs Nicholson?" She asked.

"She's our teacher, she's very good and kind."

"Though *who* is she?"

"Mrs Nicholson is the wife of…," Drina stopped herself from answering *Mr. Nicholson* and instead continued with, "a collier."

"Whatever can Charles be thinking off," the Marchioness of Studland muttered to herself.

*****

Charles Martin looked directly at his visitor, "Well, Inspector Mason…. It's not superintendent now, is it?"

The policeman laughed slightly and shook his head, "No sir, I fear I shall remain an inspector for what's left of my career."

"Surely, you're not here to ask me about Wright again?"

"The case you speak of is floating belly-up at the moment. Sir James is in America and his daughter's now a marchioness – though I suppose you'll be aware of this."

"Then why *are* you here?" Charles asked simply.

"Yet another death on your estate, Sir Charles. It's getting as bad here as it is in areas of our great cities."

"This is without a doubt, an exaggeration."

Mason smiled his agreement, "However, as soon as anything happens in Martindale that *may* involve Sir James

Wright, certain powerful, though worried persons, send for me."

"Though this latest death can't possibly have anything to do with Sir James Wright, my ex-wife or even Russian greatcoats."

"Well, sir, top-people back home become twitchy whenever Martin Hall or Martindale is mentioned. It's as though they believe that something big; earth shattering even, is going to crawl from the undergrowth and bring the whole government down," Mason nodded knowingly.

"The death of this poor boy has been laid at the feet of my gamekeeper, there would appear to be no connection to any sort of conspiracy."

"Dunnett, isn't it, I remember him, a sound chap. Perhaps I should have a word with him?"

"Well, you could, but you'll have to visit him in Durham prison, where he's awaiting arraignment for murder."

"He deliberately killed a child?"

"I doubt it, the best the prosecution can hope for is a conviction for manslaughter."

"Will he be represented?"

"Yes, I've seen to that myself, Mr Dunnett will be attended by my own lawyer, Mr Digby, who will brief a barrister."

"What defence against murder can Dunnett put up?"

"He had a drink or two at the Martin Arms and on the way home was struck from behind and knocked unconscious."

"Who hit him?"

"He has no idea, the next thing he knew was when he came to and heard the young lad, George Murphy, howling."

"Murphy, he's the pie-boy, is he not?"

"Who informed him of the death of young Mouse."

"Mouse? Strange name, don't you think."

"Poor child was a refugee from a dreadful orphanage in Liverpool where he had never been Christened. The Cooks took him in and gave him their name, but most of the time he answered to *Mouse*."

"So, to sum up, Dunnett's knocked out, Mouse is killed and found by Murphy."

"That's about it."

"What was the cause of death?"

"Doctor Grace, acted for the coroner, he persuaded Doctor Cowley to examine the body with him and they agreed that the likeliest cause of death was from shotgun pellets to the chest and stomach."

"Any other wounds?"

Charles nodded, "His body was badly scarred all over, scratches, gouges, bruises."

"New or old?"

"Mostly old, though quite a lot were very recent strokes with a cane or some such instrument."

"So, what's Murphy's story? Why was he in your woods in the first place? Not a poacher, is he?"

Charles laughed, "No, he's not that. He had some garbled story about warning Dunnett of danger from unidentified men he hadn't seen but though had heard talking."

"Has he any corroboration?"

"No, says he was keeping a watch on the premises of the Christian Workers' Education League accompanied by Mouse."

"Was he the last to see the boy alive?"

"It seems so."

"Why were they spying? Childish game, perhaps?"

"No, they were convinced that the Reverend Thomas Leakey, who they know as the *Deacon*, is behind much of the unrest in the town."

Mason shook his head, "Nothing's ever straightforward in Martindale, is it."

"Well, last year, I led a party which rescued George and Mouse from the New Church Asylum For Orphans," Charles nearly added that the boys had saved themselves but felt it best not to over-complicate his story.

"Grim was it?"

"So I've been told, but I've not been there myself."

"How was it that George ended up in such a place?"

"It's a long story, but in a nutshell he was taken to Liverpool under false-pretences by a Mrs Keogh, who's husband had stolen the petty-cash tin from the Elysia Colliery."

"Really?" Mason shook his head and thought to that it would be quieter and safer to live in some parts of wildest Africa than in Martindale.

"Yes, it's rather complicated. One thing to mention about the shooting, though, Dunnett says his gun was open, he never carries it both loaded and closed. Something I can vouch for."

"So it couldn't have gone off when he was struck down by either accident or design when he dropped it?"

"Exactly."

"Could Dunnett have been felled by a low branch or a trip leading to a bang on the head?"

"I suppose so, but it is very unlikely that the gun could load itself, snap closed, go off and hit Mouse, who just happened to pass by at the right distance and right angle to suffer mortal wounds."

"Unlikely," agreed the detective.

"In which case, a third party or parties *must* have been involved."

"I wonder where Mouse was between Murphy leaving him and his corpse being discovered in the wood," the policeman scratched his head.

"Is it possible that you could investigate a little further, on my behalf? I'm sure Dunnett's innocent of any charge and I wouldn't like him to suffer the severe consequences of a guilty verdict."

Mason shook his head, "Policemen don't like men from other constabularies interfering in their cases – especially when it already looks as though they'll secure a swift conviction."

Charles' face dropped, for he was very worried about the fate of the man who'd taught him to fish and also; though much less successfully, to stalk.

"I'm not due back to report for a few days yet, I'll see what I can find out."

"Will the local police be prepared to speak with you?" Charles doubted this.

Mason laughed, "I have in my possession a very wide-ranging warrant which they will be disinclined to ignore."

"My dear fellow, how can I thank you?"

"You could show me Mayberley's documents concerning Sir James Hannibal Wright."

Charles' face fell and showed the internal struggle he was fighting.

"Sir Charles, I said that in jest. I'm certain in my own mind that Wright is guilty of many crimes, for which it's unlikely he will ever be brought to book. Even so, it would satisfy my curiosity just to *see* them. Remember, without the papers being brought into court any evidence I related as to what they contained would be mere hearsay."

Charles thought for a while, then he smiled and promised, "Very well, I shall retrieve those I have and you shall spend an hour or two in the library with them. Though this must be on your word of honour that they will not be removed or copied in any way whatsoever."

"You have my word, sir."

*****

Frank Turner looked up from his correspondence to find that Sir Charles Martin had arrived. "Sorry, sir, I didn't hear you come in."

The baronet shook his head, "No matter, Frank, I could see you were deeply committed to tallying up our accounts."

"Should I call for refreshments, tea, coffee?"

"No, I thought we'd take some lunch together at the Martin Arms, unless you're too busy."

"I am quite peckish as it happens."

"I feel we need to discuss the current discontent in the town, for I've heard a silly rumour that the miners are accusing the ironworkers of the murder of young Mouse," Charles raised his eyebrows very high, unable to believe how such silly and vicious gossip could be created and spread.

"Aye, I've heard that too, absolute rubbish, but any such suggestion while emotions are running high could lead to unpleasantness."

"A meeting of the opposing groups to see if their differences can be resolved by the application of some common sense might help," suggested Charles.

"Something needs to be done, and there's nothing like a face-to- face meeting and the airing of actual facts to defuse a bad situation."

"At the same time, it may be a good thing if we had something to take their collective minds away from all this damn silliness," proposed the baronet.

"Aye, sir, the men always like a competition, they could sort out their differences on… Say, on a cricket pitch."

"Boxing," mused Charles, "Or is that too risky?"

"Cricket, would involve more men, the ironworkers and colliers could each put in a team."

"Why not the Balaklava and the town too?" Charles thought for a moment and then continued, "The Martindale Festival of Cricket could become a part of the Gala."

"Why not," Frank was becoming enthusiastic.

The landowner came to a decision, "Let's get representatives of the different parties together, give them the full facts about the American contract; as far as we know them, and then set up this cricket competition."

"Aye, sir, I can organise that, but do you not feel that the sooner we strike the sooner these troubles will be over?"

"Yes, I suppose so, how about the 30th of June, that's only a week or so away."

"I'll get straight on with it," promised Frank.

"Very good, now let's go and see what delights the Martin Arms can provide us with for lunch," said Charles Martin.

"Aye, sir, I'm with you there."

The baronet paused as he suddenly remembered, "Oh, by the way, those papers I asked you to look after for me?"

"Yes, Charles, you said I was to hang on to them like grim death."

"I still do, but I shall need them back for a day or two."

Frank looked suspiciously at his employer, "This is nothing to do with Hannibal Wright is it?"

Charles laughed, "No, nothing at all. It may even help Mr Dunnett."

"In which case, I'll bring them to the office in the morning," promised the agent.

*****

As soon as Inspector Roland Mason set his eyes on the Reverend Thomas Leakey, he immediately assessed him as being a *bad'un* though he didn't allow it to show in either his eyes or his demeanour.

"Well, Inspector, I wondered when you might call upon me," the Deacon spoke with a hint of arrogance.

"Yes, Reverend, there are one or two questions I'd like to ask you, if you don't mind."

"You do realise, I presume, that the local police have already satisfied themselves that I had no part to play in the death of the poor orphan boy?"

"Aye, I've spoken with them and it is as you say. However, I hope you will indulge me, Sir Charles Martin and I would be grateful."

Leakey was about to refuse, though then looked behind the seemingly slow, plodding policeman and realised that there was more to him than there appeared to be.

"Of course, Inspector, please, question away as much as you wish."

Mason nodded, "Had the boy been present on these premises at any time on the night of the killing?" The local police told me that they had found many bloodstains here."

The Deacon flung back his head and laughed, "Why, inspector, they were playing a silly game with you. Taking you for a fool, because I'm certain that they failed to mention that this shop was previously that of a *butcher*. There are blood stains to be found everywhere here, but they are those of long dead beasts and not those of a young boy."

Roland Mason smiled to himself, "Yes, I can see that I may have had a prank played upon me. However, was the boy here that night?"

"No, and as far as I'm aware he never set foot on these premises."

"You have a witness for the whole evening, I believe."

"Yes, Mister Eddy Dobson, a local colliers' leader."

"He stayed until?"

"Well after midnight, we had a long session discussing the similarities and differences between Evangelical Christianity and Marxism. Most enjoyable. Why don't you go and ask Mr Dobson himself?"

"I already have."

The Deacon was taken aback and knew he had been correct to treat this policeman with care.

Mason saw that; for a fraction of a second, Leakey's expression changed, though his facial muscles were swiftly brought under control.

"What did he tell you?" asked Leakey, keeping his voice seemingly disinterested.

"That both of you had drunk a lot of strong spirits and he can't remember much about the end of the evening."

"I see."

"Bit unusual, isn't it, a clergyman taking sufficient strong liquor to befuddle him?"

"Yes, perhaps it is."

"It's a funny thing, but Sir Charles tells me that on your visit to Martin Hall you claimed to be a non-drinker," the inspector smiled.

The Deacon was disconcerted, but he put on a frank expression and opened his eyes wide, "As a rule I do not drink, but we all fall into the grip of our own demons on occasions, inspector. On the night in question, Mr Dobson and I became so carried away by our talk that the bottle was passed more freely than would otherwise have been the case."

"Yes, this happens."

"I remember it became impossible to keep my eyes open and the next thing I recall is Dobson shaking me awake."

"Would you say you were inebriated?"

"I awoke with a headache, though I'm sure Dobson was in a worse state, for he'd drunk far more than myself."

"I see," said Mason, at the same time believing that Dobson was being used as an alibi.

"Well, inspector, I've much to do. I trust you have no more questions," again the Deacon smiled brightly.

"No, I have no more," Mason paused for a long time, his eyes boring into those of the Deacon, "Not at the moment."

Leakey was thrown off-balance, *he* wasn't used to being the disconcerted one, it was always *he* who made other people uncomfortable.

Inspector Mason left the premises of the Christian Workers' Education League with the certainty that he had just spoken with the man who had been behind the death of Mouse.

*****

"So, as I've said, there is *no* American contract at the moment, though Martindale Iron & Coal is currently in negotiation for one," Sir Charles finished speaking and waited for comments from the floor.

"Though there soon could be such a contract soon and then the ironworkers'll end up better-off than the colliers," Dobson spoke stridently.

One or two voices in the group rose in support of their fellow pitman.

"We deserve more, for workin' in heat an' grime," put in Jimmy Carr, the chief representative of the ironworkers.

"D'ye not knaw how hot it is down a pit?" queried an old miner.

"Aye, and it's so clean down there we all come back up smellin' o'roses," muttered a collier who's work had left him with a single eye and a claw-like left hand.

"Lads let's avoid picking holes in each other, we're here for more than that. Let's have some peace in the town again," Matthew Priestly spoke calmly.

"*Bosses man*," accused Dobson.

"Mr Priestly's right," said Sir Charles Martin, "We're here to bring peace back to the town. Far too much *gossip* has been taken as *fact* and some of it has been downright inflammatory. It must stop and stop now."

"Well *ye* would want that," called a voice from the back.

"Aye, Sir Charles would want that, it's obvious he would. Who wants trouble when they can have peace?" Jack Nicholson spoke boldly and he voiced the sentiments of most of the workers at the meeting.

"I'm all for peace," put in Eddy Dobson, "but not at the price of the colliers losing out t'the ironworkers."

Charles Martin shouted to make himself heard, "You all know me, you know me well."

There came a buzz of agreement from the hall.

"Then answer this. Have I ever tried to cheat you? Have I ever lied to you?"

The vast majority of those gathered made it plain that the baronet had done neither thing.

"Well, I've no intention of misleading any section of the workforce now. If and when the American contract is agreed, we'll talk again and everything will be out in the open and I give you my word on that."

"We've heard this all before," cried a disgruntled Eddy Dobson, desperate that this time the meeting would go his way.

Priestly took his turn to speak, "I say we go back to our works and collieries and pass on Sir Charles' promise. Persuade the lads that the time for discord has passed and now we should settle down to peace again."

The Association leader's words were well received by most of those present and many were getting ready to leave.

Frank Turner called them to attention, "Right lads, instead of fighting each other, Sir Charles has suggested that we arrange a *Festival of Cricket.* Sort out our differences at the wicket."

The ironworkers and colliers became interested immediately.

"Aye let's have some friendly rivalry on the cricket-pitch," shouted a collier.

"We've got men of iron t'do the bowling," gloated a puddler, going through the arm motion of delivering a googly.

"Why man, we've got Jack Nicholson on our side, ye'll be shivering at the crease," returned a hewer.

"Iron workers canna strike a cricket ball, not like a collier can," came another comment.

"Aye, we can, just you wait an' see," defended an ironworker.

"Gentlemen," Frank called the meeting back-to-order before explaining, "The plan is that the Martindale Collieries, the Ironworks, the Balaklava site and the townsfolk will all put in a team."

"*Ha, the toon,* that's a laugh, we'll paddle them," cried a foundryman.

"Aye, I can just picture the shopkeepers wi' Jack Nicholson makin' his run-up ag'in them," laughed a hewer.

Frank brought the meeting back to order and promised that details of the Festival of Cricket would soon be posted.

"They went away happy, I'm pleased to say," Sir Charles smiled as he watched the hall empty.

"It went off better than I had hoped," said Priestly, "though, there again, Dobson never really has many of the lads with him when all comes to all."

"He just likes making trouble," said Frank.

Sir Charles spoke coolly, "From what I've seen and heard of him, there's more to Dobson that just making trouble. In his own eyes he is part of a crusade to change everything we know."

"Though there are a lot of things which badly need changing," commented Priestly firmly.

"I agree, I do indeed," put in the baronet at once, "It's merely a matter of how change is to come that we disagree."

"With or without bloodshed," added Frank.

They all nodded sagely in joint agreement.

*****

Frank Turner thundered down the stairs from his dressing room having just discovered that Sir Charles' papers were missing from behind the wardrobe where he had secreted them.

"*Abigail*," he shouted, "Abigail, where are you?"

The housemaid awaited him at the bottom of the staircase, she bobbed her head, "The mistress is in the garden, sir," she informed.

Frank half-ran outside and soon stood towering over his wife who was reading the Chronicle.

"I've read that the Northerners have lost yet another battle, Chancellorsville or some other such *ville*," she commented on the news.

"Abigail, where's the papers?"

"Papers? What papers?"

"The ones belonging to Sir Charles Martin, which I kept behind the wardrobe in my dressing room."

"Why on earth did you risk; presumably important, documents, behind your wardrobe," she said airily, "the mice have probably nibbled them away."

Frank only just managed to prevent himself from grabbing his wife by her shoulders and shaking the truth from her. Instead, he forced his voice to be steady and reasonable, "They don't belong to me. They are important to Sir Charles and he wants them back. Where are they?"

"Somewhere safe," Abigail's eyes widened wrinkling her forehead as she spoke.

The agent breathed easy for he at least knew the papers hadn't vanished into thin-air.

"I've read the documents, most interesting, aren't they," Abigail said casually.

"You've read Sir Charles' *private* papers," Frank spat his words out swiftly and hotly.

"You mean that you haven't?" Abigail was surprised.

"Of course I haven't," Frank just managed to prevent himself from shouting, "You broke the seals… How will I be able to explain that?"

Abigail's voice became hard, as hard as Martindale steel, "I've got what appears to be Sir Charles' most important papers and I intend to make full use of them."

"Wright won't be interested in them, for Sir Charles will still have enough evidence to destroy him," said Frank as strongly as he could.

Abigail laughed, "Sir James Wright," she laughed again, "I've no interest in saving *his* neck."

"What you *will* get is a broken-neck, if you don't hand the package back," Frank knew that his threat lacked conviction.

His wife laughed in his face, "You'll not harm me, Francis, I've made *that* much of a gentleman of you at least."

"Charles needs those papers urgently. What shall I say when I'm unable to hand them back?"

Abigail had already considered this, "Oh, that's quite easy, *I'll* take the envelope to Martin Hall and once Sir Charles has done with the documents they'll be returned to *my* place of safety. Which will satisfy everyone."

"What if Charles sees through your scheme and begins to ask awkward questions about the seals and such like?"

Abigail merely put her head on one side and smiled in a very superior way, "I can deal with Charles Martin as easily as A, B, C."

Frank became red in the face, making his scars even more livid, and his neck bulged over his collar, "I'll.., *I'll*…"

"You'll do as you're told," she cut him off firmly, paused for a short while and then continued, "Oh, by the way, I *did* telegraph papa about Aunt Prudence, I'm sure he'll return forthwith and put a stop to her ridiculous wedding."

"You did what…," Frank blustered, it was all he could do.

"Prudence is a wanton who is certainly unfit to become the wife of a clergyman," Abigail's voice rose above that of her husband's.

"She can't be anymore of a wanton that the one I saw playing the part of Lady Macduff, not so long ago," Frank struck back fiercely.

Abigail produced a knowing, mocking smile and before her husband could reply she raised her eyebrows and said, "Another thing, don't ever again expect to share my bed."

*****

"There is a communication from the United States of America amongst the post, sir," announced Mr Rust.

"Excellent," cried Charles, who quickly took the proffered envelope and tore it open.

Metropolitan Hotel,
New York City,
1st June 1863

Sir,

I have inspected the books of the Western Supply Company at the office of their accountants and they definitely have ten-million dollars lodged there.

The accountants themselves are of solid reputation having extensive premises on Wall Street. They are, I'm certain beyond reproach.

I went through the books with Mr Everett; a very senior partner in the firm, and the Western Supply Company inspires my full confidence.

In addition I have been shown the plans of depots which are currently under construction at Omaha and Sacramento. I would say that the whole scheme is feasible and will be ready to begin the moment a victorious peace has been concluded.

I have also contacted the <u>actual</u> railroad builders and they are very interested in buying from Western Supply, in fact it has been intimated to me that the contract is in the bag.

Amelia and I intend to move on to Gettysburg, where hopefully we'll be able to meet up with Helmuth.

However, my wife is determined to remain in New York (she so likes it here!) for at least another week.

I will write again as soon as I have further information of any use.

Fred Schilling.

PS

Mr Widmark has promised that a party of his people will set-out from Omaha in the hope of finding and recovering the remains of Mr Bellerby.

The actual return of this gentleman to his ancestral home may throw some light on the genuineness of the Western Supply Company.

Should you tell Caroline of this, then it would be best not to raise her hopes too high.

Charles' face lit up with pleasure, he had his doubts about this whole scheme, but Fred had done his job well and the whole business could proceed at a pace once contracts were exchanged.

Then all the uncertainty in Martindale over the contract would disappear like mist on a sunny day and everyone would be happy.

He decided there and then he would write to the Western Supply Company confirming his interest in entering into a contract with them.

*****

Sir James Hannibal Wright lit a second cigar; because he felt that he deserved it, eased himself more comfortably into his chair and reached for the large brandy that lay to hand.

"*Ah*, Widmark, there's nothing quite so satisfying as when a scheme comes seamlessly together," he remarked gloatingly.

"It all went very well. The hotel clerk pulled off a fine *coup* when he stole the letter we required, though he had to remain on duty for a full eighteen hours."

"Well paid for it, I expect."

"He was happy, though the forger was more expensive."

"Martin won't have had the chance to make a detailed study of Mr Schilling's handwriting, anything would have passed."

"Still, best to leave nothing to chance."

"Yes, it's important that when Martindale comes tumbling down; in a year or two, my hand must not be seen to have had a part in it."

"No reason why it should, is there?"

"Martin will be suspicious and he believes he holds the whip-hand over me, however, he forgets I could easily establish myself permanently in America."

"Yes, sir, you sure could do that," agreed Widmark.

"Then, no matter what he suspects or has found out, I'd be far away and safe from anything issued from England."

"What has the baronet got which makes you fear a return to your homeland?"

Wright smiled sardonically, "This is strictly my own business, Widmark, though I'll tell you this - should I fall, there are many high-up in English politics and society who will tremble."

"Sounds like serious business."

"Aye, it is. By the way, how goes the search for the remains of poor Bellerby?"

"I received a telegram this morning, they've contacted the Clapps and were shown the grave.

"Well tended, I hope," put in Wright, who felt a tinge of regret over the sad, lonely-end to which Bellerby had come.

"Yes, sir, covered with prairie flowers and a well carved headstone."

"Good, better than I imagined."

"What's left of the gentleman is on its way to Omaha. I expect the coffin could be back to... Brakewell is it?"

"Blanchwell."

"Back to *Blanchwell* by the beginning of August. Maybe September if there are delays."

"Excellent, if the return of Bellerby's dust to his old home doesn't prove to Sir Charles Martin, baronet, that our little scheme is entirely trustworthy, then I've no idea what will."

*****

"Joe, I'm sad t'see you in here," Susan Russell brushed away a tear, her homely face a picture of concern.

"Never worry, my dear, I've done nowt an' Sir Charles has sent his own lawyer, Mr Digby to see that I'm well defended when the time comes."

"Sir Charles' *own* lawyer, fancy that," Susan was reassured.

"He's come t'see me twice he has," continued the gamekeeper.

"*No,* never, Sir Charles *himself* came here," Mrs Russell found this hard to believe.

"Aye, I'm in good hands," Joe laughed and his forehead caught the light.

Susan asked quickly, "What's that bruise on yer forehead and I can see now that yer lip's been split."

Dunnett laughed, "I've met up wi' one or two of my old poachin' friends in here and we had a bit of a disagreement."

"Fighting In here? Why, were the villains not punished for attacking ye? It's shocking that you should be treated so."

"The attendants sold tickets," again Joe laughed.

"But they should have stopped them picking on you."

"Everything that *can* happen, happens in here, love."

Susan's face became a kaleidoscope of emotions, surprise, fear, concern and worry.

Joe couldn't reach her through the grill of the visiting box but he made his concern show in his voice, "Don't worry, my dear. I've never had time to let Sir Charles know of our plans, but he'll be all for it and you'll move in with me once we're married."

"Oh, Joe, if only that could happen to-morrow, I'd be as happy as I've ever been before."

"And so will I," called Joe as he was tapped on the shoulder by an attendant and led away.

*****

"Mister Leakey *was* a clergyman, though he has been de-frocked," declared Jane Turner once she'd finished reading through the morning mail.

"I'm not surprise at this, as our suspicions were well aroused when we checked in *Crockford's*," replied Richard.

"It turns out that he was sent down from Cambridge, Rusticated from Oxford and then sought to continue his education at St. Andrew's."

"No doubt he thought a different country would improve his chances," mused Richard.

"Anyway, he was eventually ordained at York, and then went into Somerset to a boarding school for boys."

"You don't need to tell me the rest."

"Oh, yes I do, he was dismissed from service there. Do I need to tell you why?"

"No, I can imagine."

Jane ignored her husband and continued, "Paederasty and thrashing a boy, seemingly, well beyond the bounds of what is considered acceptable."

"The court didn't convict then?"

"Leakey has never seen the inside of a courtroom. As is usually the case, the school was desperate to keep the whole affair quiet. The parents were paid off and the whole thing brushed aside."

"So, he's carried on in his own unpleasant way ever since?"

"Oh, and by the way, he's never been a deacon – except in his imagination."

"Fancy that, I am surprised," commented Richard.

"In addition, he inherited quite a considerable sum when his father died, and he set up the New Church Asylum, which he runs as his own personal fiefdom."

"Very useful for a person of his twisted inclinations," commented Richard, before continuing, "It looks like we have him, but can all of this be proven?"

Jane waved a thick wad of notes, "It's all in here, my boy."

*****

"Well, it's nearly time to leave, children, and I do so hope you've enjoyed your stay at Winterbourne," said Elysia Scott-Wilson, smiling benignly.

"Oh, yes, mama," cried Bertie Martin.

"May we come again… Please, *please*," begged Alexandrina Martin.

Elysia turned her smile on to Cissy, "Do you believe they deserve to visit their mama again, Jackson?"

"Aye, my lady," the reply was a stolid one.

"The children have enjoyed themselves so much here," put in Martha von Kleist, "and they have been so good, they must be allowed back."

"In which case, children, you must persuade your father."

"And our *other* mama," corrected Bertie.

Elysia forced hot words back down her throat and continued to light up her features with her best, her most winning smile, "Your *other* mama?"

"I think they mean Lady Martin," informed Cissy.

Elysia felt that holding in her temper might choke her, so to dissipate it she knelt beside her children and took them into her arms.

"You must remember, my darlings, that it is impossible to have any more than *one* mother and that person is *myself*," Elysia explained softly.

"Though can we call our other mama, *mama* too," Drina was puzzled.

"Of course, though you must remember that I am your one and only *real* mama."

"I shan't never forget that," promised Bertie who then kissed his mother's cheek.

"I wish *I* had two mothers," interjected Warren Scott-Wilson, "I'd receive twice as many Christmas and birthday presents."

Elysia rose to her feet, "I've arranged for Kent to accompany you home."

"No need for that, your ladyship, I travelled here without trouble."

"No, no, I'll not have you overburdened. Though, perhaps, your employer will allow Kent to remain at Martin Hall for a day or two before he returns."

"Yes, my lady, I'm sure Sir Charles will be pleased to do that," Cissy bobbed her head and found herself unsure whether it was a good or bad thing for the handsome Virgil Kent to be around for another few days.

*****

"You've had too much to drink again," suggested Solly Vasey.

"I've to come face-to-face with my bride in a few minutes time and so I've not had *nearly* enough to drink," replied Roderick Villiers, who was slightly unsteady on his feet.

"I thought she looked quite appealing in her wedding costume, pink suits her," said Solly.

"She is now much slimmer and her complexion is quite clear," Villiers continued in a positive way.

Solly looked at the clock above the bar at the Martin Arms, it's ten past ten, well beyond your bedtime, I should say."

"God, the *bewitching time* is upon me. Can't I stay down here for an hour or so longer?"

Vasey's voice dropped to a stage-whisper, "Your guests are all expecting you to make a move."

"So they can have a good laugh at my expense, no doubt. Well, they can wait."

"Bobbity will be *aching* for you," Vasey couldn't hold back a little splutter of laughter.

Villiers groaned to himself, but recognised that there was a fee to be paid to be enfolded into the safe arms of Martindale, and that indemnity lay abed upstairs, awaiting him.

He raised his glass, put on his most brilliant smile and swept his arm around the room.

His action brought forth a ripple of applause and some high spirited comments.

The actor left the bar as though he was making his way off stage, stopping to show off his profile and to deliver a polite nod here and a swift handshake there.

John Fisher grabbed his brother-in-law's hand, "Thank-you, *thank-you*," he cried fervently.

Roderick Villiers paused halfway up the staircase, turned to face the assembled wedding guests and quoted, his voice, deep, clear and strong, "*It is a far, far better thing that I do, than I have ever done; It is a far, far better rest that I go to, than I have ever known.....*"

There was a short silence after which his guests showed their appreciation.

"*Bravo, sir.*"

"*Well done, Villiers.*"

"*Good for you Roddy.*"

The Director of the Martindale Theatre, accepted the plaudits of the crowded bar, made half a bow and then continued on up to bed.

"*Stairway to Heaven this isn't,*" he muttered under his breath.

Chapter Eleven

After he ran from Durham railway station, Losser had wandered around the city for many days trying to find a safe refuge, but having little success.

Most nights he slept on the banks of the Wear and had several times been drenched.

He still had some money, for the Deacon had provided his accomplices with several shillings each, though this would not last much longer.

"What then?" He asked himself aloud.

His options were stark and limited, he decided. He could go to the police, confess all and end up in prison – or even worse.

He could return to Liverpool and the asylum, to face the wrath of the Deacon and Twiss, neither of whom would ever trust him again.

Or, perhaps, he could go to Sunderland or Newcastle and attempt to take a ship away from his home shores.

He passed these options slowly through his mind, though it soon became plain that none suited him.

Then, he began to wonder whether he should return to Martindale to see if he could make his peace with the Deacon and be received once more into the fold.

The more he thought of this the more he liked it, for he was bigger and heavier than Leakey, so, perhaps, he'd be able force his will upon the clergyman if the need arose.

"The Deacon's got money, plenty of it," again he spoke to himself before coming to a decision. He may be able to squeeze money from Leakey and make a new life for himself far away from either County Durham or Liverpool.

"And if he won't give me what I want.... *Ah'll take it,*" he said to himself, and though his voice was strong his resolution was weak.

*****

"These pastries are awfully good," commented Amelia Schilling as she bit delicately into an éclair.

"Andy once worked under a *chef-de-patisserie*," explained Captain Schilling.

"They are far too fancy to suit my taste," put in his sister, Grace with very little charm.

"Amelia has the sweetest tooth I've ever known," laughed Fred.

"That's why I'm so sweet a person," returned Amelia tartly.

"*Sugar and spice and all things nice*," that's you my dear, Fred smiled adoringly at his wife.

"Anyway, whatever you may say, these are far too grand for Gettysburg," stated Grace as she helped herself to a third cake.

"How did your mission to New York go?" Queried Helmuth, changing the subject.

Fred shook his head, "To be honest, I'm not sure. It *seemed* all right, though I've a nagging suspicion it isn't. They were far too nice; especially to Amelia, and spent an awful lot of money on our comfort and entertainment."

"They're to recover the remains of poor Mister Bellerby too, which won't be cheap," put in Amelia.

"You are only having doubts because you were dealing with common Americans instead of with the fine English gentlemen you're so used to now," Grace condemned her younger brother.

"They won't insist you repay them for my shopping excesses if the contract is not taken up, will they?" Amelia sounded somewhat worried.

Fred laughed, "We'll be safe back at Blanchwell by then, so I think your dresses, cosmetics, and….," he winked at his wife, "certain other bits-and-pieces are safe."

"It is my belief that a woman should maintain a wardrobe that is sufficient for her daily needs, any excess is mere vanity and extremely vulgar," Grace released a further stream of sour grape juice.

"Enough of that," began Fred, "let's get to important business. How's the war going, Helmuth, what's happening at the moment?"

"I'm surprised Helmuth has found the time to visit us," Grace jumped rudely into the conversation, "the war is going very badly and we poor civilians are let down by our army time-after-time. Sometimes, I wish I was a Southern lady, indeed I do…."

"Don't be any sillier than you are already, Grace," Helmuth interrupted his sister sharply.

"You were saying," Fred was keen to return to news of the war.

"I'm only here because the regiment's nearby and Colonel Kellogg has friends in Gettysburg whom he wished to visit. Anyway, I badly needed a bath."

"Quite right too," Amelia supported her brother-in-law.

"I should say so," added Fred wrinkling his nose, "Though what's happening?"

"Let's start with the good news, since February, our division has had a new commander, Brigadier-General John Buford and he's a man who fully understands how to handle cavalry in a modern war."

"Well, I've never heard of him," Grace was unimpressed.

"You will, Grace, believe me, you *will*. Our cavalry are getting to grips with the Rebel horse now and sooner or later our numbers will overwhelm them."

"So, you're content with your company?" Fred asked.

"The Seventeenth are no longer a laughing-stock, I'm pleased to say and Company 'J' will do its duty, I'm certain of that."

"Though what of the wider war?"

"Lee's on the move again, he slipped across the Rappahannock early this month and is heading along the Shenandoah. We're following him; covering the right flank of the Army of the Potomac, and bumping into his cavalry every other day or so. Though who knows when Jeb Stuart will launch his men on another of his raids."

"Jackson being killed after Chancellorsville must be counted as a piece of good fortune, though," suggested Fred.

"It was, I suppose, for Lee's lost a brilliant leader. However, he can still rely on the services of Longstreet, Stuart and quite a few others."

"So, where are the 17th Pennsylvania presently?" queried Amelia.

"Near Upperville just over the border in Virginia, we were involved in a fight there on the twenty-first of the month."

"Were you heavily engaged?" Fred asked.

Helmuth shook his head, "We didn't see much of it. We never do."

"I pray that this continues to be the case, 'till you're safely home to Blanchwell," Amelia spoke with complete sincerity.

"Don't you forget that Helmuth's *real* home is here," huffed Grace.

"Can you see any end to it?" Asked Fred, totally ignoring his sister.

"No," Helmuth replied sharply.

"Well, the Union has enough men, for goodness sake, that we should all be so inconvenienced is a disgrace. A disgrace, I say," Grace complained in a long whine.

"What do you suppose will happen next, Helmuth?" Queried Amelia, who also bypassed her sister-in-law.

Helmuth thought for a moment, "I believe Lee will continue to strike north, as the Confederacy *needs* to be recognised by other countries as an independent nation."

"I can't see what difference this would make," interrupted Grace again.

"It would make a great deal of difference if; say, the French or British navies hove-to over the horizon. Our blockade would be finished and the war would end."

"Though, everyone in England is against slavery and there'd be an awful stink if the government sent in the fleet," informed Amelia.

"Anyway," Helmuth picked up the thread of his thoughts, "Lee *must* win a decisive victory, which means he will leave Virginia and continue to strike north, though to where, who knows. He could well march into Pennsylvania. The Rebs could even be here, in Gettysburg, in a day or two."

Grace shrieked and clapped her hands over her face.

"A battle here," Amelia's eyes shone, "Fred, we must stay, I do so wish to tell everyone at home that I've *seen* a real battle."

"I doubt you'd like the reality of it, Amelia," said Helmuth grimly.

"Why should Lee wish to come into Pennsylvania?" asked Fred.

"To force us to fight on his terms. Imagine it, the main body of the Army of Northern Virginia, sitting comfortably on a ridge deep in our territory and only a short distance from Washington itself."

"The army and the politicians couldn't put up with that," agreed Fred.

"Hooker would *have* to attack, probably up hill and against prepared positions."

"Fredericksburg all over again," commented Fred.

"It would give Lee the chance to win a famous and decisive victory," declared Helmuth gravely.

Then the coffee arrived after which the ladies went off to see to womanly business, leaving the men to their cigars and brandy.

"Fred, I've a favour to ask," Helmuth's voice was low and serious.

"Anything," Fred nodded.

"If the Rebs do come here in the next few days, will you be ready to run for it and take Grace back to Blanchwell with you?"

Fred's face dropped at the thought, but he smiled and said, "Yes, of course, though I don't know how she'll take to England."

"It worries me more how England will take to her," replied Helmuth dryly.

"Do you really think such an evacuation will be necessary?" Fred asked.

"Gettysburg's just across the border from Virginia, anything could happen to a town that just happens to lie in Lee's line of march. If Grace stayed on here she could be burnt out of her home or worse."

"Yes, of course."

"There is also the question of father's gold eagles."

"I thought they were just a part of family mythology."

"No, they do exist. I'll take you down to the cellar and show you which of the flagstones they lie under," said Helmuth.

"A trove of treasure beneath our feet, well, well, fancy that."

Helmuth's voice became very serious, "Should anything happen to me…"

"Never, you'll be all right," Fred interrupted, not wishing to hear any further such talk.

Captain Schilling held up a hand and his voice was low and serious, "Men are killed or die every day in this war and I have no special charm protecting me. So, should the worst happen, then papa's money is to be divided between you and Grace."

"What about Caroline?"

"Caroline… Yes, *Caroline*," Helmuth's voice broke.

Fred detected a tear forming in each of his brother's eyes.

Helmuth sniffed, cleared his throat and continued, "My wife, my darling wife, is to inherit everything else I have."

*****

Lady Marian was taking tea in the nursery with Cissy Jackson, whilst in a corner the three Martin children were noisily playing *Akbar*, an Indian game given to them by Colonel Esprey at Christmas.

"You've moved five spaces and you only threw a *three*," accused Drina with some passion.

"It was a *six*, but I thought I'd let you off with one," Bertie defended himself not altogether logically.

Alexandrina turned to her half brother, "What did you see, Robert?" She asked.

"It was a three."

"*You always side with her…. You're her sneak….. You…..*"

"Children, please," Marian's voice was hardly raised but it was effective.

"Sorry, mama," said Alexandrina and Albert together.

"Sorry, mama," added Robert.

"Very well, carry on, but please, no more arguments, remember *Akbar* is *only* a game."

"Yes, mama," the children spoke as one and then continued their game though in a much more subdued and friendly manner.

Cissy refilled the tea cups and picked up a biscuit before she said, "Oh, it's so good to be back here."

"I'm pleased to have you all returned safe-and-sound," Marian patted her nursemaid's hand and then asked curiously, "How were you treated at Winterbourne?"

"The children had a wonderful time….."

"No, I meant, how did Lady Elysia treat *you*?"

Cissy thought for a long while before she spoke, "She seemed a different person to the one we knew here. You know how she used to go on about nothin' when she was Lady Martin. Well, she wasn't like that at all. All friendliness and consideration."

"Then you believe her character has changed for the better?"

"By rights, I should agree, *but…*," Cissy closed her eyes and her head swayed gently from side-to-side a few times before she continued, "There was always somethin' inside me that doubted her. Whenever she spoke to me I was still on tenterhooks, expecting to be shouted at or even slapped."

"I know she treated the children very well. They were full of the wonders of Winterbourne when they returned and seemed very fond of their *real* mama."

"Aye, that's very true, I thought they'd never be quiet about their visit on the journey up."

"Sir Charles was very pleased with how their excursion went and seems happy to send them again."

"*Oh*, really," it didn't sound as though Cissy liked the idea of a return to Winterbourne, despite its comforts and wonders.

"Still, I doubt he'll let them go much before next summer," continued Marian.

"Oh, I forgot to mention, the marchioness suggested that perhaps Robert would like to accompany the twins next time."

Instantly, Marian's heart froze-solid and it was all she could do to prevent her whole body from trembling at what Elysia might do to her only child.

However, she managed to put on a smile and replied, "Oh, I don't think so. I doubt this will ever happen."

*****

"*Ah*, Mister Villiers, congratulations on your recent marriage," Abigail Turner caught the actor just as he was entering the theatre.

"Why, thank you."

"To Fisher's sister too, how useful it must be to have the support of your brother-in-law," Abigail waved her hands around elegantly, "here, in the theatre."

Villiers coughed, "Yes," he said, "he is indeed useful."

"Your new wife," Abigail smiled thinly, "she is no doubt a treasure. *Bobbity* is it not?"

Villiers' voice dropped several octaves, his eyes took on a pleading, hang-dog look, "It all happened so suddenly, my dear... My options were so limited."

"Your options are even more limited now, shackled to a woman no one could possibly love, though no doubt you play the part of Romeo very well," Abigail's voice was sharp. She wanted to hurt the man who had been her lover, the man who was the father of her daughter. The same man who had cast her aside without even the grace of a second-thought.

"I'd taken too much drink, it was ever my downfall," Villiers excused himself.

"You dropped to your knees and begged her to marry you, *ha*," Abigail spoke scathingly.

"My befuddled brain truly believed her to be Cleopatra," pleaded the actor.

Abigail shook her head in disbelief, "This was all your own stupid doing...," she began.

"I would have avoided it," Villiers interrupted, "but your husband had a part to play, the strength of his arms led me into marriage. I dared not defy him."

"Could you not at least have *played* the part of the hero?"

"He's so big and so...."

"*Ugly*," Abigail completed the sentence for him.

"I'm just an *actor*, I'm not *real*. There is *no real* me," Roddy was no longer playing a part.

"At last, an honest answer from you," returned Abigail sharply.

"What else could I have done?" Roddy Villiers was reduced to pleading.

Abigail laughed harshly, "It serves you right. You could have had me any time you wished. Francis is so stolid and stupid that he'd never have suspected a thing."

Villiers hung his head, "It was all a dreadful mistake. How I wish now that I'd done as you suggest."

"Anyway, I see your wife is deeply involved in the theatre and her brother is never away from the place This must be of some comfort to you," Abigail sneered.

"I have no choice. What can I do to keep them out? I am at a loss," complained the actor.

"What about me? Is my part here to be merely a member of the committee? Am I to have no further place on the stage?"

"Of course, I haven't cast yet for *The Riever Brothers*, though I've something really strong in mind for you."

"Really, what is it?"

"A new part, one that has several important lines, one which you will play to perfection...," unusually for him, Villiers dried up.

"Well, out with it, what is the part?"

Villiers thought quickly, he'd willingly come back to Martindale and all he'd had so far were people pestering him for good-parts, when every professional actor knew that no play had a *good* part in it for everyone.

"The gypsy dancing girl," he suddenly said, thinking that adding a dancing girl to the play would enhance it as far as an audience of miners and ironworkers were concerned.

"Oh, no, Roddy Villiers, I've still not regained my reputation after the shame of the way you insisted I play Lady Macduff."

"Why, Abigail, you were superb in the *Scottish Play*. Though, sadly, there are so many people about who do not recognise true art when they see it," Villiers' wonderful voice hummed persuasively.

"You think so, you think I was as good as that," Mrs Turner's tone softened and her eyes brightened.

Villiers immediately noticed the change and saw that beneath her hard shell, there sheltered a woman with needs. The sort of needs that only he could fulfil.

"Of course, there are few true artists to be found in Martindale, but *our* two minds are as one, we recognise immediately the subtle connections between form, flow and the aesthetic," Villiers was now bullshitting for England.

"Oh, Roddy, I've so missed you," Abigail found it difficult to control her feelings.

"Why don't we go up to my office," suggested Villiers, knowing that the theatre would be quiet for at least the next hour.

Abigail's lips pouted, "Why should I, you discarded me, left me with both child and a suspicious husband and all for..... *Bobbity.*"

"My dear; as I've told you, there was no avoiding it. Indeed it was your husband who drove me to my current sad-station with threats of violence," Roddy opened his eyes as wide as they would go and hung his head as he had once before when playing Iago.

"I *will* accompany you upstairs, Mr Villiers, but your attention must be fully concentrated on the satisfaction of *my* desires."

"Of course, my love."

"You will follow my instructions exactly and you may be certain that I shall ignore your animal needs in favour of my own," her voice became silky.

"Of course, my dearest, nothing would please me more," Roddy hadn't had a pleasant liaison with a woman since last he'd had congress with Abigail and if she wanted to play the dominant role, then he was happy enough with that.

"Very well, then you may go to your office and I shall join you shortly," ordered Abigail.

*****

The delegates, on returning to their works and collieries from their meeting with Sir Charles Martin, had expected their fellow workers to accept what had been agreed.

Generally speaking, the men approved, however, there still remained an undercurrent of ill-feeling, the flames of which were vigorously fanned by Eddy Dobson who was provided with a never ending flow of fuel by the Deacon.

Matthew Priestly spent much of his time visiting the Martindale and Elysia collieries talking with the men coming and going from their shifts.

He found that most agreed that there was no sense in continuing a rivalry based on gossip and innuendo. However, he also knew that Eddy Dobson rarely missed an evening with Leakey at the Christian Workers' League, which always resulted in further inflammatory chatter spreading through the town.

His only hope was that the proposed Cricket Festival didn't turn into a bloodbath.

*****

It seemed to most people that Martindale had become a peaceful place again. There were still disturbances and fighting; especially at week-ends, but this was only to be expected.

Then, the weather turned hot, or at least as hot as the sun can ever make it in County Durham. This combination of heat and plentiful drink could lead in only one direction.

The trouble began on a busy shopping Saturday afternoon. Working men representing all of the town's enterprises were making full use of the public-houses, inns and beer shops whilst their wives did their shopping.

It was a colourful scene, the women were attired in their best, whilst the men wore their favourite posey jackets and ribboned hats.

Random disagreements soon began at various watering-holes. These were over future rates of pay, the result of unplayed cricket matches.

In one or two hostelries the death of young Mouse was discussed in ever louder and more slurred voices.

Blood rose with the temperature and voices became raised at the slightest provocation.

There was no pattern to this unrest for it was not planned, no punches had been thrown as yet, but tempers were becoming increasingly frayed.

*****

The two policemen patrolling the streets of the town began to relax as the afternoon was coming to a close, knowing that before long the men would be away to their homes looking to sleep off the effects of strong ale.

The constables had expected an explosion of trouble, which was why there were two of them on duty instead of the regular one.

"Earlier on, I felt we'd be lucky t'see this day through alive," commented the first of the policemen.

"Aye, me an'all. There's been trouble brewin' here for weeks. It's that Eddy Dobson, I'd lock him up in a trice, if I had my way," answered the second.

Just then a large group of ironworkers; who were much the worse for wear, came out of the Lord Raglan.

At the same time, from around a corner, there appeared a group of ten or so colliers who also had too much drink to remain sensible. Alongside this latter group there padded a black-and-white mongrel dog.

"Oh, dear, here we go," commented the second policemen.

The ironworkers halted in their tracks and looked malevolently towards the miners, though they said nothing.

The colliers continued on their way, led by the dog which was a pugnacious sort of beast.

"*Fuckin' ugly dog,*" remarked one of the iron-men, though not particularly loudly.

"*Not half as ugly as you,*" replied the owner of the animal, though again, not above conversational level.

"*Set him off Buster,*" laughed a fellow-miner, though not seriously.

However, the dog needed no second bidding, it ran at the offending iron-worker and made a leap for his throat.

The selected victim took a step back and held his arms across his chest in a defensive move, at the same time screaming for help.

The colliers found this very amusing.

So did the policemen who were loathe to intervene until they were dutybound to do so.

A tall, thin puddler stepped forward to aid his companion and kicked out at the dog, striking it with his heavy boot on the muzzle.

The animal screeched and launched a revenge attack on its attacker's ankles.

The pitmen found this to be uproariously funny and soon found their eyes to be running with tears of laughter.

From this point the whole scene turned ugly, first one and then another of the ironworkers began to kick out at the dog whose growls turned to whelps of pain and distress.

This was too much for the owner of Buster who ran across to rescue his pet. He was instantly followed by all his companions and a vicious *melee* began.

"Should we bother wi' the rattles?" Asked the first policeman.

"They're bloody useless – anyway, we've no help to hand," replied the second constable.

Then, together, two policemen drew their truncheons and launched themselves into the fray.

The fighting men ignored the police, for they knew quite well that there were only two in the town and an old sergeant, who they suspected was currently drinking tea in the police-house.

The first man to go down was the owner of the dog, who, when bending over to collect his animal was kicked from behind between the legs. The resulting pain sent the breath from his body and he fell to his knees.

A friend of his stepped forward to protect him from further injury, when he too received an unexpected punch to the side of the jaw which sent him reeling into the gutter. He lay groaning, but soon spewed out a pool of sour beer, which was immediately lapped up by a quickly recovering Buster.

Seeing two of their men down and the ironworkers clearly in the ascendant, in ones and twos the colliers slipped away to spread the news that the trouble they'd all been expecting had broken out.

The victorious iron men re-entered the Raglan and began to celebrate their success.

"That was short and sweet, anyway," said one of the constables who was well out-of-breath.

"Shouldn't we have arrested somebody?" queried the second, delicately dabbing at a split lip.

"I think we did right enough without having *both* sides setting themselves ag'in us."

"Aye, well, let's back and inform the sergeant there's trouble afoot."

"Right, and I expect he has the sense to call in reinforcements."

*****

Jack Nicholson was walking with his wife; and as usual, was believing himself to be the luckiest man in the County.

Sarah was beautiful beyond compare, at least in his eyes she was, and just the thought of her cleverness made his head ache.

"Elinor needs new ribbons, John, so I shall pop into Murdoch's, you'll easily have time to take a small-beer if you so wish."

Jack thought about it and declined, "*Naw*, Sarah, I'll wait in the sunshine, someone may come along I can crack wi'."

*****

Roderick Villiers left the saloon bar of the *Martin Arms* and set out to return to the theatre, where he was having difficulties writing his new play *The Riever Brothers* as Solly Vasey was being awkward over the number of lines allocated to his character.

"I've only a dozen or so more than he has," Villiers said to himself, "*Vanity, vanity all is vanity*, with that man," he continued.

Then there was the problem of John Fisher demanding a leading part. He'd been offered that of third-fisherman but had refused it out-of-hand, even though there was a full line in it for him.

"Fancies himself as the Laird of Melrose," Villiers spoke to himself in an annoyed tone, "if he isn't careful he'll become the rear end of the dung-spreader's donkey."

Then there was Abigail to whom he had promised the part of a gypsy-dancer, though he couldn't see where he could fit one in, especially one who would have a line to deliver.

To top it all, even his wife had become seriously interested in the theatre. Villiers couldn't keep her away and if she wasn't interfering with the costumes, she was criticising his writing.

"*Ha*," he cried aloud, "my writing is second only to that of the Bard himself."

*****

Frank Turner left the offices of the Martindale Iron & Coal Company and hurried to-wards those of the Chronicle for he wished to hear if there was any news regarding Thomas Leakey.

He soon came across Geordie Cook who was involved in humping a huge bag of flour which; he presumed, was destined for the pie shop.

"They're all wantin' pies, far more than what we thought," explained Geordie.

"Do you need a hand?"

"I can manage, but I'm supposed t'get another...," wheedled the collier "You get on and I'll follow you with the other bag. Will two bags be enough?"

"Aye, anyone short of a pie at the end of the day will just have t'starve."

Frank soon collected the flour and set off in the tracks of his friend. Before long, though, he came across a miner who was propped up against a wall with blood streaming from a head wound.

"What's happened to you, marra?" Frank asked.

A pair of woozy-eyes looked into his, "*Ah*, Mr Turner, sir, 'tis you, I was worried ye were one o' those wild iron fellers come back. There's been trouble the day and there'll be more afore the night's ower."

Frank looked around and noticed for the first time that the street was filling up with groups of men who were forming and reforming, coming and going and eventually coalescing into larger and larger groups.

Just then, he caught sight of two sensible young men he had recently promoted to be hewers. "Hi, lads, over here," he shouted.

The colliers did as they were bidden and between them they were soon helping the wounded man to be seen by one of the town's doctors.

"I don't like the look of this," Frank said to-himself before he hefted the flour bag back on to his shoulder and continued on to Annie's Pie Shop.

*****

The sergeant entered the police house, took off his helmet and with a ludicrously small, pink handkerchief, embroidered with blue flowers, wiped the sweat from his face.

One of the constables tittered.

The sergeant looked up sharply, "I picked it up from the wrong pile of ironing, is that all right wi' you."

"You'll be in trouble the night, then," nodded the second policeman.

"Aye, it's called married-life, you two should try it an' become miserable like me."

"What did ye think of the temper out there?" Asked the younger constable.

"They're working themselves for a bust up, I wouldn't be surprised if there's not t'be murder afoot later on," wheezed the sergeant.

"Shouldn't we send for help?" Suggested a constable.

"Aye," agreed the sergeant, "I've seen young George Murphy about, he's a sensible lad," he then pointed to the constable who had spoken first, "Get yersel' ower to Annie's an' see if you can get him on his way. Borrow the postman's horse – I'll settle with him if he misses it."

The police constable put his helmet on and ran outside to do the bidding of his superior.

"Are we two goin' out or are we awaitin' reinforcements?" Queried the second constable, pleased that the decision was not his.

The sergeant thought for a long few seconds, "There's not much two o' us can do against a mob," he considered slowly.

"We'd just disappear into it an' it's not as though we're talking about poets and singers out there, they're colliers and ironworkers, hard, *hard* men, all of them."

"Aye, they are that, I think we'll stop here 'till we get help or it quietens down a bit."

*****

Thomas Leakey climbed to the front upstairs window of the Christian Workers' League establishment, from where he could watch the trouble he had helped create in Martindale bubble and boil out of control.

He was soon rewarded by the sight of a group of ironworkers fleeing for their lives from a larger group of pitmen who came howling after them.

Then, as the fugitives reached the corner of the street, the iron men were suddenly reinforced by a flow of their own fellows coming in the other direction and it was the turn of the colliers to run for it.

"*Such, fun, Oh such fun,*" the Deacon laughed to himself, "Poor Martindale, poor, *poor*, miserable Martindale."

*****

"This riot should be fully reported, so perhaps we both ought to cover it," suggested Jane Turner.

"No, certainly not, one will be sufficient" replied her husband.

"We could cover twice the ground," insisted Jane.

"You should remain here," replied Richard.

"Why don't you stay here and *I'll* go out. Even at their wildest the men wouldn't hurt a woman."

"Don't you believe it. No, I must be the one to report on this, remember you've two children at home."

"So have you."

"Though you're their mother," appealed Richard.

"You're their father, what's the difference?"

Richard said nothing more, instead he took his wife in his arms and kissed her hard, his eyes had a forbidding glint in them when he released her and he said, "*Stay here...* Please."

Jane let him go and watched as he went out into the street which was riven with trouble.

Five minutes later she put on her favourite, lumpy bonnet, checked that her notebook was in her large-reticule and followed her husband.

*****

Matthew Priestly was concerned, for from his office he could hear continuous disturbance in the nearby streets.

He went outside to look and though he could see nothing, he could still hear plenty. In every direction there came the sound of trouble.

"*Damn Dobson,*" he muttered to himself, before he set out to see if he could settle things down.

Since the meeting he had tirelessly spoken with everyone who would listen about the importance of maintaining peace in Martindale, though Eddy Dobson was always following close behind him undoing his good, sensible work.

Priestly reached the end of the street and was startled to find an angry group of colliers striding purposefully towards him.

"Now, lads. What's up?" he asked softly, raising his arms placatingly.

"Fuck off, Priestly," a slurred voice shouted from the centre of the crowd.

"Aye... Ye're nowt but a bosses man."

"Stand aside or ye'll get what's comin' t'ye."

Matthew Priestly raised his voice to be heard, "We've settled our differences, we've agreed to peace and to let bygones-be- bygones."

"Aye, but it's your peace, not ours," the voice was that of Eddy Dobson who pushed his way to the front and confronted the leader of the Association.

"Eddy, this'll do no good," Priestly kept his voice low, "people will be injured, some may be killed."

"Killed ye say?" the collier raised his voice to a shout, "As long as it's the bosses or their lackeys that die, what care have we of that."

"Haway, lads, push him out o' the way," screamed a drunken collier from deep in the crowd.

"*Fuck him,*" supported a very inebriated miner from the centre of the mob.

A powerfully built young putter stepped forward, his eyes glazed and woozy, who; with no warning, struck Priestly between the eyes.

The leader of the Association staggered back, blood pouring from his nose. He stood still and upright for a second and then fell to his knees and forward until he lay face down in the road.

"Come on, lads, there's more t'be done the day," encouraged Dobson, giving the prone Priestly a solid kick in the ribs, before he moved on.

*****

Roderick Villiers' mind was dragged back from the problems he was having with his latest production by an almighty row that was coming from just around the corner.

He froze to the spot, for he decided he'd be very surprised if a second Waterloo wasn't been fought in the vicinity.

As he watched a hewer; his clothes torn and head bleeding, came limping around the corner where he collapsed, breathing heavily and holding his head in both hands.

"My dear, man," consoled Roddy as he came nearer, "You *are* in a state, perhaps I should call for assistance."

"Best call the army in, not much less will help," panted the collier.

Just then a further small group of miners jostled around the corner, saw their marra, picked him up and began to support him along the road and out of danger.

Villiers watched them go and was about to return to the problems of staging *The Riever Brothers* when a howling mob of iron workers ran into sight and very nearly knocked him flying.

The actor outstretched his arms as far as they would go, "Gentlemen, gentleman, some courtesy, *please*," his voice was strong and as masculine as he could make it.

"Push him out the way, it's just that actor feller."

"Aye, just give him a knock."

"Puff of air'll blow 'him ower."

"Gentlemen, *please*, your enemies are vanquished, look they flee," again the stage trained voice of Villiers carried to each and every one of the ironworkers and they slowed their pace.

"Haway, man, they're getting' away," shouted the leader of the mob, desperate that they get on the move again.

Villiers clasped his hands together as though in prayer and then began to recite, coolly and calmly, "Peace, gentlemen, let us have peace, for remember, *Peace hath her victories no less renowned than war*."

"I put tuppence in t'the fund for him, but I didn't want him back t'be canting at us," shouted the leader, "knock him out o' the way."

Villiers expected that by now the fugitive colliers would have disappeared, so he stepped to one side, took-off his hat and waved the mob onwards.

"Gentlemen, advance, *Was none who would be foremost to lead such dire attack; But those behind cried 'Forward' and those before cried 'Back!'* the actor spoke encouragingly.

"Nothing like a good quotation when times become difficult," he said as he watched the iron workers hurrying off looking for further trouble.

*****

Jack Nicholson heard the mob coming long before he saw it. Then, just as it appeared, Sarah came back out on to the street.

"Go back in there," he shouted urgently, "I'll join ye in a minute."

Sarah hesitated and then withdrew as she had been told.

The mob rolled forward like particularly troubled waves pounding on to shingle, the eyes of each man on the look out for some way he could make trouble for and strike out at his perceived enemies.

Jack took a step forward and folded his arms across his chest, he smiled and shouted, "Now lads, have we not had enough o' this?"

The rolling mob came to a restless, grumbling halt.

"I thought all-sides had agreed to an end o' this silliness," Jack had to shout to be heard.

"Naw, we haven't," yelled a voice from the rear.

"Charlie and Priestly might ha', but we never did."

This shout was taken up by a score of others.

"Ye all knaw this bother is all over nowt, it's the drink takin' ower yer minds," John Nicholson remained as cool as ever.

"Bastard's just another collier, knaws nowt about smelting," cried a further inflammatory voice safely embedded in the middle of the crowd.

"So, ye're all lookin' for a fight?" Nicholson asked a rhetorical question.

"We're gonna scrap 'till all the colliers is down an' out."

"Aye, that's right."

"Ye'd better shift."

"We're not afraid of you."

Nicholson smiled and raised his arms high above his head, "All right," he called out conversationally, "Tell, ye what, I'll take ye all on, one man at a time. How's that? That's fair isn't it?"

The crowd began to smile, one or two laughed at the idea of any man being daft enough to take on the great Jack Nicholson by himself.

"Who's t'be first?" Asked a still smiling, unfazed Nicholson.

The mob quietened and became less restless.

"Come on, ye can't all be shy, and I could do wi' a bit exercise," Jack laughed

Nicholson's easy good humour was irresistible and most of the mob joined him in laughter.

"Come on lads, I've not had a proper to-do for weeks,"

"Tie a hand behind yer back, Jack," shouted yet another voice from the safety of the mob.

Nicholson laughed again, for all the world as though he was really enjoying himself, "Tell ye what, I'll cover me eyes wi' a blindfold an'all."

The mob went from sullen and mean to sweet reasonableness in seconds.

Apart from, that is, one hulk of a man with fists like steel-blocks and the brain of a small-child.

From inside the shop and joined by the other besieged customers, Sarah Nicholson watched the way her husband was able to effortlessly cool down a large and angry crowd.

She shook her head gently in disbelief that he would have the nerve to try something like this. One day, she thought to herself, I'm sure that he will become a *great* man.

Out on the flank of the mob the very large iron worker with a grudge and a lot of beer in his belly, hefted the iron-bar he carried from hand to hand. Nicholson had humiliated him outside the school to show off to the fancy schoolmistress he married. His workmates and his own wife had given him nothing but grief over this ever since. His befuddled mind now believed that this was the moment to get his own back.

"Time t'go home lads but maybe have just one more drink on the way," coerced Nicholson.

"What about your collier friends, will they knaw we're callin' it a day?"

"I'll fight any of them too if need be. Once I'm fighting I divn't much care who it's with," Nicholson flung back his head and roared in good-hearted merriment, the richness of his laughter spreading across the crowd like a mantle of goodwill and most of them joined in.

Though the huge child with the iron-bar did not.

As the working-men stood in the late afternoon sunshine, their shadows lengthening and now enjoying some quick-witted repartee, the man with the iron bar; using other men as cover, edged ever closer to John Nicholson.

One of the puddlers saw what was going to happen and lunged forward in an effort to prevent a tragedy, shouting, "*Jack, man, look out.*"

Arriving just across the street at the same time, Frank Turner had seen how Jack had taken the mob into the palm of his hand and he began to breathe easier.

It was then, on the side of the mob away from him, that he saw a massive ironworker easing his way around to get behind his friend.

"*Jack*," he shouted as loudly as he could, "Jack, t'the back of you..." though his words were drowned out in the general hubbub.

Sarah Nicholson's hand went to her mouth, "*Oh, no, Oh, Jack, Jack......,*" she cried.

The iron bar descended and struck John Nicholson across the back of his head. His brain recorded the strike as a blinding, yellow flash which was immediately followed by an all-engulfing blackness.

Two or three of the iron workers grabbed the culprit and began to pummel him, pushing him to the earth and kicking him.

"Ye, coward... Ye're nowt but a coward."

"Hitting a man from behind when he wasn't looking."

"Ye're nowt but a piece shit."

Sarah Nicholson ran past them all and cuddled in her arms the bleeding head of her husband, her lover, her wonderful man, "John, hold on, *hold on*, please, help's coming." She cried with all her might, though she knew that he had already gone to a far, *far* better place.

Jane Turner arrived on the scene just seconds too late to see the end of John Nicholson, hewer of Martindale.

She came to a dead halt as soon as she realised what had happened, her heart seemed to have shrunk to the size of a walnut and was pounding her ribcage out of shape with the wildness of its beating.

"There is *no* God. There can be *no* God," she confirmed to herself, "There is *no* hope when a life of such promise can be so randomly, so uselessly wiped out."

She then sat huddled on the street her features contorted and tearful.

*****

As soon as Losser arrived in Martindale he knew the day there hadn't been an ordinary one. There was an unfathomable hush in the air and the few people he saw hurried about their business with heads downcast.

He came across a young miner, sitting in the gutter, his face gloomy, "Hey, what's on here – somebody died or somethin'?"

The pitman jumped to his feet, legs apart, fists raised, "You an iron-man wantin' t'make summat of it?"

Losser jerked backwards a step or two, "Naw, naw, I was just askin', honest."

"Jack Nicholson's killed," said the collier, much deflated, shortly before he returned to his seat on the kerb.

"Who killed him?" Losser asked quickly, wondering if it had been the Deacon. This thought was quickly dismissed, for Leakey never carried-out his own dirty-work.

"A big ironworker, massive bugger – he could have made two o' the pair of us."

"Not a clergyman then?"

The colliers hackles arose again, "You being funny?"

"Naw, sorry, I was thinkin' o' summat else," again Losser made amends quickly and set off in the direction of the Christian Workers' League.

*****

George Murphy was riding the postman's horse without a saddle or stirrups and thus was forced to lean backwards, whilst at the same time holding on to the reins for dear life. He was certain his brain was turning into porridge by the jogging he was receiving.

"Come on, gal," he encouraged, but the beast; used to the ways of mail delivery, carried-on at no more than a brisk walk.

Murphy had; as requested, informed the police-office at Oakland that reinforcements were required at Martindale and then he'd wasted no time in setting off for home again.

The journey gave him no time to think of his own troubles, so concerned was he for his own safety.

Though as soon as the horse's gait settled to a reasonably predictable motion, thoughts of young Mouse and the jailing of Joe Dunnett fought for the attention of his mind.

Annie had persuaded him; over a number of difficult days and, especially, nights that everything which happened had been part of a pattern set in motion by people other than himself.

Anyway, he was eating again, sleeping for a part of the night and the bakery kept him busy.

He was no longer the same lad he had been, but he was moving on – as Annie had said he would.

*****

As soon as he received news of the murder of John Nicholson, Sir Charles Martin mounted his horse and rode into the town.

He had believed his intervention, along with the good offices of the delegates, had defused the situation.

"I've never been more wrong," he said to himself fiercely as he trotted on.

On entering the High Street he came across the forlorn figure of Frank Turner, leaning against a lamp post with a hand covering his eyes, unseeing, having no care for anything that was happening around him.

"Frank, dreadful news," called the baronet.

Turner looked up, his scarred face livid and tormented, "Damn this town," he uttered, "I wish I could return to the simple, plain, farming life again. Live somewhere were nothing ever happens, except the measured progression of the seasons."

Charles dismounted and joined his friend, "Yes, I've often rued the day I set out in search of coal and improvement."

"What's done's done. Jack's dead and there's an end of it," Frank felt like crying, like howling in fact, but he couldn't, he just stood stony-faced.

"Mrs Nicholson must be bereft."

Tears again attempted to form in Frank's eyes, but he fought them off, "Till the day she dies Sarah will have to live without the love of her life. She knows she'll never find another and what's she to do? Her home isn't even hers."

"Yes, well, that's no matter she can remain where she is for as long as she cares to."

"Aye, though hers is an overman's house, it'll be needed," even his sorrow couldn't subdue Frank's Turner practicality.

"There's no rush," insisted Sir Charles, who's soft-heart was beating strongly.

"It'll be needed for who ever replaces...," Frank sniffed and stopped speaking.

"We'll not try to fill his place.....," began Charles, who found that he too couldn't continue and wished his agent would leave the subject be.

"We can't do the impossible," Frank's words were uttered with finality.

*****

Just as he entered the High Street George Murphy was told by several people of John Nicholson's demise.

At first, he couldn't believe that such a thing could happen. Jack was indestructible, everyone knew that, and yet, he had been taken by surprise and felled with a single blow.

A *single* blow.

He then considered how impermanent life was and how quickly the soul could be sucked from the living body. Life was not forever, he concluded, so it could not be wasted and had to be taken advantage of.

There and then he decided he would waste no further time continuously recalling past events. Mouse was dead and though he would never forget him, he had to let him be.

Just at that moment he caught sight of Losser and at first his heart was full of fear, but just as he was about to pull the head of his mount around he was filled with a new resolve.

He encouraged the postman's horse into, if not a gallop then at least, a trot.

Losser heard the sound of approaching hooves and looked up to see his old victim, George Murphy, trying to ride him down on a scraggy, brown and white horse.

At first Losser laughed, for George was hanging on to the reins as though his life depended upon them, the horse was unwilling and not achieving anything above a canter.

"Losser, I'm not afright o' you now. I'm goin' t'…" screamed George just before he rolled backwards from the saddle and landed with a heavy bump in the road.

Losser had stopped laughing when he had seen Murphy's face which was filled with determination and hate and for a moment fear had overtaken him.

Winded, George didn't move for long seconds and then he opened his eyes to see Losser staring back at him. He pulled himself into the defensive foetal position, expecting a hearty kick at any moment.

"Murphy are you all right?" asked the orphanage bully.

"Aye, I think so," replied George, climbing dizzily to his feat.

"Do ye need a hand?"

Murphy was puzzled for there was something different in his old tormentors voice which he'd never heard before.

"George, I'm terrible afraid. I've been afraid since that night in the goods yard. I ended up wi' a terrible beating there."

"You well deserved it," began George, who couldn't help his words.

"Yes, well, I'm frightened of everything now, just like Mouse was. I know what it was like being him."

"Not good and that's a fact," replied Murphy, who, by now was back on his feet looking for the postman's horse which had disappeared.

"No, then there's the Deacon, you know what he'll do t'me."

"Why, man, you're one of his gang aren't you?"

"I was till... Till...," Losser couldn't finish his sentence.

"Mouse was killed?" Murphy finished for him.

"Aye," Losser said, his tone deadpan, his eyes reliving the moment.

"So, what are ye doin' here?"

"I ran off, like you, I ran off. Been in Durham for days, but my money's run out, so I thought I'd find the Deacon an' see if I could come to an accommodation wi' him. Get him t'leave me be, 'cos I'm not going back to the asylum."

George considered for a moment, thinking how useful his old enemy could be, and then offered, "Tell, ye what, before you find the Deacon, come an' have a pie. Then you can tell us *exactly* what happened to Mouse."

A look of abject fear crossed Losser's face and his eyes danced with alarm, though after a moment he nodded, "Aye, which might be for the best."

*****

"This is Losser, mam," introduced George Murphy.

Annie Cook looked surprised, "Ye mean, this is the one that beat ye up when ye were in that awful home," as she spoke she curled her hands into fists and looked about ready to strike.

"He's got a lot to tell us, he'll tell us about Mouse," said George meaningfully, before he offered Losser a seat.

Geordie Cook entered from the bakery, "Who's this?"

"It's the lad what hurt our George at Liverpool."

"He'll help us," put in Murphy quickly, before his surrogate father had time to become aggressive.

"With what happened t'young Mouse," added Annie.

"I'm awful hungry," appealed Losser.

"Will a pie suit ye?" asked George.

"Aye, anything, a bit of bread an' dripping, anything at all."

Annie hurried off to find some repast for her visitor whilst Geordie settled himself on the bench opposite the two lads. "Now, then, what can ye tell us?" he asked in a friendly, companionable way.

"He knaws enough t'get Joe Dunnett out o' clink."

Geordie smiled and nodded, "Ye don't say."

Annie came back with a plate loaded with two pies, a huge pile of mashed potatoes and a soft, green swamp of mushy peas. "Here ye are, son, eat up and start talkin'," she commanded.

Losser set-too with a will, taking in massive forkfuls at a time, interspaced with gulps from a pint pot of tea.

"Well, lad what happened t'young Mouse?" Annie asked when Losser had finished his meal.

He looked up from the table and belched softly, "That was the best pie I've ever had."

"Aye, and ye shall have more, but only after ye've answered our questions," said Geordie.

Annie put on her fierce-face and her eyes locked on to those of Losser, "And mind you, I divn't want any lies."

Losser rubbed his eyes, for he'd had little sleep since running off from his mates at Durham station, "Can I not sleep first?" He appealed.

"*Naw*, we need to know now," said George with determination.

"All right, but can I have another pot o' tea?"

Tea was quickly brought and Losser began to drink it with the other three sitting expectantly by.

"I wanted nowt t'do with any of this, ye understand?"

"Aye," Annie answered for all of them.

"The Deacon planned it, we just followed his orders, you realise that?"

"We know he's the chief villain," said George.

"He's obsessed with getting his own-back on the gamekeeper and the hewer who give him a good caning back at the asylum."

"He's a nasty man, that Deacon," confirmed George.

"The plan was that we'd wait for Dunnett in the woods, set on him and give him a good beating," explained Losser.

"What about Mouse, tell us about Mouse," demanded Murphy.

"Twiss caught Mouse outside the League and brought him along to the Deacon."

"Who's Twiss?" Asked a puzzled George Murphy.

Losser looked up and continued grimly, "He's Peter Twiss, and mind, he's dangerous, he'll do owt the Deacon wants."

"Was Mouse much hurt?" George was determined to know everything that had happened to his friend during his last hours.

Losser looked shamefaced, "He was roughed up a bit at the shop, but that was 'cos he tried to escape. Then; as we were leaving, the Deacon handed him over to Twiss telling him to take the boy upstairs."

"Then, Mouse died in the shop," suggested Annie.

"*Naw*, Twiss brought him into those awful dank woods later on."

"So, it was Twiss that did the killing?" Queried George.

Losser shook his head vehemently, "The Deacon was behind it from the start. Just as we were going out I heard him say to Twiss something, like, '*Here, take him, you know what to do*'."

"And what do you think it was that Twiss was supposed to do?" Queried Annie.

Losser shook his head, "I didn't know at the time, but in the woods, Mouse became tired and dragged back. Twiss threw him along the path, kicking him when he wouldn't get up. Eventually, he drove him along bashing him with a springy branch of wood he'd found."

"So, you got to the site of your ambush and waited for Joe?" Geordie was raging inside but forced himself to keep calm in order to make sure that Losser confessed everything.

"Aye, that's about right, we waited ages and thought we'd missed Dunnett and wanted to go."

"So why didn't you," queried George.

"Twiss wouldn't let us, said he'd trailed behind Dunnett an' he would be along shortly."

"Then Joe came?" Asked Annie.

"Aye, we heard him whistling as he came, so we hid."

"Yer plan must have worked 'cos Joe was knocked out," surmised Annie.

"Didn't Mouse try to give a warning t'Joe?"

"Aye, but Twiss gave him such a knock t'the head, the little lad was more-or-less senseless."

"Joe's gun didn't go off itself, did it?" George was sure that he already knew the answer to this question.

Losser shook his head again, "Mind, none o' what follows was of my doin', ye believe me, don't you," he appealed.

"Aye, gan on, son," encouraged Annie

"Twiss picked up the gun, snapped it shut, nudged Mouse into the path and fired. He couldn't miss, being only two or three yards away."

"Did you look to check that the boy wasn't just wounded?"

Losser put his head in his hands, "Knaw, I took fright and legged it. We all did."

"Twiss as well?" Murphy was curious.

"No, he joined us later."

"Though Twiss killed Mouse? It was definitely him?" Asked Annie.

"Aye, it was him all right, I'd swear on my mother's grave – if I ever had a mother and knew where it were."

"What do we do now?" wondered Geordie Cook.

"Ye'll not give me t'the police, will yer. I might be hanged and I'd never have shot Mouse, or anybody," begged Losser.

Annie thought for a moment, "Geordie, you'd best find Frank Turner, and I think Sir Charles himself will want to know of this an'all."

"Aye, he could get Dunnett out o' Durham goal straight away," Geordie caught on at once.

"What about me," Losser whispered.

Annie patted his head, "Queen's Evidence, son, *Queen's Evidence,* that's what you are now."

*****

Later that evening, returning from a deathly quiet Martin Arms, the Deacon flung himself into a chair and poured a large whisky. He took a sip and then said to himself, triumphantly, "Dunnett in prison and Nicholson dead. Even in my wildest dream did I expect so great a success?"

Five-minutes later Leakey drained off his drink and smashed the glass into the fireplace.

"Time to go and thank the Lord I'll never have to tread the streets of this dreadful town again," he spoke quietly to himself as he picked up his bags and made for the front door.

He paused for a moment there and said aloud, "Unless I can find some way of making life difficult for Martin and Turner."

*****

Sarah Nicholson sat quietly with Elinor asleep in her arms. Beside her was Peggy Nicholson who'd hardly spoken since the death of her son.

The house was morbidly dark as all the curtains had been pulled together and there was a silence so deep that it could nearly be touched.

To Sarah, the streets outside felt to be as remote as China and she was sure that; for her, an every-day life would never again be attainable.

Sarah, Peggy and Elinor lay besieged by death, thoughts of death and the consequences of death. It hung over the three of them like a cloud, a cloud which would never lift.

Elinor snuffled and pushed further into the bosom of her mother.

Peggy Nicholson opened her eyes and said, "I suppose we'll have t'get out o' this house in a day or two. It'll be wanted."

Sarah's reply was short, "I suppose so."

"I'll find lodgings for m'sel' over at Queen Mary or Queen Ann Street. I should be fine there," said Peggy doubtfully.

Sarah's eyes opened wide, "It's awful there. Why should you move at all?"

"I'll be nought but a burden t'ye. I don't want to be that. Jack wouldn't ha' wanted it."

"How could you possibly be a burden?"

"Why, woman, ye've got prospects. You're a teacher, away up t'the big house every weekday. Ye don't want me in yer way," Peggy began to sob.

Sarah breathed deeply and comforted, "*I'm* the burden, Peggy, not you. How could I manage without my washing done, food on the table and a house always as clean as can be?"

Peggy Nicholson sniffed, she found these words comforting, but were they sincere, she asked herself.

"We'll continue as before, just as though Jack were still with us, still bringing his dust and mess into the front room and demanding his tea."

Mrs Nicholson senior began to cry, "*Aye..., Aye....,*" she sighed between sobs, "That's how it'll be...."

Elinor woke up, "What's wrong with Nana?" She asked.

"Nana's fine, she's just a little tired," replied Sarah.

"Why is she crying, then? And where is my daddy?"

Sarah's voice broke as she replied though she managed to hold back her own tears, "He's gone a long way away, my dear. You will see him again, I promise that you *will*, but you must be patient."

Elinor considered this for a moment and then said, "You and Nana aren't going to this far away place too, are you?"

Sarah shook her head, "We'll both be going there eventually, but not for a long time yet."

"I don't want you to go, I don't, I don't, I *don't*....."

Sarah smoothed her daughter's hair, "Hush, my lovely, believe me, you will soon understand everything."

*****

Richard Turner finished writing and handed to his wife his leading article for a special Sunday edition of the *Chronicle*

She read quickly, nodding in agreement with the sentiments he expressed.

Yesterday, all of Martindale was both stunned and shamed by the murder of Mr John Nicholson. His was a pointless slaying, carried-out in the street in a devious and cowardly way.

Mr Nicholson was a stalwart of this town, a founding member; if you like, a man who could not be ignored, a man who could be relied upon in any situation. He was that rare creature, A Man For All Seasons.

John Nicholson's working life was spent in the pits of County Durham, where he quickly became a hewer of great renown.

However, it soon became evident that he was also a leader who held the respect of everyone he met in the palm of one hand.

It is the opinion of many who knew him that when Parliament is next reformed and the franchise extended much more liberally than it is now, then John Nicholson was man enough to be sent as a representative of labouring men.

Thus a promising and productive life has been cut needlessly short, his going a great loss to everyone in Martindale.

Jack leaves a wife and daughter behind. His marriage to Sarah was a love match. He himself could never believe that she; a teacher, would agree to marry a common hewer. Conversely, she always recognised in him the promise of greatness.

It is the intention of this journal to begin a fund for the dependents of Mr Nicholson with a donation of £150. Surely, if this town can find hundreds of pounds to bring Mr Villiers back from exile, then it can donate double that for the family of a true and worthy son of Martindale.

My eyes are full of tears as I write this and I expect yours will be too as you read it.

Jane sniffed, "I didn't know him at all well, but I wish I had."

"He was one of those who everyone takes for granted, though as soon as they're gone they are missed beyond measure."

Chapter Twelve

In the days which followed Jack's death, Sarah Nicholson disciplined herself not to cry. Her face, the colour of creamy marble was not allowed by her to show any trace of emotion. She held her body gracefully erect and when she spoke her tone was both soft and gentle.

However, *inside* she seethed. Everything she had ever believed in was in ruins. Around her lay only desolation and a loneliness which was only relieved by the presence of her child. Jack's child.

She desperately, indeed craved, to find a path, no matter how narrow and twisting, which would lead her away from the wreckage of her life.

"Sarah, dear, how are you," the voice of Lady Martin broke into her thoughts.

Sarah allowed the ghost of a smile to appear on her lips, "I am well enough, Marian," she replied firmly.

"I'm not so sure that you should take-up your post again so soon after....," Marian's throat lumped and she found that she could not continue.

Sarah took her friend's hand, "I must," she said, "the education of your children cannot be delayed any longer."

"Jane, Caroline and I have done our best with them and we can continue as need be, if you'd prefer a little longer."

The same slight smile appeared on Sarah's face before she replied, "I'm sure you have done wonderfully well, but I made a commitment to the children from which I cannot and *shall not* withdraw... For any reason."

Marian smiled, stepped forward and hugged her friend, "You'll get over this my dear," she whispered, "you are too strong a person not to."

Sarah tried to respond to Marian's touch and words of encouragement, but she could not, apart from a slight nod of agreement.

Lady Martin was worried, for she could easily recall the state she had found herself in on the death of Gareth. She hoped that Sarah would be spared the depths of despair that she herself had suffered but doubted that this would be so.

"You need not be unduly concerned for me, Marian, I shall continue until my works makes up; to some little extent, for my loss."

"As you wish, Sarah, then the children may expect you at the beginning of next week?"

"Yes. Next week and the week after and the week after that."

*****

"Frank, love, I've just made a pot of tea an' there's an apple pie due out o' the oven," Rosemary Spence's delight showed both in her voice and in the smile which lit up her face.

"Why, a pot of tea and a slice of pie, what more could a man want," said Frank as he took what had become his customary chair.

"What have ye been doin' the day?" asked Rosemary as she carefully retrieved the pie from her very hot oven.

"We've been very busy getting the mines and works back to normal after all the trouble we've had.....," Frank's voice croaked to a stop as the memory of John Nicholson came into his mind.

Rosemary came and stood behind him, squeezing his shoulders as she said, "Best, ye don't over-dwell on it, Frank. Jack was just unlucky, an' ye only need t'be unlucky once."

Frank's right hand reached up and patted her left one lying on his shoulder, "Yes, I suppose so."

"Think how lucky you've been – it could easily have gone the other way."

"Lucky? Me lucky? With a face like this and my legs aching and smarting for half the night?"

"Aye, *lucky* I said an' *lucky* I mean. You're alive, aren't ye? Many a man would change places wi' you, Frank Turner. First ye lose the farm but fall on yer feet, then ye get a big house where ye're waited on hand-and-foot. Besides which ye marry the daughter of a vicar and become the friend of a baronet."

Frank smiled, "Aye, I suppose you're right, Rosie, you usually are."

Rosemary laughed aloud, though it had within it a hint of bitterness, "I wasn't right nor lucky when I allowed my folk t'turn me away from ye. We could ha' been happy, Frank."

"Which is more than I am now, with all my money, house and possessions," it was Frank's turn to sound aggrieved.

"Aye, well, drink yer tea an' don't let that pie get cold, then ye'll feel better."

*****

As Captain Helmuth Schilling rode into camp on his return from his visit to Gettysburg, he was greeted by the unpleasant sight of two of his troopers bound tightly to the wheels of the regimental quartermaster's wagon.

He dismounted outside the tent which served as his company's headquarters and called for Second-Lieutenant Carter Gibson, determined to know the reason for the punishment he'd seen.

"Sir," said an out of breath Gibson as he entered the CO's quarters.

"*Field punishments*, Mr Gibson? Field punishments in my company? For what crime, may I ask?" Helmuth made it obvious that he was very annoyed.

"First-Lieutenant Matheson is back," informed Gibson, emphasising his brother officer's superior rank.

"Yes, I see, this would be difficult for you," the Captain's tone made clear his understanding of the situation. "Then his uncle has sent him packing, has he."

"No, Hooker has sacked Eldred's uncle," continued Gibson.

"So he no longer requires the services of Lieutenant Matheson," Helmuth caught on at once.

Then his mind began to assess the problems associated with the early return of his second-in-command.

"Oh, by the way, the word around the camp is that Joe Hooker is going to resign and will be replaced by Meade," informed Gibson.

Helmuth's ears pricked up, "So the Army of the Potomac's to have yet *another* new commander. How many is that we've had?"

"I've lost count," Gibson shook his head.

"So have I," replied Helmuth before he sent for his second-in-command.

On arrival, and understanding he was in trouble, Matheson brought himself to a stiff-attention, though this was marred by a gentle swaying of his body and eyes which were finding it difficult to focus.

"What's the meaning of dealing out field-punishments without my consent?" Schilling's voice was cold and sharp.

"As you were absent at the time, I *was* the commanding officer," Matheson was much put-out and his tone indicated this.

"Nonetheless, what crime could Coburg and Larson possibly have committed to deserve such punishment?"

"Both troopers were insulting and insubordinate to me personally," Matheson sounded aggrieved.

"In what way?" queried the company commander.

"They laughed openly when I tripped over the guide-rope of my tent," Lieutenant Matheson defended his actions.

"He fell flat on his face and the whole camp laughed," added Gibson, his tone deadpan.

Helmuth turned to Gibson, "So you witnessed their *crime* too."

Carter Gibson nodded, "Yes, sir. I saw it all."

"I may well have enjoyed the scene myself, had I been there," commented Helmuth, who went on to say, "However, I do not believe their crime serious enough to warrant immobilisation for several hours."

"I was in command. I was the judge of their actions," Eldred Matheson, slurred his words and punctuated them with spittle.

"Well, I've returned now," said Captain Schilling before turning to Gibson, "Set the troopers free and tell them to take more care in future with what they find amusing."

The second-lieutenant saluted smartly and went about his business.

"You're letting them off, I shall become a laughing-stock," Matheson's voice was raised high.

"You already *are* a laughing-stock, though I don't find you at all funny myself."

"Funny or not, I was in *command*."

Helmuth sharpened his tone, "You had no business dealing with silly behaviour as though it were a major breach-of-discipline. You also knew fine well that I'd never have condoned so brutal a punishment."

Matheson hung his head, looking very much like a small boy who's prank has gone wrong but who is determined not to apologise.

"Anyway, enough of that, for we've more important business to discuss. In your absence the company has been re-organised. Lieutenant Gibson commands the first half-company and the other will continue to be led by Sergeant Crittenden."

"I'm superior in rank to both of them and Crittenden's not even an officer. You're giving them what's mine by right," Matheson's voice was raised high and his facial colouring had shaded from pallid-green to bright-pink.

"You do realise, I hope, that our regiment will soon be taking part in a major battle," Helmuth spoke harshly, "I will not make risky changes at so dangerous a time."

"Then what am I supposed to do?" Matheson began to rage.

"You, Mr Matheson, shall act as my adjutant."

"You can't do this, Crittenden's only a non-com, I'm an officer, for Christ's sake…."

"You've never even vaguely resembled an officer and I'll not have you lead my men into battle," Helmuth couldn't have been more forthright.

"You're still blaming me for Occaquon," shouted Matheson, "You ran too… Don't you dare to forget that… You ran too."

"I *did* run and I'm still ashamed of it. However, remember, I came into camp many, *many* minutes after you."

"I'll see Colonel Kellogg about this. My father's a big name in Philadelphia, knows Governor Curtin well… You can't do this, I'm an officer by Act of Congress," by this time Matheson was virtually howling.

"Then damn well *behave* like an officer. *Lead* like one. And should it become necessary *die* like one," Helmuth's voice also reached a high pitch.

"My 'pa will see to this," threatened Eldred, "He knows *everyone*, your life won't be worth livin' once he's through with you."

"We'll see," smiled Helmuth grimly, "Now get out before I kick you out."

*****

Sir Charles Martin dismounted, handed the reins of his horse to a groom and was making his way inside when he came upon Virgil Kent.

"Ah, Kent, I hear you've successfully introduced the children to riding?"

Kent brought himself to a stiff attention, "Sir."

"How have they taken to it?"

"Very well, Sir Charles, both born t'the saddle I'd say."

"Well, anyway, you've done well, they look much more comfortable on a horse than I ever do."

"It helps if you learn young, sir… Or join the cavalry."

"You were a cavalryman?" queried Charles, noticing the footman's military bearing for the first time.

"Yes, sir. Ten years sir. With the *Cherrypickers*."

"*Ah*, they're the 11th Hussars, are they not? You charged with the Light Brigade, then?"

Kent's rigid stance relaxed slightly and he gave an almost inaudible sigh, "Aye, sir, I did."

"You must have been lucky to survive," suggested the baronet.

"Cannon ball disembowelled my mount about half-way down the valley. *Clarion* he was called, a fine gelding."

"Lucky for you, unlucky for your mount."

"Looking back now, if my old charger had carried-on much further down the valley...," Kent shook his head in remembrance of close friends and a special animal.

They stood in silence for a moment and then Charles asked, "Would you have *'Gone again'* as it was reported some trooper offered?"

Kent's face took on a bitter smile, "No, sir, if that man ever existed, which I doubt, then he'd just been released from a lunatic asylum. I wouldn't have gone again, no not for free beer for the rest of eternity."

Charles pondered for a while and then said, "Bertie and Drina are loathe to lose you. Can you stay a little longer and continue with their riding lessons? Perhaps you would introduce young Robert to the secrets of horsemanship too."

"I believe my mistress would raise no objections to my remaining here for another fortnight or so. She's keen to see her children become confident riders."

"Excellent," replied Sir Charles, "I also hear that you're a particular favourite of their nurse, Miss Jackson."

"She's a fine lass, sir," replied Kent soberly, but his thoughts differed considerably from his words.

*****

As he walked from Jack Nicholson's funeral, Matthew Priestly was filled with dismay and foreboding.

He came to a sudden stop at the bottom of the steps leading to the entrance of Martindale Methodist Church, paused for a moment and then gazed heavenwards before shouting, "Damn you God, damn you, damn you, *damn you*."

As he became aware of the angry looks other funeral goers were directing against him, his face pinkened slightly and he shook his head, half-in-apology and half-in-sorrow.

As far as the leader of the Miners' Association was concerned the death of John Nicholson was a disaster. Jack was the leader the men listened to, not only colliers but working men of every description too. He was the perfect foil against the mischief of Eddy Dobson.

Priestly cleared his throat and took a deep breath before he whispered to himself, "And what good were *you* in this?"

For during the riot a group of colliers; his own men, had ignored and then trampled over him.

Not long after, Jack Nicholson had a belligerent group of ironworkers laughing *with* him, safely held in the palm of his hand. A short time later he would have persuaded them to go to home.

Though this was not to be, for he was struck down from behind by a stupid oaf who was certain to hang.

It was at this moment Priestly became determined to show the qualities of a leader, though it would require him to discarding an oath he had made to the woman he'd both loved and lost.

*****

Lieutenant-Colonel Esprey watched as his wife, Elizabeth, was handed down from their carriage after attending the funeral of John Nicholson and he very much liked what he saw.

She turned to face him, her green eyes and copper hair set off by the black-silk of her mourning outfit.

"Shall we have luncheon, or perhaps wait for an hour or so?" She enquired.

"We'd best have it now."

As he spoke Elizabeth recognised in his eyes that his mind was set on more than food.

"Carew," shouted Esprey as they entered Merrington Manor.

The soldier-servant came from the shadows, "Sir?"

"Luncheon, Carew, luncheon in half-an-hour," ordered the colonel.

"Sir," Carew nodded.

"Is there to be steak-and-onion pudding?"

"I believe so, colonel."

Esprey rubbed his hands together, "Good, tell cook to cut me an extra-large slice and send what remains of the dish straight up to the dining room."

"As you say, sir," replied the corporal before he headed towards the kitchens.

Elizabeth entered her dressing room and removed her veil and bonnet. Then, with the help of her maid, she began to remove her jacket, dress and crinoline.

Colonel Esprey entered his wife's *boudoir* without knocking, his face intent.

He then nodded towards the maid. who had just unlaced her mistress' corset, "Mrs Esprey can do without you now," he said, his voice soft."

The servant bobbed and looked shyly towards the lady of the house.

Elizabeth nodded gently and then smiled at her husband.

As soon as the servant had gone Jervis Esprey took his wife in his arms and began to rain kisses laced with passion upon her lips, neck and shoulders.

"*Oh, Jervie,*" she cried, buckling on to the bed beneath him.

Before much longer he was tearing at her underwear, renting open the separate parts which covered her vagina. Then, before she expected it, he had entered her and was thrusting long and hard.

"Oh, I do love you, I do want and need you, Lizzy," the colonel cried aloud and passionately.

Elizabeth recognised that no lady should *ever* pant with animal abandon, though she was happy to flout convention and did so.

"*Lizzy, Lizzy,*" continued Esprey as he kissed and caressed his wife, at the same time attempting to pull away her chemise to give his fingers access to her breasts.

"*Wait,*" she ordered hoarsely, before she tore off the offending garment herself and flung it on to the floor.

The colonel set too again with a will and soon had his wife near to howling with the vigour of his strokes.

Then, all at once, it was over and they both sank back on to the mattress, gazing at the ceiling their breathing heavy.

"God that was good," said Colonel Esprey.

"Indeed it was, my love," agreed Elizabeth.

"I always have a craving for food-and-fornication after a funeral," he observed semi-seriously.

"When's the next funeral to be, do you suppose?"

*****

"Nicholson's was a very well attended funeral," commented Solomon Vasey to his fellow actor, Roderick Villiers.

"Assemble the right cast and people will turn up in droves."

"I can't think who will bother to stand at my graveside," said Vasey thoughtfully.

"I shall be there come rain or shine," promised Villiers.

Vasey laughed, "Why, you'll be gone long before I."

Villiers came to a sudden stop and faced his friend, "*I know death hath ten thousand several doors For men to take their exits...,*" he paused for precisely the correct length of time and then continued meaningfully, "*But none of us knows the when or the where of it.*"

"First quotation was good, the Bard perhaps?"

"Webster, the *Duchess of Malfi*."

Vasey shook his head, "All dead, they all end up dead in that."

"It's a dreary play, though popular in certain quarters."

"The Angel of Death hovers constantly above our heads," Villiers remarked solemnly, "we must never forget this"

"Either of us could be taken at any time. Suppose we were to go at the same time? In a train crash, say."

"What a disaster that would be for the English Theatre," suggested Villiers seriously.

"Indeed, yes," Vasey nodded vigorously in agreement.

"The Martin Arms may not be a bad place to be snatched from this earth," suggested Roddy Villiers.

Vasey nodded, "Indeed it would not, let us see if they have a bottle or two of the brandy they keep especially for you."

*****

"Did you notice Caroline's face at the commitment?" Jane asked of her husband.

"She looked very pale, I don't believe I've ever seen her so washed out."

"She already fears for Helmuth and I believe Mr Nicholson's death, coming so suddenly, has unsettled her further."

"You could well be right."

"Don't you think you ought to visit her more often?"

Richard didn't like where this was leading, "We'll visit Blanchwell together, when next we have time."

"Perhaps, though as this is a very trying time for her. Frequent visits would be best."

"We haven't the time."

"Perhaps we should go separately."

There was a long silence and then Richard's voice was raised, "Jane, why must you *test* me like this? How can I convince you that any liaison there was between myself and Caroline was never consummated. I have you and the children, for what more could I wish?"

Jane's face became fixed and immobile as terrible thoughts of loneliness-and-loss tumbled through her mind.

Richard crossed the room and took her in his arms and gently kissed each of her eyelids.

She responded by cuddling as deeply into his chest as she could and remained there for a long few minutes. Then she opened her eyes and looked into his face, "How can you care for me when I'm so ugly... It's impossible... It's ridiculous, I'm ridiculous."

"You have never been even close to ridiculous – unlike my good-self."

"You can't deny that I'm ugly."

"You are ordinary on the outside, there's no denying this, though inside you are truly beautiful."

"You think so? I do not repulse you?"

"We have two children and have coupled many more times than *twice*," Richard laughed gently.

After a moment, Jane sniffed and then joined his laughter with her own.

"We're a curious couple," observed Richard.

"Very curious," agreed Jane before she added, "Perhaps we should go to bed."

*****

"I was especially struck by the courage of Mrs Nicholson," observed Charles Martin as his carriage rumbled towards Blanchwell.

Marian grasped her husband's hand, she shook her head as though it were herself suffering the pain of bereavement, "I don't know how Sarah was able to face it so well. I know I couldn't have."

What little colour remained in Caroline Schilling's face, left it as she thought of her husband, enduring goodness knew what dangers on the battlefield that America had become.

Charles gripped the hand of his wife firmly, "There, there, my love, these things happen, even so, I could hardly hold back the tears myself."

"Do you think Sarah will recover?" Asked Marian.

"How can she," Caroline's tone was flat and it was obvious that she was thinking of herself in the same situation.

Charles reached across the space between them and took both of Caroline's hands in his own. "Helmuth will be all right, you'll see, he'll be back before you know it."

The baronet's words were of little comfort to Mrs Schilling, for the war in America seemed it would go on endlessly and if this were the case, how could her husband be home soon?

"Yes, the Union has the numbers in both men and materiel of war, they're sure to triumph sooner than we think."

"It'll go on for months, if not years, yet. Helmuth sees no hope of an early end to it," Caroline's tone was deadpan.

"We must wait for and accept the Will of the Lord," even as she spoke, Marian felt a hypocrite, for her own belief in God had been badly shaken after the death of Gareth.

Caroline merely smiled, "You're both very kind to me and I much appreciate it, but *please*, no more words of comfort."

*****

"I really don't know why we should have had to attend Nicholson's funeral," Abigail Turner was in full, spiteful, spate.

Frank looked at his wife in amazement, but before he could begin to speak she continued on.

"For, after all, Nicholson was a mere hewer of coal. On top of which not so long ago, we were expected to attend the interment of the Russell boy."

"Jack Nicholson was a good man, a brave and honest man."

Abigail laughed sharply, "Why, he was such a paragon of virtue that his own wife was unable to shed so much as a single tear over him."

"Mrs Nicholson behaved with the greatest dignity, I thought she was truly *magnificent.*"

Abigail pulled up short and stared at her husband, "*Dignity?* To show no sorrow at the graveside of her husband."

"In public; were I to die, you'd go through handkerchiefs galore though inside you'd care nothing," Frank laughed harshly.

"How can you say such a thing," Abigail flung her gloved hands up to her face in simulated horror.

"It's easy, Abigail, it's very easy."

"Then you do not deserve to have me. When I think of what I've helped you become, the struggle and travails I have endured on your behalf, why I'm nearly struck dumb."

Again Frank laughed, "Struck dumb, is it? If only that were the case."

"You're no more a gentleman than is a beast of the field," Abigail turned on her husband, her eyes reflecting her anger.

"Yes, well, if I'm *no* gentleman, then you're *no* lady."

Abigail was affronted, "How *dare* you say such a thing."

"Should you truly desire to be a lady, then look at the examples set by Sarah Nicholson, Caroline Schilling and by my sister too, if we're coming down to comparisons."

Abigail cut off her husband furiously, "Your sister? *Little Molly,* or perhaps I'd better refer to her as Lady Marian."

"Yes, perhaps you should as she has more true gentility in her than you've ever possessed."

"*HOW DARE YOU*," Abigail sputtered in rage.

"I dare because I've discovered what you are, I know you inside-out and the whole is not a pretty picture. For all your airs- and-graces, for all the trouble you take with manners and the way things should be, you've lost the humanity you were born with. Shame on you, Abigail, shame."

"Why, I've never been...," Abigail began strongly though her husband cut short her words.

"Don't think *I'll* ever wish to share my bed with *you* again either," he cried forcefully.

Abigail could find no reply, but with her self-esteem smarting, she pulled herself to full erectness, straightened her hat, gazed with something close to hatred at her husband and then strode off without glancing back.

*****

Geoffrey Hodge saw that Prudence Urquhart, his fiancée, was hanging back in order to be the last of the congregation to leave Evensong. This quickened his pulse rate considerably.

"My dear, will you tarry a while?" He asked as she came up.

"Of course, my love," she stopped beside him and tilted her head until her face was bathed in the pink-light of the dipping sun.

"Perhaps you'll come to the vestry, for I've much to discuss with you," he suggested persuasively.

"That would be highly improper without a chaperone," her tone was sweet but her purpose firm.

"But, *but..*," stuttered the Curate, "We have been alone together before. We... *We..*," he dared not finish what he wished to say.

"Though this was prior to our engagement to marry. The situation has completely changed now," stated Prudence soberly, though her eyes twinkled.

Hodge found himself to be very disappointed. Prudence had given him a brief sight of paradise though was now denying him further access to its fruits, even though they were formally joined as the last of the banns had been read.

Prudence reached up and kissed him gently on the cheek, "Be patient, my love," she whispered, "Allow me to play the blushing bride, it's a role I've long waited for."

Geoffrey Hodge kissed her chastely back and then looked into her eyes, where he saw in them great promise, a promise that made his knees weak and his loins shiver.

"Shortly, my love, you shall have all you desire," she whispered before leaving for the household of Mrs Brass.

"Shall I call for supper?" He asked hopefully.

"Certainly, not, Geoffrey," replied her retreating figure.

*****

Cissy brought all the children into the schoolroom and handed out to each of them the work they had begun the previous week.

"I'm sick of this," complained Bertie Martin, "When's Mrs Nicholson returning?"

"Yes," put in Drina, "we may as well be out riding with Kent than doing this old stuff."

"Oh, it's all right," put in Robert Martin, "mama gave us it."

"*Ha*, she's not our mama," said Drina sharply.

"Lady Martin is your step-mother," said Cissy, and then; wishing to change the direction of the conversation, "Do you ride well with Mr Kent?"

"Oh, yes, and I'm much faster and more daring than Bertie," Drina pulled a face at her brother.

"That's of no matter, for I shall become a cavalryman," reposted Albert, "You're nothing but a *girl*, you can't be a soldier."

"You've fallen out of the saddle many times more than I. You'll begin your first charge as a brave lancer and end it as a plodding foot-soldier covered in dust," Drina laughed, finding her jibe to be an extremely amusing one.

"I shall be a cavalryman *and* a baronet."

"*Ha*, the army won't have you at *any* price."

"Papa will buy me a commission."

"No he won't."

"He will and I shall become a *general*…," began Bertie, then he noticed how quiet the room had become and turned to see that Mrs Nicholson had entered.

The room remained still, as though under a spell, with each child instinctively understanding the frame of mind that their teacher was in and what her needs were.

Sarah reached the chair she often used when she wished to read to them and sat down.

None of the children spoke, but they came and gathered around her, calmly waiting.

The widow, Mrs Nicholson, sat serenely, her countenance immobile.

Slowly and quietly, one by one, the children edged closer to her feet, the face of each child tilted towards their teacher, waiting for her to speak, to tell them what she wanted, to tell them what she *needed* to tell them.

Young Maud Turner shuffled along on her bottom until she was very close, then she got to her feet and buried her face into the crook of Sarah's arm, "*I love you Mrs Nicholson,*" she whispered hoarsely.

"I love you too," added Martin Cowley, his face serious and full of concern.

"We all love you," confirmed Guido Turner.

An even deeper silence enveloped the room, it was as though their actions had been planned and agreed to by every child present.

Sarah's whole body began to tremble and her eyes filled with the tears she'd managed to hold-back for so long.

"It will help if you cry," advised Robert Martin.

Sarah gulped, sniffed and then began to sob ever more deeply, each extended gasp expressing her rage, hurt and loss.

"Don't worry, Mrs Nicholson, we'll look after you," promised Bertie Martin.

The tears flooded rapidly down Sarah's cheeks and kept on coming as; one by one, the children left the room, knowing that their teacher needed to be alone for a little while with her grief.

*****

"Well, missy, I'll be staying on at Martin Hall for a while yet," stated Virgil Kent confidently.

"Is that so," returned Cissy Jackson trying to keep her response completely neutral.

"It is indeed so. Sir Charles wishes me to carry-on with Bertie and Drina's riding lessons. Wants me to teach young Robert too."

"What ever will Winterbourne Abbey do without you?"

"The children always come first with the Marchioness," Kent wasn't certain this was indeed the case, but he felt it was the right thing to say.

"That's all fine-and-well then."

"Isn't it time you took me to meet your mother? I bet she's curious why you're so cheerful now. Not at all like the squeaky little mouse I first met."

"Don't flatter yourself, Mr Kent," replied Cissy, her tone decidedly moderate.

Kent caught her hand, pulled her into his body and planted a fierce kiss directly on to her lips.

Cissy tried to pull free of him but found that he was far too strong for her meagre eight-stones.

"*Let me go,* you've no right," she managed to gasp once her lips had been released.

"I've every right, I'm the man for you and you know it," Kent's left hand supported the nape of her neck and again he pulled her towards him, kissing her even more urgently.

Cissy had no choice other than to return the caress of his lips, but she was still disconcerted by his attentions. For there was something about him of which she was unsure. She then came to the realisation that he reminded her of her captor, the man who had bound her to a chair and had taken liberties with her that should only be allowed to her future husband. She trembled at the thought and pulled her lips away.

Kent, feeling a shiver run through her body mistook it for reciprocal passion and smiled to himself at the thought of how pleased the Marchioness of Studland would be that everything was going so well at Martin Hall.

*****

Sir Charles and Lady Marian were taking their ease in the rose garden when Inspector Mason called upon them.

"Thank you for the work you've carried out on my behalf," greeted the baronet, "in fact, for the whole of Martindale."

"And I must thank you for allowing me to peruse certain very interesting documents, Sir Charles."

Marian wondered which documents these could be, but thought it best not to ask.

"Anything new on Leakey?" Queried Charles.

"As far as I can make out, he's flown."

"Gone?" Charles was surprised that the impostor clergymen has gone so suddenly.

What about the Christian Workers' place?" Questioned Marian.

"Shut down, empty as far as I could see," replied Mason.

"It is a great pity that so useful a place should have been established by such a rogue," considered Charles.

"Perhaps it could be resurrected," suggested Marian.

"Properly constituted it would be of great value to the town," agreed Charles.

"Anyway, the place is currently closed and our suspect has gone. I'll telegraph colleagues at Liverpool and ask if Leakey's turned up there," offered Mason.

"Will proceedings begin against the Losser boy?" Marian hoped that they would not.

"Until the Law catches up with Deacon and Twiss, there's not much more that can be done," replied the inspector sadly.

"Yes, well, at least Martindale's rid of him and his cohorts," nodded Sir Charles.

"For good, I trust," put in Lady Marian.

"You'll dine with with us, Inspector?" Offered the baronet.

"I believe I shall, Sir Charles, thank you."

*****

"Welcome to the Board of the Martindale Iron & Coal Company, Colonel," Sir Charles greeted.

"Very pleased to have something to do at last," replied Jervis Esprey as he firmly gripped the baronet's hand.

"We're quite a small group here, there being very few individual shareholders," continued Charles who went on to introduce everyone present, "Frank Turner, whom I'm sure you know."

The colonel nodded and smiled at the man with the ruined face who stood before him, "And how is Mrs Turner?"

"Very well, colonel," replied Frank.

Esprey doubted this, as Turner's woman; as the whole town knew, was a harridan of the shrillest sort.

"Mister Digby, who also acts as our lawyer," continued the landowner.

"I believe we've met before," the colonel smiled.

"Mrs Schilling, who, of course you know, is here representing her husband," introduced Sir Charles.

"I suppose; by rights, I'm representing my wife, for at present I have no shares of my own," informed the colonel.

The meeting was called to order and Charles began with the most pressing business before them.

"We only have one item on our agenda and that is the proposed contract with the Western Supply Company."

"I've received a letter from Mr Fred Schilling, which I will now pass around the table. Perhaps, after you've read it, we shall continue." Charles sat down and took a sip of water.

A few minutes later, Lieutenant-Colonel Esprey was first to speak, "Why do you suppose that the Union Pacific and Central Pacific companies would wish to make purchases through the services of a third party? Seems strange to me."

"The Western Supply Company hopes to persuade them that working through a single supplier will cut their costs as well as increase their efficiency," commented Digby.

"I suppose that is possible, but it's something I too have wondered about," added Frank.

"You're sure this letter *is* from Mr. Fred Schilling?" Queried Caroline.

"Yes."

"I've not seen too much of Fred's handwriting, but this doesn't look like his. To begin with it's far too carefully written."

Sam Watson looked up sharply, "Mrs Schilling has a point, he's a careless devil with a pen is Fred."

"Even if it is his, can we rely on so young and inexperienced a man?" Colonel Esprey asked.

"He's a good'un, knows his business, but I must admit that he *is* inexperienced," commented Watson.

Charles sighed deeply, "Well, we were happy enough to send him to America and it's only when he's done as he was asked, that we're beginning to have doubts over his level of experience."

"Which we already knew was minimal before he went," put in Caroline.

"We'll have to come to a decision, for there's a lot of money to be made here and the Western Company are hoping for our tender to reach them soon. Also, keep in mind that the paperwork must cross the Atlantic, so whatever we decide to-day isn't going to get to New York to-morrow," warned the lawyer.

"There's no harm in actually tendering, though, is there?" Asked Charles Martin.

"No, it don't mean we have to sign anything binding," put in Esprey.

"To myself it has a strong stink of fish," said Caroline, "but, as you say, there's no need to risk any investment just yet."

"Though suppose a contract is won and we find we can't deliver because we haven't increased capacity?" Enquired Digby.

All the members of the Board looked to Sam Watson.

The Viewer thought for a moment and then said, "The lad's will have to work harder and for longer."

"That could lead to further trouble," protested the baronet, desperate to avoid another disturbance.

"They'll receive more pay through it, that should sweeten them," mused Frank.

Esprey nodded, "Money can smooth most rough edges."

"Suppose things go wrong at the collieries or the iron works? Accidents happen, as we all know too well," Caroline opened her eyes wide as she spoke.

The room became quiet as everyone thought of the consequences of not being able to deliver the contracted goods.

Eventually, Frank spoke up, "Why don't we start-up some production now? Build a stock-pile even before we have the contract?"

Digby's lawyer's soul was outraged, "The rails would lie rusting, we may never be able to sell them, we're talking of many thousands of pounds."

"It's a risk, I admit, but there's always a market somewhere in the world for our products," replied Frank Turner.

"Could they not be melted down again and transformed into something else at a later date?" Queried Caroline.

"Possibly," replied Watson with little enthusiasm.

"Business is like war, risks must be taken to achieve success," said Jervis Esprey.

"Should we vote on this?" Sir Charles asked the Board.

"No, let's not, for we've time to ponder further," said Caroline.

"Aye, give us a little while longer to think on it," was Watson's opinion.

Colonel Esprey merely nodded his agreement.

*****

Thomas Leakey settled himself comfortably into his carriage which was taking him to London. He had decided to spend a day or two in the capital before leaving for Dover, there to take the Calais-Packet and safety in Europe.

It seemed that Losser had changed sides and was being sheltered by the dreadful Cook woman. On top of which, the policeman, Mason, was still snooping around, asking awkward questions here, there and everywhere.

"It's a great pity the other reprobates should be so easily free of me," Leakey muttered to himself as he realised that he would have to give up any thought of taking further revenge on those who had degraded him.

Though he smiled to himself in a satisfied sort of way as he thought of Nicholson lying dead in the street and Dunnett incarcerated.

It's best I stay away from Liverpool, he thought to himself, shaking his head sadly, as the New Church Asylum had very much suited him and he was loathe to let it go.

However, he would remain abroad for a month or two and then discover from Cruikshank how the land lay. Were all well, then he might return as there would be a further crop of fresh, young faces he could take his pleasure from.

Fortunately, he had considerable means and so could travel anywhere he wished.

"*Mmm*," he considered to himself, "Florence or Rome perhaps, for the streets of Italy are strewn with willing street urchins. I may visit both countries. Indeed, I believe that I *shall* go to both and see which of them suits me best."

*****

"Well, Hodge, I see you've played the Judas, the viper in the nest, the treacherous crocodile slinking in the mud….," Edwin Lander struggled to find any further illustrations of treachery.

"Prudence and I are to be married on Saturday next, 27th June, at Holy Innocents. I hope you shall attend and, indeed, we would be greatly honoured if you would agree to conduct the service," Geoffrey Hodge stood calmly, his steady gaze not being deflected in any way by the anger of his visitor.

"How dare you, sir, suggest such a thing. You take-up with a vulnerable woman of middle years and entice her away from the bosom of her family."

Venetia Lander came behind her husband and took his arm firmly, "I'm sure Mr Hodge would much prefer to discuss this inside, rather than at the doorway of Kirkby Vicarage, well within the hearing of most of his parishioners."

"Of course, please, come in," Hodge immediately felt that Mrs Lander had some sympathy with his position.

Edwin Lander was about to refuse, but a gentle push from his wife ended his complaints and he followed the curate into the drawing-room.

Lander sniffed and looked about, "Where's Marshall? What does he say about this? He'll not be happy, I'll be bound. Bring him in, I need to speak to him."

"I'm afraid the Reverend Mr Marshall has gone to his reward. His funeral was yesterday."

"Oh, I'm so sorry to hear that. He was so sweet an old man," Venetia spoke softly.

A much-deflated Rector of Holy Innocents coughed, nodded, shook his head and said, "Regret to hear of it, very sad indeed."

"I'm to take his living and Prudence is much looking forward to becoming the Mistress of Kirkby Vicarage."

"The Cathedral has agreed to your appointment? In so short a time? They knowing what you have engineered?" Lander was flabbergasted.

"Edwin, my dear, Mr Hodge has committed no crime and where else could the Dean & Chapter find a more suitable candidate?"

The Reverend Lander spluttered and tried to find a reply, but before he was able to his wife spoke again.

"Mr Hodge's marriage must have been favourably looked upon by the Cathedral, for do they not prefer married clergymen," Venetia's tone was persuasive.

"But, Venetia, *Prudence... Prudence....*"

"Prudence is very happy, very happy indeed. Have you spoken to her?" Enquired Mr Hodge.

"No, we have not," a tinge of irritability came into Venetia's voice, "Mr Lander *insisted* that we come here first, even after undergoing an *exhausting* journey of many hours."

"Then you must take refreshment," offered Geoffrey Hodge at once.

"No, sir......," began Edwin Lander.

Venetia forced her husband into a comfortable seat and took one herself, she tilted her head, smiled at Hodge and replied, "That would be so very kind and so very welcome."

When Hodge had left the room to speak to his cook, the Rector of Holy Innocents turned angrily on his wife, "How dare you....," he began.

"Edwin, *Edwin*," Venetia's voice was chilly and full of warning, it was a tone she had only used two or three times previously in the whole of their married life.

"Yes, Venetia," his temper was cooling quickly.

"The die is cast. Prudence is to be married and there is nothing you can do about it. Accept it. Do you hear me? *Accept it.*"

Mr Lander's chin dropped on to his chest, "Yes, my dear," he replied sheepishly.

*****

Eddy Dobson and two of his stalwarts entered the office of the Miners' Association and confronted Matthew Priestly.

"We're takin' ower here, ye'd best get yersel' away."

Priestly looked up unfazed, "Oh, really? Where's your legitimacy? In your back pocket, I suppose?"

"Divn't call us illegitimate," cried an outraged young tub-filler.

"Aye, I wasn't birthed on the wrong side o' the blanket neither," shouted a hewer of no great reputation.

Eddy raised his hands to calm his associates, "Leave it t'me, lads, ye've got the wrong end o' the shovel."

"Aye, well, if ye sez so, Eddy."

The leader of the radical delegation turned his attention once more to Priestly, "Get out, get out now while ye've the chance. The Association is turning in the right direction t'day."

"Aye, we thought ye'd ha' been away by now," said the tub-filler.

"There's no room for ye in Martindale, we're goin' to change all that's wrong," added the hewer.

Matthew Priestly rose to his feet and briefly scanned each of the faces before him, "Have you three even the vaguest idea of what you've inflicted upon this town?"

"Aye, we have, we're leading the masses to the liberty they've earned by the sweat of their brows," returned Dobson zealously, certain of the rightness of his cause.

"Yer right there, Eddy," supported the tub-filler shrilly.

"Dobson, you are a pathetic disgrace to the cause you claim to follow. Your revolution to date has amounted to a few broken windows, one or two broken heads and..," Priestly's throat was choked with emotion for a few seconds and then he found his voice again, "And the murder of a good and true-man who was; unlike yourself, a *leader of men*."

Dobson replied quickly, "Why, leader is it, you're no leader, anyway. Ye're a yellow milksop, that's all ye are."

Matthew Priestly was now struggling to control his temper. He was raised in a violent society and had been deeply involved in violence himself – until through it he had lost the love of his life.

"After all that has happened I cannot believe you *dare* to attempt to make further trouble. It is preposterous, utterly preposterous."

"We're goin' t'sweep away the likes of you, Priestly on our way t'gaining true liberty."

"And we're goin' t'get what we want," shouted the hewer.

"No matter what it takes," cried the filler.

"How they must already be shaking in their shoes down at Westminster," Priestly laughed ironically, "Dobson on the warpath."

Eddy cut in, "We just want the best for the lads, the pity is, ye dinna see it that way."

"You want the best for the lads? You then man who led them on a pointless rampage which ended in a murder," Priestly was exasperated.

"I had nowt t'do wi' Jack's killin'," Dobson defended himself.

"Did you *not*, though? You and that damned Leakey fellow, who has since disappeared."

"Leakey's Cause was our Cause," Dobson defended the clergyman stoutly.

Priestly shook his head in disbelief, "How could you; a radical, ever have believed that such a man would have sympathy with the cause of labouring men?"

"Aye, well, he said he was......"

"You are an idiot. The stupidest man with a decent brain I've ever had the misfortune to come across," Priestly declared with some fervour.

"He canna' call ye that," shouted the filler.

"Knaw, ye're not puttin' up wi' that, are ye," added the hewer.

Dobson balled his hands into fists and thrust forward his chin pugnaciously, "I'll toss him out of office m'sel', you see if I don't," he shouted, stepping forward at the same time.

Matthew Priestly stepped deftly to one side and caught Dobson's outstretched chin with an uppercut. This was quickly followed by a second punch which puffed up the radical's left eye and then by a third heavy blow which winded him.

"*Sorry, Nan, but you see how it was,*" under his breath, Priestly apologised to his long-dead sweetheart.

Dobson, meanwhile, lay groaning on the floor.

Priestly stepped forward and pulled the radical leader to his feet and pushed him into the arms of his fellow conspirators.

"I shall call a meeting of the Committee to-morrow. We will discuss your part in the recent troubles and I will propose that you are expelled from the Martindale Miners' Association forthwith."

"Ye canna' do that," complained the hewer.

"I can and I shall."

"The Committee won't back ye," said the tub-filler.

"I believe they shall."

Eddy Dobson hung his head, "They will, they'll back him all the way, they've no fire in their bellies t'do owt else," he spoke morosely and then made went to the door.

Priestly called after him, "Eddy, you've a good brain, you're a clever man, don't waste it on pointless acts of sedition."

Dobson turned, "Everything I've done is for the *Cause*, I've nowt t'be sorry for."

Priestly shook his head as the delegation departed, "Such a pity," he muttered.

Chapter Thirteen
30th June 1863

After a considerable amount of work, Fred Schilling managed to lift the paving stone which had been pointed out to him by his brother. He knelt forward to see into the cavity and found it to be nearly filled by an ancient wooden-chest.

Fred took a grip on the box and gave a good heave, "*Ugh*," he groaned when it refused to budge even so much as an inch.

He tried a further three times with similar results and then decided to open the chest where it was instead.

This took a further ten minutes of pulling, levering and some downright vandalism. Though, eventually the top sprang open to reveal the box contained a dozen canvas bags of similar size. He chose one at random, opened it and shook out a stream of coins.

"*Phew*, Pa' was always awful mean so this must be where his money went," Fred muttered to himself as the light of his single lamp lit up the coins and reflected their bright yellowness into the dark of the cellar.

With difficulty he then withdrew a further bag and plonked it on to the floor beside him.

"Fred, what on earth are you doing? I thought the whole Rebel army was down there with you and fighting amongst themselves," It was his wife's voice.

"Come down here and bring Grace with you," he shouted his return.

A few minutes later all the Schillings were staring incredulously at the treasure-trove which lay before them.

"Pa' can't have hoarded all that himself," considered Grace, "he never had that much money to buy gold eagles."

"No, these must have been secreted away for years. Probably grandpa' or even great-grandpa' began the collection."

"We're rich," cried a dumfounded Grace Schilling.

"Yes, you are," agreed Amelia, who, after having been brought up in the daughter of an impecunious clergyman, had a great respect for wealth and the comforts it brought.

"We can't leave it here, the Rebs may get it," stated Fred.

"Can we carry it all?" queried Amelia, her voice indicating that she doubted it.

"It will be too heavy for the springs of the buggy," replied Fred thoughtfully.

"I think we should cover it up and sit-tight until this trouble is over," Grace was determined not to leave her family home without a fight.

"Helmuth wants us to get away, the war is nearby and anything could happen. A stray artillery shell may take our heads off as we sit having coffee tomorrow morning. The house may be plundered and burned, and you ladies… Well, soldiers who've been without their womenfolk for a long time….."

"Their officers wouldn't allow such behaviour..," Amelia didn't like to even think such thoughts.

"Their leaders are Southern gentlemen, so of course they would not tolerate any beastly behaviour, especially involving white gentlewomen," even in the face of so shocking a threat, Grace remained determined to stay where she was.

Fred shook his head, "It matters not, the thing is Helmuth wants us out of here, and I need to visit the offices of the railway companies, wherever they may be."

"I'm *not* moving," stated Grace.

"Yes you are," replied Fred forcefully.

"*Humph*, you're my *young* brother, I've no need to take orders from you," stated Grace forcefully.

"Would you have disobeyed papa?" Fred asked.

"Of course not," replied Grace sharply.

"Well, Fred currently the acting-head of the family, so you must obey him."

Grace became suddenly lost for words.

"We're going. Have I made myself clear?" Fred pushed his advantage.

"Only should it become absolutely necessary," Grace conceded ungracefully.

*****

"What on earth is that noise?" Queried Grace Schilling, straining her ears.

"Sounds like the whole town's in the street," said Fred.

"Let's go out and see," put in Amelia, excitedly.

Standing on the front porch, they could see that the whole town had come out to welcome the arrival of General Buford's First Cavalry Division.

"See," said Grace, "We need not flee, the Union Army is here."

Singing broke out spontaneously as the population of Gettysburg welcomed the sight of their boys-in-blue.

"Yes we'll rally round the flag, boys, we'll rally once again,

Shouting the battle cry of freedom……

Even though they were being joyously received by the local people, Fred noticed that the cavalrymen hardly had the energy to smile, so dog-tired were they.

"They don't look very smart, not soldierly smart," complained Grace.

"Well, they're not on a parade-ground holding a review, they must have been marching for days on end," defended Amelia.

"Helmuth is bound to be amongst them somewhere," said Fred and then he pointed excitedly, "yes, there's the regimental flag of the 17th Pennsylvania."

Amelia began to rigorously scan the faces of the troopers as they trotted past and looking further down the street, she shouted, "Look, there by the hardware store, isn't that Helmuth."

"We will rally from the hillside, we'll gather from the plain,
Shouting the battle cry of freedom..."
"The Union forever! Hurrah, boys, hurrah,
"Down with the traitors, up with the stars.....

"I can see him, I can see Helmuth," cried Amelia.

"So can I," added Grace, "but he doesn't look very happy."

"While we rally round the flag boys, we rally once again,
Shouting the battle cry of freedom...."

Helmuth saw his family waving to him and urged his horse forward. He dismounted and approached Fred, his face expressing his unhappiness, "Why on earth are you still here?" He demanded to know, his irritation obvious.

Fred shrugged his shoulders, "It's the gold, I'm not sure we can move it, at least not all of it," he spoke loudly to be heard above the singing and general hub-bub.

Waiting on his horse behind Helmuth, the ears of Lieutenant Eldred Matheson picked up the word *gold* and he suddenly became interested in both the family and financial standing of his superior officer.

Captain Schilling led Andy Jackson into the house and slumped down into a chair. "I'm whacked, we've been riding since sun-up, trying to keep in contact with Lee."

"Are the Rebs indeed *so* close?" Fred asked.

"Yes, they could be here within hours."

"Then I expect you will be in action shortly," said Amelia.

"Sooner or later the main bodies *will* collide and they may just as well fight here as anywhere," said Helmuth, accepting a glass of water from the housemaid.

"I think we'd best stay safe where we are," said Grace with some determination.

"Of course you won't be safe if the fighting rolls through Gettysburg, how *stupid* can you be," Helmuth half shouted and his tiredness, anger and frustration came out in his voice.

"Papa would never have allowed you to speak to me in such a way."

"Papa is dead and I'm head of the family. You will leave as soon as you can," Helmuth turned a strict gaze on to his brother, "Fred, see to this, I'm relying on you."

Fred nodded, "It'll be best to leave the gold behind," he suggested.

Helmuth nodded his agreement, "Do what you think best, but get yourself and the womenfolk away from here."

"I will, Helmuth, I promise."

"Good," muttered Helmuth before he rose, kissed the cheeks of both women, shook hands with Fred and left.

Amelia and Fred ran out on to the porch where they watched as Helmuth trotted off towards Seminary Ridge.

*****

Wednesday, 1st July 1863

"Hour before dawn, Cap'n," Andy Jackson gave Helmuth a hearty shove and pulled the blanket from him.

Schilling, blinked a couple of times, rolled over and planted his feet on the ground by his camp bed.

"Misty I suppose," he queried.

"Yes sir but looks like it'll come t'be a fine July the First."

"My horse saddled?"

"Yes, sir."

"Lieutenant Matheson awake?"

"Took some doin' but I reckon he'll be up an' about by now."

Helmuth nodded, swallowed coffee and began to pull on his boots. He had slept in his clothes, expecting to have no time to dress should the call to action come.

"Andy, I need a favour of you." Helmuth's tone was serious.

The ex-slave turned from checking his commanding-officer's revolvers, "Yes, captain?"

"You're aware, of course, that Gettysburg is only a mile or so behind us."

"Sure am."

"I want you to take my spare-horse along with your own, go down there and check that my family have left."

"Miss Amelia's mighty keen t'see a battle," Andy Jackson nodded.

"Yes, this is exactly what I fear. On top of which Miss Schilling is determined not to leave either."

"So, what do you expect me to do if they're still there and won't go? I got no power over them."

"I'd deem it a great favour were you would try," smiled Helmuth, "and having your support will make Fred's task much easier."

Andy Jackson laughed, "Anything for you Cap'n Helmuth, I owe you and Miss Caroline."

"If the family are still at home, tell them the Rebs will be in the town by this evening at the latest. They must go *now*, tell them to take the Hanover Road, for Stuart passed that way yesterday, so he's probably moved on by now in an attempt to re-join Lee."

"Right, sir, I understand," put in Andy.

"Offer them the spare animal, for the sooner they get away from; what I'm sure is to be the site of a long and bloody battle, the better I'll be pleased."

"Then I'm t'come back to find you?"

"Only if the house is empty."

"Even if it ain't, I'm comin' back," determined the ex-slave.

"Andy, our paths must part for a little while."

"No sir, remember, I aint *in* the army and don't need to take no orders. I'll come and I'll find you, battle or no battle."

"Please, do as I ask."

"I ain't makin' no promises on that score, sir," Andy pleaded. "I need t'be here, I want t'see the slavers whipped and whipped good."

Helmuth relented, for he knew how important this battle was going to be, not just for himself and Andy, but also to the many millions awaiting their long-promised freedom.

"Very well, come straight back, but take care that you don't run into any marauding Rebel cavalry."

"Yes, sir, I'll be setting off from camp as soon as you do."

*****

"I'll go forward and bring in the vedettes," Captain Schilling spoke softly.

"Usual escort, Captain?" asked the recently promoted Second-Lieutenant Crittenden.

"Yes, the adjutant will come with me with eight troopers. Have the rest of the company ready to move at a moment's notice."

"I'm the senior lieutenant," complained Eldred Matheson, I should remain in charge here."

"You're the adjutant, it is your duty to remain at my side," said Helmuth dismissively as he mounted his horse.

Even though the countryside was quiet, Helmuth could still instinctively sense the movement of the many thousands of men who were concentrating all around him.

To the west and north were the soldiers of the Army of Northern Virginia, which was, probably, the finest fighting unit in the world. On top of which the redoubtable Robert E. Lee commanded it.

To the south and east he knew that the whole of the Army of the Potomac was on the move, it being composed of slightly more men than that of their enemies and was also their equal in courage. However, the difference in skill and experience weighed heavily in favour of the South.

The two armies were on a collision course and Helmuth was sure that this particular Wednesday would be decisive.

Upon what happened on this soil depended the future of the United States. Defeat would mean the downfall of Lincoln, the continuation of slavery and the ruin of his country. Victory would certainly bring about an early return to Blanchwell and Caroline.

*****

Eldred Matheson reined-in his horse and turned in his saddle to speak to his commanding officer, "I'm sure this devil's thrown a shoe."

Helmuth took a quick-look down, "Seems all right to me," he muttered with some irritation.

"I don't want to be sat on a lame horse with a battle going on," complained Matheson, climbing from the saddle.

Helmuth halted the little column he was leading and shouted, "Private Miers, Private Kaley, stay here with Lieutenant Matheson until he's seen to his horse."

The named troopers closed up on the lieutenant and dismounted, looking with interest at the front left hoof of his horse.

"Seems OK to me, sir, and my pa's a smith," reported Kaley as the rest of the party rode on.

"Dammit, mind your own business. My pa's a lawyer but it don't mean I know anythin' about litigation."

"Just saying, sir."

Matheson found himself to be in something of a dilemma, for he hadn't expected Schilling to leave troopers behind with him. He had intended to wait until all was clear and then find some hidey-hole in which to spend the day. Then, the next he would be able to make up a good story to fob off his company commander.

"Look, sir, your mount's standing up fine now," this time it was Miers who interfered.

Eldred Matheson pulled out the claw blade of his knife and began to work on the hoof of his animal, he scraped out some dirt and one or two very small pebbles. Then he allowed the beast to put its hoof down before he stood back and surveyed the situation. "Looks like that did it," he said as though he was very pleased with his efforts.

"Yes, sir, looks fine t'me."

Without further ado, Matheson climbed into the saddle and set off at an easy pace in search of his company commander.

Just then, to his left, and seemingly quite close he heard the crackle of carbine fire.

"Looks like it's started," commented Miers.

"Sure does," replied Kaley.

Matheson said nothing for his stomach had cramped and his bowels were running out-of-control.

He had to get away from what was soon to become a battlefield, he just *had* to.

*****

Captain Schilling reached the line of vedettes he'd set out the previous evening and was told they had been observing enemy movements to the north since it had got light.

"Skirmishers so far, I think," informed Lieutenant Carter Gibson, "but the Rebs don't appear too keen to press on forward, they're probably as mystified by our presence as we are by theirs."

"It could be Ewell's corps, coming down from Carlisle," mused Helmuth.

"A full corps, you reckon. In which case isn't it time we moved on?" Gibson sounded anxious.

"Let's see if we can first send some approximation of numbers and direction back to Colonel Kellogg."

"Where are they exactly?" queried Helmuth.

Gibson pointed to a group of trees around a barn, "I'm sure most of them are there," he informed before swinging his arm further around to a tiny knoll, "There maybe some using that as cover too."

Schilling scanned the countryside and his eyes alighted on a rocky outcrop a couple of hundred yards or so forward and to his left.

"I may be able to see more were I to go over there," he suggested mainly to himself.

"You might get yourself killed too."

"Look, there's a gully going part of the way, it may well give a mite of shelter."

"The gully you're talking of is a mere fold in the ground."

"It'll still give some cover," mused Helmuth persuasively to himself.

"It's not deep, it's not even shallow, it's shallower than shallow."

"Even so, our flank of the battle seems quiet enough."

"This is what all heroes say before they get shot, and I've seen a few."

Schilling laughed gently before he urged his horse forward to leave the cover of the rail-fence and shrubs where his vedette had spent the night.

The slight gully he was using exposed the top half of his body and he had never before felt so vulnerable, not even when the slave hunters were in hot pursuit of him.

Once he gone fifty yards he dismounted and in a hunch, he led his horse onwards to a point when the questionable safety of the gully had to be left behind.

He paused for a minute or so, his heart racing and his eyes never still, darting from side to side. Though it turned out that he could see nothing of the enemy.

Could he possibly go back? He asked himself. No one would know, nor even care, but then his resolve stiffened again and he prepared to cross open ground to further observation point.

Coming to a decision he continued to walk his mount, he wishing to keep as low a profile as he could.

As soon as he set off from the gully he expected to hear bullets buzzing around him, however, he heard nothing apart from the muted sounds of battle coming from his left-hand side.

Breathing heavily, he took out his binoculars and began to crawl to the summit, hoping his horse wouldn't decide there was better feed to be had elsewhere.

Taking off his hat he edged forward until he could view what was happening to his right front.

There he was rewarded by the distant sight of a long column of Rebel infantry marching down the Chambersburg Pike; they were mainly dressed in butternut brown, but with a heavy sprinkling of grey uniforms amongst them.

"It's Ewell's corps all right," he muttered to himself after attempting to make an estimate of the enemy's numbers.

Just then a piece of earth was flung into his face and he heard the whine of a bullet as it ricocheted off a rock which lay close beside him, this was instantly followed by the crack of the rifle which had fired it.

Helmuth hugged the earth and sweat began to pour from him, prickling every part of his body beneath his uniform. He slithered further down the rise, his field-glasses banging against his chest in time with his fast-beating heart, until he believed that he was out of sight of the sharpshooter who had fired upon him.

He suddenly realised that he had already been within six inches of death and dawn hadn't long broken.

"Dear Lord, please look after me this day," he prayed fervently and with more meaning than he had for many years.

Just then he was startled by another *bang*, but this time it was much closer. He turned and caught a glimpse of a brown clad man who was just lowering his rifled-musket to re-charge it. Behind him were two or three others in the process of raising their rifles to their shoulders.

Helmuth pulled out his revolver and took three carefully aimed shots in the direction of the enemy. He knew that he was too far away for accurate handgun fire but hoped his bullets would at least disconcert and slow-up the Rebs.

"*Time to go*," he muttered to himself, after a further couple of random shots passed over his head.

Jamming his hat back on to his head and keeping his body as low as he could, he collected his animal and climbed into the saddle.

This was done with some difficulty as the creature was disturbed by what was now an almost constant exchange of gunfire, again, mostly from his left-hand side.

He decided not to waste time and go hell for leather, collect his vedette and get back to his company.

*****

Lieutenant Matheson rode up to the vedette post and exchanged salutes with his junior, Carter Gibson.

"Where's Schilling?" he asked.

Gibson pointed two hundred yards or so to his left, "He's out there reconnoitring. Thinks it's Ewell's corps coming down the road."

"*Ha*, he won't see no better there than we can here," Matheson was dismissive.

Just then the Confederates, ranged out to their front and opened fire.

Soon their bullets landed all around, slashing through the undergrowth, thudding into trees and clattering into the rail fence.

Gibson watched as a leaf, which had been detached by a passing bullet, slowly flutter-and-twirl its way to the ground. He seemed transfixed and couldn't force his eyes away from it.

It didn't seem right or even possible to Matheson that something so ordinary could happen while he was in such danger. His horse bucked at the noise and nearly threw him.

He dragged the animal's reins around so that the snaffle bit deep into its tongue whilst at the same time he thrashed its hide with his riding whip.

"Bitch nearly had me off," his voice was high pitched and panicky.

"Shouldn't we return fire?" Gibson was itching to make some response, even if were just to settle his own nerves.

"We should get out of here," chattered Matheson, before his words were cut off by the sounds of a further volley from the enemy.

"Give fire boys, aim low and steady now," commanded Gibson, giving up all hope that his superior officer would settle down to his duty.

"Aihee..."

"Yahhhhooo....."

"Whoooo... Whoooo.."

The Rebel yells were loud and seemed far closer than they actually were, then the racket made by a third volley added to the general confusion.

"Get out, they're coming, get up, *get out*...," Lieutenant Matheson lost control of himself, he also realised that his bowels had released their full contents into his pants.

Some of the men turned to look at their officers and wondered what to do. Most of them were prodded into movement by the instinct of survival, to get away from danger, to get clear and find somewhere safe to go. Several began to shuffle backwards.

"No boys, *stick* to it," Carter Gibson's voice was calm and unhurried, he took out his revolver, stepped a yard or two forward and began a deliberate fire upon the enemy.

The men settled at their posts and began to return the enemy's fire with everything they had. Action helped to fix the minds of the troopers on where their duty lay.

Matheson, his face drained of all colour was caught in a dilemma. The men had not joined him and Gibson had held firm. If he ran, it would be judged desertion an act of cowardice in the face of the enemy. He would be shot-at-dawn.

"*Ohh. Oh, mother,*" cried Gibson as he was struck fairly in the chest by a Rebel minnie-ball.

He crumpled to the ground, falling as though he were merely a sack of corn and lay still.

The vedette corporal rushed to the fallen officer, checked his wounds, looked at Matheson and said, "He's dead, Lieutenant. You gonna get off that horse or not?"

Just at this moment the Rebels fired a further volley, began their war cries again and seemed about ready to charge.

At this instant, Matheson flew like the wind away from danger, tears pouring down his face, for he knew this act of cowardice had changed his life for ever.

As he rode on he had never felt so useless and the stench from his riding-britches filled his nose, making him sure that his life would never again be sweet.

The Corporal watched the adjutant go, glanced to his left and saw that the company commander was on his way back.

"Right, boys, let's show them what we got. You two men with the Spencers, give 'em your full magazines."

There came a growl of agreement from the vedette line.

"*FIRE,*" screamed the corporal.

They let loose together and to their delight saw that they had completely disrupted the enemy who were just beginning to come forward.

*****

The dull boom of distant cannon-fire brought Amelia Schilling fully awake. At first, she thought a thunderstorm was imminent, but then realisation the true meaning of the sound brought her out of bed in a single action.

"Fred," she shouted when she'd noticed that he wasn't lying next to her.

Dressing quickly though taking as much time with her hair as it required, she made her way downstairs to find her husband drinking coffee.

"The battle's started, hasn't it?" She asked.

"Yes, we've got to get away, though Grace won't shift from her bed. The maid's tried and tried again, but she won't budge."

"We already know she's determined to remain here," said Amelia.

"Go up and see what you can do, won't you," begged Fred.

Upstairs, Amelia found the serving girl gently pushing at the body of her mistress who was covered from head to toe by her blankets.

"Grace, you must get up. The fighting has begun and so we must be away before it's too late," Amelia put as much urgency into her tone as she could.

Grace grunted but said nothing.

"Please Grace, get up," cried Amelia.

"She won't move mum, I've tried all ways," the maid was frightened and it was obvious that she too wished to leave Gettysburg as quickly as possible.

Amelia glanced around and saw Grace's ablutions set of bowl- and-jug. She picked up the pitcher and with some pleasure poured the whole of its contents over her sister-in-law.

"*Aghh... Aww.... How dare you,*" Grace sat bolt upright in bed, trying to wipe the water away from her hair and face.

"Fill that up," ordered Amelia passing the jug to the maid, "If she hasn't moved she'll have more of the same until she does."

Grace saw the flinty look in Amelia's eyes and decided it might be better to move away from the incoming water.

"All right, though you've ruined my bed and look at my hair."

"It could be more than your hair that's ruined if we remain here much longer," replied Amelia tartly before she went off to rejoin her husband.

*****

As he galloped across open ground back to his vedette, Helmuth closed his eyes and imagined himself to be back in England, riding with Caroline, tearing across the countryside at full tilt in the company of the Zetland Hunt.

He heard the whistle of one or two shots as they came near him, though his engrossed mind ignored them.

However, he was brought back from his dreams when his horse; without warning, bucked and plunged dramatically.

He had to fight hard to stay in the saddle, though his mind was working at super-speed and realised that his animal's left ear had been snicked off by a bullet. A bullet which may just as easily have hit himself.

He steadied the creature and continued onwards at a gallop.

As soon as he pulled up at the vedette-line he leapt from the saddle to find that young Carter Gibson lay dead.

"Where's Lieutenant Matheson?" Helmuth queried, though he was sure that he already knew the answer to that.

"Skedaddled, sir," replied the corporal shortly, "They got poor Lieutenant Gibson."

"So I see," returned Helmuth.

The corporal nodded towards the Confederate line and said, "There's more of them now, with hundreds coming up and they're plannin' t'charge."

"Very well, corporal. Get the men to mount up though tell those with the Spencers to hold fast and give the Rebs a full magazine or two as we ride off."

The corporal went about his business whilst Helmuth wrote down his observations as precisely as he could regarding the position of the enemy and their estimated strength.

He then chose the best horseman in the company, "Private Schultz, take this note to Colonel Kellogg, you'll find him by John Forney's barn, next to the Mummasburg road."

The trooper grabbed the despatch, saluted and galloped off on his mission.

"Matheson ran off, you say," asked Helmuth of the corporal as his eyes followed the despatch rider down the road.

"Shit his pants, if you don't me sayin', sir."

Helmuth shook his head, "Felt like doing that m'self at least twice so far to-day."

The corporal laughed, "Me too – but neither of us has run."

"No, we haven't," agreed Helmuth, "When, and if you get a moment, write down all you remember of the adjutant's behaviour."

"Sir," replied the corporal shortly, his tone indicating that he would be more than happy to place Mr Matheson in front of a firing-party.

Helmuth sat and watched as the vedette galloped off towards the company-lines a mile or two away.

Then he gazed back towards the enemy who where now in an extended straggling, brown line marching towards him.

"*So far and till alive,*" he whispered to himself, before he began to mumble yet another silent prayer, just proving that atheists are rarely to be found on battlefields.

*****

Andy Jackson rode into Gettysburg to find that most of the population was on the move. Those who had a wagon or carriage had them on the road, whilst tramping alongside straggled those citizens who were not so fortunate.

Of the excited, singing, patriotic townsfolk of the previous day there remained no sign.

"That's good," he said aloud as he approached the Schilling house, which appeared to be deserted.

He dismounted, ran up the steps and hammered on the door, expecting it to be locked. However, to his surprise it was flung open and he found himself looking at three surprised Schillings and their maid.

"*You've not gone yet!*" He exclaimed.

"Grace has been difficult and we can't decide what to do about pa's hoard of coins," explained Fred,

"Leave 'em here," Andy's solution was a simple one.

"I'm not having any *uppity* Black man telling me what to do in my own house," Grace spoke in an aggrieved half-shout.

"Someone needs to," said Fred before he stepped forward and shook Jackson's hand, "Helmuth sent you, I suppose?"

"Yessir, he sure did. Wants you out o' here before the battle overwhelms the town."

"We've been hearing the noise of it for an hour and more, I've got the buggy out but...."

"It's the gold," Andy cut him off.

"Yes, Grace insists that we take it all, even though the carriage is too light for three people and a hoard of gold."

"It's my family's money, they worked and saved for it, so I'm not leaving it here," declared a defiant Grace, folding her arms across her chest.

"Put it back where we found it and let's get up to the next ridge and watch the battle," said Amelia, her eyes well-lit at the excitement of it.

"Sounds the best plan," said Fred.

"Yes, it probably is," agreed Andy before continuing, "and once you're on your way I can rejoin Cap'n Schilling."

"I'm not leaving without my fortune," Grace's awkwardness knew no bounds.

"You're out voted," said Fred, who then turned to his wife, "Send the maid off and join us in the cellar."

"Better get to it, gold's awful heavy," said the ex-slave.

*****

Eldred Matheson was deeply depressed by his situation as he galloped towards Gettysburg, for as he went his ears were assailed by the rumble of battle, most of it far distant and then he suddenly noticed that his horse was panting and her flanks lathered.

He didn't know what he should do, nor where he should go. At first he had thought of fleeing to his home in Philadelphia, but there could well be Confederates blocking off that direction.

Eldred allowed his mount to rest for a while and sat idle in the saddle, "Suppose I became a prisoner-of-war?" He suggested to himself, but dismissed this notion as it was likely to involve a great deal of deprivation and discomfort.

Then he thought of his father who was a lawyer. Could his pa' get him out of this? He wondered. Then he realised that as a prominent lawyer with strong political connections, his pa' couldn't afford to have a son who ran away from battles.

A son who is a coward, tears of frustration welled up into his eyes as he spoke and only by screwing them up tightly could he keep them at bay.

Eventually, the deserter urged his horse onwards, though at a slower pace for he needed time to think before he reached the centre of the town.

"Will the railroads still be running?" he queried to himself, before answering his own question, "I doubt it, the Rebel cavalry seem to be *everywhere*."

He breasted a rise and the small town of Gettysburg lay before him and again he pulled his beast to a halt.

"Canada?" he suggested to himself, realising that he could be over the border in no time, "With luck a couple of days will see me safe in Queen Victoria's Realm."

Pleased with this thought he nudged his knees into his horse and set-off at a half-trot, which continued only for a minute before he dragged his animal to a sudden stop again.

"Money? Whatever shall I do for money?"

Then he remembered the talk of gold coins he'd heard the previous day which were somewhere to be found in the Schilling house.

He came to a quick decision, he would ride into town and if the family were about he would rob them at gun-point. If not, he would scour the house from top to bottom to find any gold they may have left behind.

If the Army of the Potomac or that of Northern Virginia came through and he was still in Gettysburg he would hide. Surely, neither side could spare the time to thoroughly search every house in the town.

Satisfied with his plan, once again he urged forward his mount, "I'm already a deserter, I may as well add robbery to my portfolio of crimes," he paused for a long moment and then continued, "Maybe, even *murder* if need be."

*****

Nearly four thousand miles away at Blanchwell Hall, Caroline Schilling was preparing for lunch. It was to be a lonely one as she'd made no effort to invite friends.

Anyway, she knew that Jane was busy with her commercial interests, whilst Elizabeth Esprey was sorting out a tangle between Villiers and Vasey over their parts in the *Riever Brothers*.

Marian Martin was helping poor Sarah Nicholson with the children and there was no one else she cared to invite.

"Abigail Turner or Roberta Villiers would perhaps accept an invitation to dine," she smiled to herself, shaking her head at the same time.

She then decided to take lunch in the hot-house, it being a pleasant day but with not enough sunshine to make it overly stuffy.

Caroline had just finished her soup when she was assailed by a violently sharp pain in her stomach, which spread quickly up through her body to strike into her heart, from where it leapt into her throat, which became blocked and she found it difficult to breathe.

Her face whitened and her hands began to tremble, with her fingers rising and falling almost as though she was playing her pianoforte.

"*It's Helmuth, Oh, my God, it's Helmuth, I know it is,*" she managed to utter.

She jumped from the table, upsetting her soup plate and sending a red stain across the whiteness of the table cloth.

Appalled, she gazed at the freely flowing, blood coloured liquid, her hands went to her face and covered it. Helmuth was hurt, she knew it, she was certain of it.

"*Please, God, let it not be so,*" she had never prayed so hard since she was a little girl.

*****

Helmuth looked down from the ridge across which his company was deployed, towards a line of advancing Confederate infantry. The regiment had managed to hold the Rebs off for some time now, but enemy numbers were now overwhelming and it couldn't be long before they were forced to pull-back to the next defensible position.

"Those Spencers are working well, Johny Reb must think we're a whole division," Lieutenant Crittenden said cheerily as he came up to his commanding officer.

Helmuth turned and smiled, "Best forty-five bucks worth I've ever spent," he said.

The lieutenant's face became serious, "Even so, we can't hold them for much longer and it seems to me they're feeling their way around our right flank."

"Perhaps I should send a messenger to the colonel," considered Helmuth, though his eyes were caught by a galloper coming towards them and he continued, "Maybe I don't need to."

"Pull back, Captain, we're ordered back t'the next ridge," the despatch rider flung a hasty salute and then sped-off further down the line.

"Bring 'em forward," Helmuth shouted to the horse-holders behind him, "Get ready to move. Pass it down the line but wait for the command," this order was directed at the men a few yards in front of him.

"*Phew*, that came just in time," remarked Crittenden.

"It shows that we have a *real* commander at last, I take my hat off to General John Buford for, who knows, he may have saved the Union's bacon this day," commented Captain Schilling before he took the bridle of his charger.

As he watched, Helmuth was pleased to see that the withdrawal of Company 'J' of the Seventeenth Pennsylvania Cavalry was very orderly indeed.

He then waited until the last man in the line had passed him and then turned his horse to follow them. He was well pleased with the behaviour of his troops under fire.

The battle still raged around him, but the Confederates had made little progress and he'd heard that General Reynold's First Corps would soon be up in support of the hard pressed First Cavalry Division.

Hearing an unusual, shrill, whistling sound coming from behind him, he wondered what it was and turned to see.

*****

As he entered Gettysburg, Lieutenant Eldred Matheson was worried as he found himself amid the men of General Reynolds's Corps.

He'd even passed the general himself who was leading his staff up to the Seminary. They'd given him some curious glances but were too pre-occupied to otherwise bother with him.

However, there were now column after column of blue-coated soldiers on either side of him. He knew that at any moment he could be challenged and asked what his business was. Especially as he was so dishevelled and stank worse than a slurry of backwoods pigs.

He dismounted and led his horse in an attempt to look less conspicuous, at the same time making his way towards a street which looked quieter than the main thoroughfares of the town.

Reaching his goal, he felt relieved and seeing that the houses appeared to be deserted, he decided to find some civilian clothes which would fit him.

The first house he came to had a dog, which made so much noise and commotion that he was happy to give up and try another.

The next one was solidly locked and barred and he didn't wish to break a window in case the noise brought out nosey people to investigate.

He was finally lucky when the fifth door he tried opened without so much as a squeak. He entered cautiously and listened for a while. All was silent except for the nearby tramp of marching feet and the damped-down noise of distant battle.

He ran upstairs and checked the closets and wardrobes, at last coming across clothes which were those of a man. They were slightly too large for him, but the cloth was of good quality.

Rapidly, he stripped himself and looked with revulsion at the state of his britches. He splashed his nether parts with water from the dresser jug, and then pulled on a shirt, followed by a pair of trousers, vest and jacket.

His ensemble was completed with a round, low crowned hat. The shoes available turned out to be far too large for him, so he had to stick with his riding boots.

Feeling cleaner and considerably safer he decided to risk moving on, "Now for Schilling's gold and maybe that pretty little sister-in-law of his too," he said to himself.

*****

Five hundred yards from 'J' Company's position, Confederate Corporal Benedict Glazier was looking for a vantage point from where he could gain a clear view of the Yankee lines. However, the terrain was against him, with the enemy holding the higher ground and there being no buildings that could negate their height advantage.

"Damn, Yankees," he muttered to himself, "Won't stand still but for a minute,"

Then he spotted a stubby, gnarled tree twenty yards or so to the front of him. He eyed it up professionally and decided that if he were to climb it, he might just about get a view level with that of the Union positions.

The day was a hot one and it was with some difficulty that he reached the uppermost crook of the old tree.

"Just as well the old Whitworth don't weigh much," he said to himself as he adjusted the sights of his rifle.

Glazier was one of the few who had been provided with a telescopic sight, so he pulled it from his satchel and scanned the Union line with it. He soon saw that the Yankees were moving off the ridge they'd occupied for most of the morning.

"*Dammit,*" he cried, greatly irritated.

He pushed the thirty-three inches of the Whitworth's barrel through a supporting branch and tied it in place with a piece of string he carried for that purpose.

Glazier then used his telescope again and to his dismay saw the ridge-line was bare of movement.

However, he did pick out a lone figure who appeared to be using his hat to wave his men away from the field of battle. This fellow was obviously an officer and if he could get a bead on him it would be his first kill of the day.

He thought about fitting the telescopic sight to the side of his rifle, but reckoned he hadn't the time.

"Besides, I sure don't want another black and bruised eye," he muttered to himself, recalling the last time he'd used the sight when the recoil had sent the eyepiece into his head causing him considerable pain and much joshing from his fellows.

Sweat was pouring down his face as he set the sights of his rifle directly on to the target. His bullet had five hundred yards to go and the spread at this range was over four inches.

"Maybe it'll hit the horse, if I'm lucky," he muttered to himself.

Glazier allowed for windage; not that there was much of that, squeezed the trigger and hoped for the best.

The resulting recoil nearly sent him sprawling out of the tree, but he managed to hang on to a branch and stayed secure where he was.

As soon as he had recovered he used his telescope again, though of the officer or his horse there was no sign.

*****

Feeling much happier as a civilian, Eldred Matheson rode confidently through the advancing troops of the Union First Corps towards the Schilling family's house.

Nestled in his pocket a Colt revolver was ready for use. He fingered it nervously, wondering if he had the courage to use it.

The sounds of battle had by now driven nearly all the townsfolk away and he half-hoped he'd find the Schilling home to be empty.

In this he was to be disappointed, for he saw a light buggy was standing outside loaded with trunks and cases.

Is the gold on there, he considered to himself.

However, as the front door stood open he entered. No one was about, but there seemed to be a lot of activity coming from the cellar.

He went to investigate, slipping silently down a narrow wooden staircase until he could see, by the light of a single lamp, four figures.

The black man, Jackson, was heaving bags which Matheson was sure contained gold, into a wooden chest which stood in a pit dug in the cellar floor.

Behind him, getting in the way, was Schilling's brother. Standing watching behind the men were the ugly sister and her very attractive, sister-in-law.

"I still think that we should take all of it," complained Grace.

"We've been through this and it can't be done," replied, Fred, greatly irritated.

"Oh, dear, what a to-do," said Eldred conversationally as he stepped into the light, gun in hand.

Andy Jackson dropped the bag of gold dollars he was holding and stood up straight, "Lieutenant Matheson," he said, "Run away ag'in, have you."

Matheson swung the barrel of his revolver until it covered the ex-slave and pulled the trigger.

The *boom* of the pistol filled the small space of the cellar with an echo which seemed to go on for minutes.

Andy cried out and his right hand clapped on to his left arm, where the bullet had grazed it, drawing blood.

The faces of all three Schillings were immediately filled with a combination of fear, shock and concern.

"That'll teach ye to respect your betters, you Black scoundrel," shouted Matheson, who nonetheless was surprised that his shot had very nearly missed so near a target.

Amelia made as if to cross the cellar towards the ex-slave.

"Stay where you are, all of you, stay still. The Black ain't in any danger I won't hesitate to shoot if I need to."

"Mr Jackson requires attention, please let me see to him," appealed Amelia.

Matheson shook his head, "No, ma'am, the slave boy can bleed to death for all I care."

Amelia shook her head and took a tentative step forward.

"You move any closer I'll shoot him some more," threatened Matheson.

"Then you are no officer and certainly not a gentlemen," Amelia's voice was clear, sharp and full of contempt.

Lieutenant Matheson laughed nastily, "You British, how you love the idea of the officer-and-gentleman, yet around the world you hold millions under your sway. With how much gentleness are they treated, do you suppose?"

"We bring peace and justice into lands where they did not exist before….," began Amelia.

"Shut up, just shut up and do as you're told," Matheson interrupted, "I've no time for this."

As he stood waiting, Andy quietly tore away a sleeve from his shirt and used it as a make-do bandage.

"I suppose you're after my gold," cried Grace.

"You'll never carry it all," said Fred conversationally.

"*Dammit*, shut up, I'll take as much as I can."

"You shouldn't have shot Mister Jackson, he could have helped move the gold, now you've only two women and a slightly built man. What a stupid mistake to make," said Amelia.

Matheson aimed his pistol at Fred, "Keep your wife in order. If she says another word she'll find herself short of a husband," he said furiously.

"Do as he's said, Amelia, I believe that he means it."

"Damn right I do."

"Then what are your intentions?" Fred asked as calmly as he could.

"The two women will come upstairs with me and I'll have this here Colt covering them. You will carry a bag at a time to the street and into the buggy.

I'll be watching, so say nothing to anyone nor make any signals, or else it'll be bad news for the women."

"What about Mr Jackson, he's hurt," appealed Fred.

"Once I've gone, you can see to the Nigger and live happily- ever-after as far as I'm concerned."

"It's my family's gold," wailed Grace, "you can't take it."

"It *was* your family's gold and I *am* taking it, or as much of it as the buggy will hold" sneered Matheson before continuing, "Do you all understand? Remember, I'm desperate and have nothing to lose."

All three Schillings nodded their understanding, after which Matheson climbed out of the cellar and ordered the women to join him.

Fred Schilling checked that Andy was as well as could be expected, before he began carrying the heavy bags up to the hallway.

*****

The dusty brown line of the 3rd Alabama Infantry, Rodes' Division, Ewell's Corps of the Army of Northern Virginia, made their way up the ridge which overlooked the town of Gettysburg and were halted there.

They'd been marching for days now and were thirsty, hungry and desperately tired.

"Hey, lookya' here," shouted one of the corporals to his friends, "There's a dead Yankee officer. Cava'ry, too by the look o' him."

"Seen a lot o' them, aint worth commentin'," shouted back his sergeant.

"This one's fresh. Got a fine pair o' riding boots on."

A skinny, very young private jumped to his feet, "Ah'm just about bare foot, I reckon I'll take them."

A nearby comrade grabbed the passing ankles of the skinny one and brought him to the ground, "You just hold on an' wait your turn," he advised.

"Yeah, you hardly seen a Yank yet, never mind killed one," commented another of the group.

"This Yank's got pistols and a ring on his finger too," the corporal provided further useful information.

Very soon the body of Captain Helmuth Schilling was stripped of every item of value he had.

"*Ohh…*," this groan was both loud and long.

The Confederate soldiery jumped backwards in surprise.

"Why, he's alive," pronounced the sergeant.

"Son-o'-bitch," commented the corporal shortly.

"Shoot the damn Yankee," suggested the skinny private.

"*Naw*," returned the corporal, "Use a bayonet or a knife on him. He aint worth wastin' a bullet on."

The young private pulled out the long knife his father had given him and approached the prone, but still groaning body of Helmuth Schilling.

"Make sure y'slip it clean under his ribs, then twist an' pull out," advised one of the group.

The young soldier paused and found himself to be trembling, for he'd been brought up strictly on the Ten Commandments and found himself to be on the verge of breaking a major one of them.

"If ye're gonna do it, do it," a weary voice shouted from the group.

Riled, the skinny private drew back his arm and prepared to plunge the knife into Helmuth's stomach.

"*You men, there, what are you doing?*" The voice was one which expected to be obeyed instantly.

The group stood back from the body they had looted.

"Steady boys, it's Colonel O'Neal himself," advised the sergeant.

The commanding officer of the 3rd Alabama rode up and took in the scene immediately. "You rogues taken what you need?" He asked.

"Sir," replied the sergeant with great respect.

O'Neal nodded towards Helmuth, "He still alive?"

"Yessir, but just about dead – might be a kindness to finish him off."

"I can't see he has much of a wound, there's very little blood," Colonel O'Neal by now was an expert on the dead and the dying.

"Hit in the head, maybe he's just knocked senseless," suggested the corporal.

The colonel considered for a moment, "Sergeant, detail two of your men to get this Yankee boy back to the regimental surgeon."

"Yes, sir."

The commander of the 3rd Alabama pointed towards the town spread out below them, "They reckon there's boots to be had there, best to get on down in case there's none left."

The promise of boots galvanised his men and they began to get to their feet.

O'Neal saluted smartly and then rode off about his business.

"I aint walkin' back down that ridge just t'walk back up again, and then maybe get ma head shot off," complained the skinny soldier.

"Might put some sense in t'it," commented the corporal.

"All right," commanded the sergeant, "Corporal, you found the Yank, so, you an' skinny there can carry him back."

"Why, that ain't fair," complained the corporal.

"Who ever said that soldiering was fair?"

"Was a god' dam liar."

With much grumbling the corporal took Helmuth in charge and set off to find the regimental aid post.

Meanwhile, the sergeant plonked himself down, took his ease."

"Don't ya want new boots," asked a very young private.

"Nope, 'specially as I don't believe they exist," returned the sergeant as he pulled his campaign hat over his eyes and dropped immediately off to sleep.

*****

"Buggy's as loaded as it'll take," Fred reported unwillingly.

"Good, now you can go and see to the Nigger."

"I'll take the ladies down with me," said Fred lightly, though more in hope than expectation.

"Nope," replied Matheson shortly.

"You could lock us all in the cellar."

Matheson shook his head, "I'll keep the pretty one here, but y'can take the other one."

"How dare you, I'll not stay alone with you," declared Grace loudly.

"I said the *pretty* one, not the *ugly* one."

"Well, I've never been….," began Grace.

Eldred waved his revolver in her direction, "Shut up," he ordered.

"Quiet, Grace and come with me," commanded Fred, eager to get this whole affair over and his wife returned to him.

Eldred watched closely as the siblings left the room and he could hear them descending into the cellar.

"Why don't you just go?" Amelia spoke dismissively.

"Very much the English lady in charge, aren't you," sneered Matheson, "'Cept, you ain't in charge here."

Amelia said nothing though continued to deliver a glacial stare.

Matheson walked casually over to his hostage and took her by the arm, "We're going into the buggy now, just you and me. Make a sound, try to pull away or attract attention, I'll kill you and throw your body into the road," Matheson's instructions were coldly delivered.

"Very well, anything to be rid of you," replied Amelia calmly.

"Get in and take the reins," ordered Matheson.

"I can't drive a carriage, I've never been taught."

"You're an English lady, of course you can."

"My father's an impoverished clergyman, who could never afford a carriage of any description."

"Well, you're gonna learn today, 'cos I need both hands to keep an eye on you. Remember, my gun is in my pocket and, as the Nigger well knows, I'm not afraid of using it."

Amelia had no choice other than to do as she had been bidden.

The street was still full of Union soldiery marching towards the sound of the guns. However, they were too concerned over their own futures to take much notice of the young couple fleeing from the endangered town of Gettysburg. In fact, more than a few of them were wishing that they too were moving *away* from the scene of the battle.

*****

Fred helped Andy up from the cellar, by this time the freed slave had his wound cleaned and properly bandaged and he looked considerably the better for it.

"Did he get much o' Mr Helmuth's money?"

"Our money," corrected Grace quickly.

Fred ignored his sister, "About a quarter I'd say, but it was worth it to get rid of him."

"*A quarter,*" Shrieked Grace."

Fred cut in, "For goodness sake, be quiet. I'll make it up to you from my share."

Andy reached the drawing-room doorway, "They've gone,

Fred ran to the door, "Oh, no, *Dear God, no.*"

All three came on to the porch to gaze up the road, though of the buggy and Amelia there was no sign.

*****

"Put him on the table there, I'll have a look at him," ordered the surgeon.

"He's a Yankee," informed the skinny private.

"Makes no difference to me, put him down," replied the doctor sharply.

"D'ye need us, sir?" Asked the Corporal hopefully, he looking for a nice safe-billet in which to sit-out the battle.

The surgeon turned on them, "What on earth use could you pair be to me?"

Taking this as a refusal of their help, the two soldiers turned and began the long trudge back to their regiment.

"We might ha' missed the fighting," suggested the thin private.

"Let's take our time," replied the corporal.

The surgeon examined Helmuth and spoke conversationally to a nearby orderly, "Something's stopped the full force of the bullet, it's taken part of his scalp away, but he's not lost much blood. He shall probably live."

"He'll end up a prisoner-of-war, lucky devil," said the orderly.

"Yes, unless some infection sets-in."

"The Lord giveth and the Lord taketh away," droned the orderly.

The doctor sniffed and looked up the ridge to find that a further group of casualties were about to descend on him. Some limping, some senseless whilst others were being carried on the shoulders of their comrades.

"Will this *never* end," the surgeon shook his head.

"What about the Yankee?" Queried the orderly.

"Find a place he can lie-up and bandage his head."

The orderly called for help and took Helmuth away.

*****

Amelia halted the buggy at the top of Benner Hill and looked back at Gettysburg. Behind her and to the left there came the constant sound of battle, and to her right column after column of blue-clad troops marched towards Cemetery Ridge.

"What'ya stopped for?" Demanded Matheson.

"Horse is blown, you're supposed to be a cavalryman so you should be aware of this."

"Damn it, I've no time, get going."

"We shan't get much further if the animal drops in the traces," replied Amelia sensibly.

Matheson was about to make a hot reply when the wisdom of what his prisoner was saying struck him, "All right," he said, "but no more than five minutes."

Matheson kept a sharp watch on Mrs Schilling and saw she frequently looked backwards, he laughed "That skinny boy of a husband o' yours ain't coming, he's not got the belly for it."

"Young he maybe, however, he's not the one running for his life from a battlefield," pointed out Amelia, defending Fred strongly.

Matheson scowled but said no more as his eyes were taken by the various groups of troops seemingly approaching them from every direction.

Amelia also noticed that some of the advancing formations were less than a hundred yards away. Could she jump for it and be away from her captor before he could take an a shot at her? She asked herself as she prepared to try.

"Don't think of running," It was as though Matheson could read her thoughts, "I might be a coward, but I have a gun."

"Jump down and escape?" Cried Amelia, "Have you ever worn a corset, numerous underclothing a crinoline, high-heeled boots and a heavy dress?"

Matheson laughed nastily, "Why should I?"

"You'd look better than you do in that *dreadful* suit you're wearing. Besides which, the very *idea* of wearing riding-boots *under* trousers," Amelia shook her head distastefully. "You know, you really ought to change your tailor."

"Just you wait, Missy, just wait till it's quiet aways up the road, then we'll see who's cutting the fine figure," threatened the deserter.

Amelia managed to keep the fear from her expression, but inside she trembled and realised that if anyone was going to save her from this dangerous situation it had to be herself.

*****

Caroline Schilling awoke with her heart pounding and a cold sweat drenching her body. She tossed off her bedding and attempted to breathe more slowly.

A full moon suddenly lit up her bedroom with a ghostly silver light, the sight of which brought palpitations to her heart.

"It's Helmuth. I know *it's Helmuth*. Can he have been killed? Is he trying to contact me?"

She tossed and turned, rolled over and buried her head deep into her pillows and tried to cut out the gloomy thoughts which were assailing her.

Just then, an owl hooted from a nearby tree. Its call was so calm, familiar and natural that it seemed to cut through and clear away the mist of gloom which was enveloping her.

Suddenly, her husband came to her. At first his image was fuzzy and ill-defined, though it eventually became sharper and in better focus until it seemed he was truly at her bedside.

"Helmuth, Oh Helmuth, I do love you," she cried, "*I do, I really do.*"

It was at this point it suddenly occurred to her that Helmuth *was* truly the love of her life.

The truth of this brought about a feeling of great peace within her. She lay back and closed her eyes, pleading softly, "Please, Lord, keep him safe and send him back to me."

*****

"I've got to get after Amelia," Fred Schilling was desperate.

"I'm with you there, Mister Fred," said Andy Jackson.

"What about me?" Asked Grace.

"You'll have to stay here."

"What, with hordes of Rebels about to tear through the town, you must take me with you."

"I shall need two horses to have any chance of catching up with my wife."

"I want t'get Miss Amelia back too," put in Andy.

Fred shook his head, "I need you to stay here with my sister."

"What if the Rebs come an' they want t'send me back South?" As he asked this question Andy shivered.

Fred thought for a moment, "It would be best if you both were to go around to the church. The enemy won't harm folk in a church."

"No," Grace disagreed at once.

"You shall do as you've been asked," Fred's tone indicated that he'd put-up with no further nonsense.

Just then the firing they'd been hearing all morning seemed louder and much closer.

"Very well, have it your own way," agreed Grace quickly as she herself became aware of the imminence of battle.

After seeing his charges off to the Lutheran College Church, Fred took his horse and with his brother's tied behind him, galloped away from the embattled town of Gettysburg.

*****

As she drove to-wards Hanover, Amelia considered seizing the whip and belabouring her loathsome kidnapper about the head with it. The more she thought about it the better she liked this idea.

"Don't even think about touching that horsewhip, you cunning bitch, my gun is ever ready," again, Matheson appeared to have access to her thoughts.

"*Tibi deformis, stultissiumum hominem cadere,*" Amelia's words were laced with contempt.

"*What?* What did you say," Eldred Matheson was puzzled.

"Surely, you have at least a modicum of learning?" Amelia was in superior mode.

"Dammit, I went to good schools. I recognise Latin when I hear it."

"Though, no doubt you were thrown out of every one of them."

"Think you're so superior don't you, damn you British….," Matheson was working himself up into a rage.

"*Imperitos barbarus parum fetura,*" she continued unabashed.

"*SHUT UP,*" he shouted raising his hand.

"*Et procul dubio comeuppance occurrere*" she continued unabated.

Matheson reached across and struck her across the cheek with all the force he could muster, leaving behind a deep, red impression of his fingers and some bleeding where his nails had penetrated her flesh.

"*Ohh,*" cried Amelia, putting her free hand to her cheek, "*Vos ignave vos awful bruta.*" She knew her Latin had become a bit rusty since she'd left the rectory, but was certain that it was still better than that of her kidnapper.

Matheson raised his hand again but then saw something in Amelia's fiercely lit eyes that made him hold back, "All right, all right, enough of that, just keep quiet and drive."

*****

It wasn't very often that Lady Marian Martin was to be found out riding. It wasn't as though she was unused to the creatures, but the farm ones she had known in a life long past were beasts of burden and not much given to excessive speed nor frisky behaviour.

However, Caroline Schilling had come to visit and had begged Marian to keep her company on a canter across the Park.

"I know you are not fond of riding, Marian, but I truly need fresh air and an accompanying friend," Caroline spoke quietly as they passed through the stables gate.

"Of course, my dear. The stress upon you at the moment must be almost unbearable."

"It is."

Before Marian could develop their conversation any further, Caroline had nudged her mount into a trot and was heading for a rise in the ground which was a favourite viewpoint of theirs – one which did not include the sprawl, mess and stench of Martindale.

Marian followed as best she could, the side-saddle which convention required her to use, did not suit her at all.

"I've always enjoyed the prospect from here," Caroline greeted as her friend joined her.

"Yes, I believe it to be the finest the Martin Estate can offer," replied Marian as she brought her mount to a halt.

For a moment they gazed at the glittering silver line of the River Wear and the green hills rolling upwards towards the Pennine Chain.

Then Caroline's words came out in a flood, "I had a feeling last night, a strong feeling about Helmuth…."

"My dear, feelings mean *nothing*, it's facts that matter," Marian thought she knew what was about to come next.

Caroline turned to her companion, "You once lost a husband, Marian, didn't you."

"Yes, I did."

"Did you have any fore-warning of it? Any premonition?"

Marian paused for a moment, knowing that her friend would expect a thoughtful reply, "No, none at all. Gareth was struck by a fall-of-rock, but when they brought him out of the colliery I believed he would live. Then the cholera took him, I wasn't expecting, nor had I any warning of it."

Caroline nodded slowly and waited for a long time before she said, "I'm certain something *dreadful* has happened to Helmuth."

"You cannot be certain of that."

Caroline turned to face her companion, "Nonetheless, he has come to harm, I'm sure of it."

Marian smiled, "He's probably in camp as we speak, having a hearty-meal prepared for him by… the slave you freed…"

"Mr Jackson," Caroline helped her friend out.

"You know," began Lady Martin calmly, "we women often fear unknown phantoms which we're sure lie just around a corner waiting to pounce and ruin our lives for ever."

"I wasn't dreaming, there was no spectre. I *saw* Helmuth, he was *real*," cried Caroline, her face turning ashen and her eyes becoming as wide as eyes can become.

"Then, at least in your mind, you saw him fall?" Marian asked.

"No, nothing like that. I saw him smile at me and then I was overtaken by a feeling of great peace."

"Then he is fit and well and aching to return to you," Lady Martin spoke with great confidence, "His love is so deep that it has crossed the wide ocean to reassure you."

Mrs Schilling rapidly shook her head, "Though this morning my mind was assaulted by wave-upon-wave of dread."

"I'm sure your dream was no more than Helmuth, in America somewhere, drifting off to sleep with his mind full of love and somehow transmitting it to you at Blanchwell."

"You really believe so?"

"His love for you is so strong that anything is possible."

"Yes, I know that… Though…, though… He believes that I do not return his love," replied Caroline her final words coming out in a rush.

This did not shock Marian, for she well remembered Jane Turner's belief that Richard *was* Caroline's lover.

"I do love him, I *do*, but I have never made my feelings as plain as I should have."

Marian shook her head sadly, "Poor Gareth," she reminisced, "I was overcome with guilt after his death, for he had gone before I had had the chance to fully express my love for him."

"Really? Was there someone else in your life at the time?"

"No one else, my guilt was all of my own making, for I can be stupidly stubborn at times."

Caroline thought deeply for a moment and then said, "Though love is so capricious, is it not."

"Yes, indeed. I remember you were once destined to become Lady Caroline Martin, it was the talk of the district when I was a girl."

Caroline laughed lightly, "Yes, this is true, for at that time I believed such a marriage was the future life had in store for me. However, looking back on it, the relationship between myself and Charles was always one of friendship, there was never any passion in it."

Marian caught the eye of her friend, "Was there no one else before Helmuth?" She asked pointedly.

Caroline bowed her head, "I once hoped..," she began slowly.

"Please, don't break any confidences on my account," Marian interjected.

"No, it's all right. The fact is I fell in love; or at least believed I had at a time when I'd never felt so alone nor so frightened."

"Was this when your father was suffering difficulties?" Asked Marian.

"Just so. The affair never came to anything and I was still a maiden when I married Helmuth. Though my heart belonged to someone else."

"Does it still?"

"Is it possible to love two men at the same time?" Queried Caroline.

"I never have, but then I've never met another man who could pull at my heartstrings and make them sing."

Caroline stamped her foot, "Unfortunately, *I* have."

"Is one of them, Richard?" Marian's words came out in a rush before she could stop them.

"*Yes*... It began on the wedding day of Charles and Elysia and developed on from then," now she'd begun to confess, Caroline couldn't stop herself.

"Though our love has never been consummated."

Marian was pleased to hear Richard had not betrayed Jane. Her brother and her friend had been strong enough not to extend their affair further.

Caroline sobbed gently, "I'm sorry, so sorry about everything."

Marian reached across and took Caroline's hand, "Neither Jane nor Helmuth have been betrayed, so this is much in your favour."

"I'm sorry, so sorry. I cause confusion wherever I go. What ever can I do? I'm hopeless, I set my mind on the right track and then am derailed at the mere sight of Richard."

"Time will eventually clear your mind," Marian said at last, "It cleared mine and I had come very close to disaster."

"The dreadful Love fellow?"

"Yes, he made my life so miserable. He attempted to rape me you know," Marian felt sure that the confession of her own secret could help settle her friend.

"Never, I knew he was obsessed with you and wished to carry you off, but rape… No, I was unaware of that."

"No one else knows, apart from Charles, who saved me from dishonour."

"Charles would, ever the gentleman."

Marian smiled, "Yes, he is the perfect gentleman and I know how lucky I am to have won his love."

*****

Helmuth was puzzled, for as he lay he could see misty shapes continuously flitting past him. When he attempted to focus his eyes on them they became less distinct, rather than sharper.

Then, on several occasions, his brain had politely requested his limbs to make some movement to ease the cramp in them, and though he could vaguely *see* their movement, he couldn't *feel* that they were moving.

When he groaned he could not hear any sound of it whatsoever.

What's my name? He asked himself.

Who am I? He wanted to know, *Where am I? What am I doing? Where do I belong? Why does my head hurt?*

These questions came thick-and-fast and his befuddled brain could give no answer to any of them.

Then there floated into his mind the picture of a lady. At first she was arranging flowers in the hall of a large house, next she was riding with him across fields, jumping brooks and all the while they were laughing together.

The sight of this unknown woman helped him to relax, he wished himself to sleep deeply in the hope that when he awoke this dreadful nightmare would be over and more importantly, he would remember who on earth this woman was.

*****

As she gazed ahead, Amelia noticed that they were speeding down the slope towards Cress Run, where the road narrowed to cross a bridge.

"Slow up, damn you," shouted Matheson angrily.

Amelia ignored him and urged the horse on, then, just before they came on to the bridge, she veered sharply to the left and had them bumping across tussocks of grass towards the steep, tree lined, bank of the creek.

"*Agh*," cried her captor as he desperately took a tighter hold on to the side of the buggy.

Amelia used the momentum of the side-ways shift of the vehicle to push her shoulder hard against her tormentor in the hope it would knock him from his perch and leave her free to make an escape.

"*Oh no you don't*," shouted Matheson as he avoided her blow and instead took an even firmer grip on the side of the seat.

The hostage tried again, but she had lost the advantage of both surprise and impetus.

Then the horse careered wildly away from the creek and began to pull its burden back towards the road, slowing steadily down as it did so.

Seeing that her escape plan had come to nothing, she grabbed for the horsewhip, managed to pulled it from its socket and tried to lash out at her captor with it.

Matheson quickly realised what she was attempting and soon grabbed the whip from her before she could deploy it.

"*You bitch, you damn bitch*," he shouted angrily at the top of his voice.

Amelia broke away from him and launched herself as well as she was able, considering the burden of her clothing.

She was closely followed by her captor and before she could even clamber to her feet, he had taken hold of her hair and was wrenching her to her feet with it.

"You want whips, do you? I'll show you whips," he shouted as he began to lead her by the hair towards the trees that lined the bank of the creek.

"Let go, you beast, you were never ever fit to wear uniform," Amelia struggled, but she'd been winded in her fall and he was too strong for her.

They entered the cool, shadow of the foliage and Eldred flung his prisoner to the ground at the base of a tree.

"*Strip*," he commanded shortly.

"Certainly not," she replied as coolly as she could, filling her eyes with venom at the same time.

"Strip or I'll strip you myself and then I'll shoot you dead."

Sensing that he meant what he said, Amelia began to comply, but only very unwillingly.

"Come on, make more of a show of it," demanded Matheson, his face wearing a leer of intent.

Amelia ignored him and continued at her slow pace.

Becoming impatient, the deserter crossed to her pulled her arms away from her chest where she was attempting to undo buttons, and ripped open her dress, quickly followed by her chemise.

"*Ohh*," Amelia was shocked and felt ashamed, but only for a moment, for she was certain that the burden of any improbity lay with her attacker.

Soon, Eldred Matheson had his prisoner's breasts fully in view, he licked his lips and said in a low voice, "Take the rest off, I want you naked."

"No, please…..," she begged.

"Get rid of every scrap of clothing and maybe I'll go easy on you with the whip."

Amelia had no choice other than to do as he asked, her skirt floated down around her ankles which was quickly followed by the cage which supported it.

"I can't undo the corset by myself," she pleaded, at the same time her hands attempting to cover her breasts.

"Leave it be then, but get those off," he pointed to her drawers.

"Oh, no, I can't….. *I can't do that.*"

Once more Matheson waved his pistol around, "Do it, or else."

Amelia unfastened the drawstrings of her underwear and allowed the garment to join the rest of her underclothes around her ankles.

"Good. Very good," Matheson's voice sounded like hot, hissing slime running down a privy wall.

"*Please*," she pleaded.

"Not so much of the proud lady now, are we?" Gloated her captor.

Amelia nodded slowly, subserviently, though her brain was working frantically to find a way out of the trouble she was in.

For the first time that day, Matheson was enjoying himself. He had gold, he was well on his way to safety and he had this very attractive, virtually naked woman awaiting to obey his every command.

"Loosen your hair, let it hang down, right down as far as it'll stretch," he ordered.

Without replying Amelia's hands reached behind her head to remove the combs which held what was left of her coiffure in place.

Matheson licked his lips, for her movements tautened her breasts and forced her nipples to become erect. As well as this, he was offered an unobstructed view of the pink gash at the bottom of her belly.

"Might just give the whipping a miss, ye see how nice I can be," he said, moving towards her, "Now that I've got other things on my mind."

Amelia took a step backwards until she was supported by the trunk of the tree. She gave a little cry of fear and began to sob gently, "Oh, don't hurt me. *Please don't hurt me*," her voice fell to a whisper.

Matheson reached out and began to fondle his prisoner's breasts.

She trembled and she forced her breath to become quicker.

"You like this, don't you? You like it rough, all you supposed lady creatures are the same."

Slowly and carefully, Amelia brought her hands from behind her back, and in each of them there was grasped a hair comb with long, sharp steel points.

"Oh, honey," smarmed Eldred, "You want me, don't you. I know you do."

"*Yes...., Oh, please, yes*," her tone was silky-soft, "take me, take me *now*. Oh, *please*, now, I cannot wait...."

Eldred Matheson undid the belt buckle of his pants and began to push them down his thighs, though his eyes never left hers.

"Oh, do hurry, get it out, quickly, *quickly, please...* I can't bear to wait," Amelia spoke urgently.

It sounded to her captor that she wanted him desperately, he paused for a second while he considered carrying her off to Canada with him.

"*Oh*, do come on," Amelia began to tremble in what she hoped would appear to be anticipation.

"Just you stand easy, I'll be in you soon," he said, his voice gruff, as he looked downwards in order to be able to remove his combinations.

Amelia waited until he was struggling with the buttons of his underwear and then she struck upwards with the combs straight towards his eyes.

"*Argh..*, *Yaa...*," he screamed and howled as the points struck home. Blood streamed down his cheeks and his hands scrabbled towards his eyes, desperately rubbing them in the hope of being able to regain his sight.

Amelia wasted no time in pushing him over on to the ground, the fact that his trousers were around his knees helping her enormously.

As he rolled, writhed and screamed in the grass, Amelia went through his jacket pockets and soon withdrew his revolver. It weighed comfortingly heavy in her hands.

"I may well shoot you dead as you lie there you craven, cowardly swine," she stated with some heat.

Matheson continued to squirm in agony and terror. Afraid that he might be either shot or permanently blinded.

"Oh, *please*, I'm sorry... I can't help how I am.. I told my pa' I couldn't do it – be a soldier... *Oh, I'm hurt bad...*"

"My dear man, you were never *ever* a soldier," said Amelia in the manner of a strict school ma'am, at the same time taking the opportunity to pull on some of her clothing.

Matheson groaned and then struggled to his knees, his hands, which were still covering his face, were covered in the blood which continued to seep through his fingers.

"Put down your hands so that I can see how serious your wounds are, but don't forget I have the pistol handy."

The deserter slowly did as he was told and Amelia was shocked by how much damage she'd done to his face. One eye was swollen up out of all recognition and blood was seeping steadily from it. She saw that she'd missed the other one, but the steel prongs of the hair comb had gouged a series of deep ravines down his cheek and it was from these that most of the blood was leaking.

"What do I look like?" Matheson was almost too afraid to ask, "Does it look bad?"

"Your wounds are deep, but I believe that you can still see out of your right eye. Is that so?"

"Yes…. A little…," his voice trembled.

"Close it and try to open the other one."

"I can't," he groaned and whined, "it hurts too much."

"Do it, unless you do want to remain blind."

The ex-lieutenant groaned in pain but Amelia could see that he was trying to lift his eye lid.

"I can't, I've lost the sight of an eye, I'm a one-eyed man…."

"We don't know this yet," Amelia was now feeling somewhat remorseful.

"Oh, God," moaned Matheson, "Oh, Dear God, help me…."

Amelia glanced through the trees and could see that the horse and buggy were still in one-piece, the animal contentedly chomping the grass.

"I'll get you to a doctor, there are bound to be hundreds of them around with a battle going on only a few miles away."

"*No…* They'll have me shot…"

"You're in civilian dress, I'll vouch for you and say you're my brother."

Eldred Matheson fell to his knees again; his trousers still crumpled around his thighs and began to howl piteously.

Amelia's conscience began to prick, she dropped the revolver and then hurried across to the stricken deserter, thinking to lead him down to the stream to bathe his wounds.

Matheson was crouching with his forehead touching the ground, his arms spread out in front of him as though he were a praying Muslin.

She bent down and gently touched his shoulder, "There, there, It'll be....," she began but was interrupted when Matheson grabbed her naked ankles and pulled her to the ground. He climbed on top of her and began to punch her.

"You ain't going to look too good either, by the time I've finished with you," he said, his voice rising above her screams and his blood splashing on to her face.

*****

Grace and Andy struggled to reach the Lutheran Church through the streams Union troops retreating from Seminary Ridge.

However, Miss Schilling set about her task with some vigour and they eventually reached their destination and went inside.

"Good grief, look at the mess they've made in here," Grace was horrified.

Just then she was even more displeased when a recently amputated leg flashed across her line of sight, before it was flung through a nearby open window, fresh blood from it splattering the white-washed walls of the church as it passed.

"Why, they've turned it into a hospital," she was able to say at last.

"Looks like it's a slaughter-house," amended Andy.

"There's sure to be a surgeon here who'll see to your scratch," muttered Grace.

A Union officer swept towards her, "Good," he said, "excellent, a ministering angel has come amongst us, just when we need all the help we can get."

A confused Miss Schilling looked rapidly about her to see who this paragon of virtue could be and concluded that she was the only possible angel present. She smiled and suddenly became very pleased with herself.

"Wait here, I'll find you a smock, your dress is far too fine to be ruined," continued the officer.

"Are you a surgeon, sir?" Queried Grace.

"No, my dear, no I'm Horatio Howell, I'm the chaplain of the 90th Pennsylvania Infantry."

"But you're carrying a sword," pointed out the sharp-eyed Andy Jackson.

"Purely, ceremonial, my boy," replied Chaplain Howell who then noticed Andy's wound, "Come with me, we'll soon have that seen to."

Looking around, Grace saw that there were well over a hundred wounded men lying on beds which had been erected using wooden boards and the church pews.

"*Ugh....,*" screamed an agonized soldier who was in the process of losing his right arm.

Grace knelt down beside him and began to wipe the perspiration from his brow with her 'kerchief.

"Can you hold his shoulders down, do you think?" Asked the harassed surgeon who was removing his fifth limb of the morning.

"Of course, do you suppose me to be useless," replied Grace sharply before she did as she was asked.

"*Next,*" shouted the surgeon who was very quick with knife and saw.

Grace took a deep breath and prepared herself for another patient.

"*The Rebs are here already,*" the shout came from the doorway and was made by one of the many walking-wounded who were rapidly increasing the number of inmates.

Chaplain Howell looked up from the soldier he was trying to comfort and said to a nearby surgeon, "I'll step outside for a moment and see what the trouble is."

Grace watched him go to the door and her natural curiosity got her to follow him.

Outside, it appeared that the last of the retreating Union troops had passed by and they were being closely pursued by Rebel forces.

Howell took in the scene calmly for a moment and was about to return inside when a Confederate soldier appeared at the bottom of the church-steps.

"Hey, you, Yankee, come on down here, you're a prisoner now," he shouted.

The chaplain loosely waved a deprecating hand and was about to turn away.

The Rebel soldier shouted again, "Git that sword off," he commanded.

"I *can't* be taken prisoner I'm a….."

The Confederate infantryman not understanding and having suffered a morning being shot at by Union troops, was not prepared to discuss the situation. He raised his rifle and fired. The bullet struck the chaplain square-on and killed him instantly.

Grace shrieked and ran inside, "They've shot the padre," she shouted.

The interior briefly became a riot of noise and trouble, though most of the patients were in too great a state of shock to take notice and the discarding of amputated limbs through the church windows continued apace.

*****

Fred crested Benner Hill and looked back towards his hometown where he saw that some of the property, belonging to outlying farmers, had been destroyed or were on fire.

"Poor old Willy Bliss," he shook his head sadly, "he's going to need a new barn."

Seeing his horse had got its breath back he set off again at a gallop, planning to change mounts after a mile or so.

A few minutes later, he came into sight of the small bridge over Cress Run and saw the Schilling buggy off the road and beside the stream, with the horse feeding alongside it.

He pulled his mount to a halt and glanced around though could see no sign of his wife and an uneasy feeling overcame him.

"*Amelia,*" he shouted though there came no reply.

As he got closer he heard the screams of a woman coming from the trees by the creek and was sure it was the voice of his Amelia.

Fred hurried forward and came upon the awful sight of Eldred Matheson sitting astride his half-naked wife punching her without mercy.

Though Fred had never been anything of a fighter, the sight of this enraged him. He sped forward and flung himself bodily at his wife's attacker.

Matheson, taken by surprise, was flung across the glade and banged his head against a tree-trunk, where he lay momentarily dazed.

Amelia rose slowly to her feet, her face puffed-up with the beating it had received, her body caught in a violent shuddering fit, "*Oh, I'm sorry, I'm so sorry,*" she cried.

Fred took his wife in his arms and kissed her forehead, "You've nothing to apologise for, my love."

Amelia cut off his words, "I have... *Oh*, I have... I've been *shamed*... Look at me..." She was distraught.

Fred hugged his wife as tightly as he could, his voice was soft and full of concern, "Though I have you returned to me, this is all that matters. I do love you so."

"*I'm ruined*," she pulled away from her him and pointed towards the still dazed Matheson, "Ruined by that *thing* over there."

"There, my love, whatever he's done to you, it means nothing to me, nothing at all."

"Yet you will always wonder what happened, whether I am virtuous or immoral and sinful…," Amelia's mind was driving her to a dark place.

"I shall never mention this day again. *Never ever*," cried Fred desperately.

"Though I may *need* to talk about it," Amelia shook her head as she spoke and her voice was filled with despair.

"Then you shall, my precious, you shall. What ever you need to say or do, I'm with you," Fred continued to comfort his wife.

"*Ugh*," the groan came from Matheson who was struggling to his feet.

"I wish I *had* blinded him," Amelia's voice suddenly became fierce and filled with rancour.

Matheson's single good-eye caught sight of the pistol which had been left lying in the grass. He leapt to it, scooped it up, "I'm going to kill you both," he cried, waving the revolver about erratically.

Fred held up both hands in a conciliatory sort of way, "No, there's no need….," he began.

Matheson's damaged, grinning face was contorted into an image of villainy, "You're gonna be first, you bitch. Your husband can watch you squirm once I've shot you in the belly."

Fred moved quickly to place himself between the pistol and his wife.

"*Ha*," cried Eldred Matheson sardonically, "Her hero."

"Don't, there's no need for this," appealed Fred.

Enjoying the moment, Matheson carefully aimed his gun and then his finger began to squeeze the trigger.

Fred closed his eyes, whilst behind him, Amelia began to sob.

Just then a single shot rang out.

Fred turned around to look at Amelia, his expression one of dread, but found to his relief that she still stood and was unharmed.

At the same time, Amelia glanced towards her husband and saw that he too was unhurt.

Then they turned to see that Eldred Matheson was lying crumpled on the grass with blood bubbling from a single, dark hole in his chest.

Then from the trees they heard the sound of horses and turned to see a Confederate officer and three men walking their mounts towards them.

"Looks like the cavalry arrived just in time," drawled the officer.

Amelia grabbed some of her remaining discarded clothing and attempted to cover herself with it.

Fred stepped forward and held out his hand, "My wife and I cannot thank you enough, sir."

The officer took the proffered hand, "My pleasure, Mr...?"

"Fred Schilling, of Blanchwell Hall in England, but lately of Gettysburg."

"Major Gideon Sturgis of the 5th Virginia Cavalry, Ftizhugh Lee's Brigade, at your service."

"Hey, Major, ain't it time we were on our way?" Asked one of the troopers.

"Battle goin' on all around, we plannin' t'be in it?" Queried the other.

Sturgis turned to face his men, "Why, I'm surprised at you. Virginia gen'lemen wanting to leave a lady in distress, *tut, tut*."

By this time Amelia had managed to pull on enough clothing to fully cover her nudity and this action seemed to help calm her tightly stretched nerves.

She nodded, "I thank you for your concern, sir. I am Mrs Amelia Schilling."

The Major took off his hat and flourished it, "Now, that ain't a local accent, I take it."

"I am English, sir."

The Rebel officer nodded towards the corpse of Matheson, "Who's he and what's this all about?"

"It's a long and complicated story, but basically you shot a deserter from the Union Army who kidnapped my wife and when I caught up with him he was attempting to…," Fred found it hard to finish.

"Lieutenant Matheson planned to dishonour me," Amelia helped her husband out, her words coming in a rush.

"An officer-and-a-gentleman, forsooth," Sturgis shook his head, "He was obviously not a West Point man."

"Hey, Major, we ain't got time for this, there's Yankees all over that hill yonder," again one of the troopers intervened.

Sturgis ignored his men, "Well, it turns out that I've played the Good Samaritan at last. Why my folks back in Petersburg will be fair 'mazed at that."

"Do you suppose it would be safe to carry-on our way now?" Asked Fred anxiously.

"How do I know that your story ain't the other way round? You could be a Union Officer, in which case I'd have to take you prisoner," Major Sturgis spoke playfully.

"The British Embassy would soon hear of it, for my husband is an engineer on important business," Amelia spoke firmly, "besides, I can confirm everything he has said."

Once again the Confederate officer doffed his hat, "Wouldn't want to upset an English lady, nor her government, that's for sure."

"We gonna take their horses, Major?" Asked a trooper, "We sure can do with them."

"No, we couldn't leave a pretty-lady and a civilian gentleman without transport in the middle of a battlefield."

Fred and Amelia both breathed sighs of relief.

Sturgis sent his men off to the north and then said, "Hopefully, we'll be able to find our own lines, we've been cut off for three days now. Had a fight with Union Cavalry and got separated."

"I hope you do find your regiment and that you come safely through this battle and the rest of the war," said Amelia.

"I thank you kindly, ma'am," for a third time Major Sturgis flourished his hat and then set out after his men.

Fred took Amelia in his arms, "You know, in spite of all which has happened, I doubt we'll ever be so lucky again.

*****

"What do we do with him," asked the orderly, pointing at the prone figure of Captain Helmuth Schilling.

"Leave him be," ordered the surgeon shortly, he being involved in other delicate work.

"They're asking for all walkin' prisoners," informed the orderly.

"He ain't walking."

"We don't know for sure, he might be able t'walk a hundred miles."

The surgeon straightened up and stretched his arms, he looked into a wooden tub which contained the arm he had just detached, the hand of which lay grey, cold and repulsive.

Suddenly a wave of tiredness overcame him, he was sick of this war. Hell, he was sick of any war.

"D'ye want I should send him off? It'd be following orders."

The surgeon shook his head wearily, "No, this boy's head's no good, no good at all. It may never be again. We'll send him down to the field hospital the Yankees set up in a Gettysburg church."

The orderly said nothing.

"Well, get on with it," the surgeon commanded, greatly irritated.

"Yes, sir, I'll pack him into the ambulance with the others."

"We do still hold Gettysburg?" Queried the doctor.

"Yes, sir, took it this mornin'. Looks like Bobby Lee's set t'give the Union boys another shellacking' in the mornin'."

"*Mmm*," muttered the surgeon, "Not that it matters much."

*****

Fred and Amelia Schilling found the road to Hanover to be strangely quiet, especially as a battle was obviously still going on and Jeb Stuart's cavalry had ridden that way only the previous day.

"I hope we don't come across any more soldiers," remarked Amelia.

"I thought you wished to see a battle," said Fred.

"All I wish for now is to forget, for I've learned more about myself to-day than ever I have before. I've done things; *bad things*, that I never dreamed possible."

"You're still the same girl to me and always will be," put in Fred stoutly.

"I was brought up to be ladylike, to have sound Christian values and yet I deliberately tried to blind a man," Amelia's whole frame shook at the thought.

"Though, you had the right to defend yourself, for think what he was trying to do to you," Fred spoke softly.

"I was raised in the household of a clergyman and I never had the need or cause to hurt anyone, except with my sharp tongue at times. I was safe, secure, and no one ever tried to do me harm. I never believed that...," Amelia began to sob quietly.

Fred drew the buggy to a stop and placed a comforting arm around the shoulders of his wife, "There, my dear, there. It will all be over soon. We have two spare horses, so in a short while we'll arrive at Hanover Junction and if the cars aren't running to-day, they will be to-morrow or the next day."

She cuddled into him, "Oh, Fred… Shall I ever return to normal? I'm so worried I won't. Especially as…"

"As what?"

"I believe I'm with child," her words came out in a rush.

"*Oh, my God*," Fred frantically looked around, "Where can we stay? We must find a place for the night? No draughty rail depot will do for you."

"I'm not planning to give birth to-night, a station hall will do me nicely, as long as a train arrives going in the right direction soon thereafter."

Chapter Fourteen
Thursday, 2*nd* July 1863

Working in the field hospital, Grace Schilling felt needed for the first time in her life and she revelled in it.

Though she had no particular nursing skills she found herself to be easily capable of providing succour to the wounded and giving aid to the surgeons.

She became sure that she'd found a role which suited her, and in a small way, she was in charge of events.

Previously, her mother and father had controlled her every action and then this function had devolved upon Helmuth. More recently, even Fred had tried to tell her what to do. No more would this be the case, she promised herself as she rolled bandages.

"Boy over there askin' for you Miss Grace," As Andy Jackson's wound was not a serious one, he was giving what help he could to the wounded.

"The one with the smashed ankle? Or the soldier whose jaw's been shot away?" Queried Grace.

"The jaw one ain't capable of much speech," Andy couldn't help his reply.

"Finish rolling bandages while I go and see to him."

As the battle had progressed wounded from both sides arrived in a constant stream. There were so many that some had to be deposited in the street until such time as a space became available.

Unfortunately, it had begun to drizzle, the very fine kind of wetting rain which soaks a person in no time, making their lives even more uncomfortable.

*****

Helmuth Schilling woke-up to find that he had no idea of who he was or where he was.

None-the-less, the pretty lady in the big house lit up his mind like a beacon, one that he felt he should follow until he found her.

Around him, in the field hospital men groaned and screamed as though they were members of the cast of a production of Dante's *Inferno*.

Unknown to him, a few yards away his sister was sleeping uneasily, her smock heavily stained with blood-and-pus, her snoring heavy with fatigue.

Similarly, just outside, attempting to take away the heaps of discarded limbs that littered the lane, Andy Jackson was wheeling a hand cart. He was hoping to find an open space where he could make a bonfire of these body parts.

Inside, Helmuth had decided to begin his quest. Rising quietly he made his way to the doorway and walked outside. No one stopped him for they had no reason to – for apart from a bandage around his temple - he looked fit-and-well.

He stepped out on to Chambersburg Street, but didn't recognise it, or even the church in which he had spent most of the Sundays of his youth. There was no feature of the town he had grown up in which struck him as even vaguely familiar.

Helmuth set off walking to find the beautiful lady, the light from whom cleared the darkness from his mind.

*****

Andy Jackson kept well into the shadows as he watched Confederate troops stream through the town towards their positions for the resumption of the battle as soon as it was light.

He was terrified that he might be questioned about his previous life and if the Rebs believed him to be a runaway slave, they would send him back to his master. The consequences of which were too terrible for him to contemplate.

A battery-of-artillery rumbled past, the caissons swaying and gunners swearing at the horses. One or two of the riding men had their heads bowed in fitful sleep.

Once the last of the guns had passed, he looked down the alley and saw a familiar figure, he took a step or two closer and became convinced it was Captain Schilling.

Discarding his caution, he hurried on to the street, "Cap'n, *Cap'n...*," he whispered hoarsely as soon as he was close enough.

Helmuth stopped and looked into the face of the ex-slave, however, the light of recognition did not enter his eyes.

Andy knew immediately that something was wrong and then; seeing the bandage, realised that Helmuth must have taken a head wound and was dazed.

"It's Andy, sir, Andy Jackson. I looked after you in the old Seventeenth."

Jackson's words were having no effect apart from bringing a look of bemusement to Helmuth's face.

Though Schilling did not recognise Jackson in the slightest, he thought he may have been sent to help him find his beacon lady.

"Yes," he managed to croak.

Andy now breathed more easily as the captain had obviously recognised him. He took his officer by the arm and began to lead him across Chambersburg Street, "I'll take ye home cap'n," he said.

"*Home,*" repeated Schilling. This seemed a good idea, for his new partner knew where home was and perhaps the pretty lady would be waiting for him there.

*****

Grace Schilling felt exhausted, previously she'd often claimed to have been *exhausted*, though it turned out that she'd never known *true* exhaustion at all. The Lutheran Church field hospital brought for her both understanding and change.

Though casualties were still coming in, even after three days of battle, the raging stream had become a trickle and many of the wounded were taken off to military hospitals in Washington or elsewhere.

She looked at her smock and found it to be shockingly filthy, covered in blood, excrement and; in fact, with all of the materials the human body needs to dispose of.

"Hey, Miss, *Miss...*," the voice was hoarse and barely above a whisper.

She looked down to see; stretched out on a pew, a Confederate major of cavalry. At first she bridled at the sight of a damned Reb, and her old personality attempted to take a grip on her again. However, she'd seen and learned much in the previous three days so she held back haughty words and asked, "Yes. What can I do for you, poor boy?"

"Don't let 'em take my leg off... Please, I'd rather be dead than lose ma' leg."

Grace knew the surgeons were prone to amputating limbs, sometimes before they'd looked properly at the damage done them.

She leaned forward to have a closer look and saw that there was a neat bullet hole towards the top of this officer's thigh.

"It looks like a flesh wound to me, but that's of no account, I'd never looked upon any wounds 'till three days back."

The major seemed satisfied and lay back, breathing easier.

Grace decided she would look after this man and pester the surgeons until they agreed that amputation was not required.

"I'll bring you some nice clean, fresh-water, she promised, setting off to seek the surgeon she felt was most amenable, the one who didn't appear to be similar to a careless butcher in a rush.

Chapter Fifteen
Saturday 4th July, 1863

Andy Jackson had spent two taut nights at the Schilling house watching as Confederate troops continued to march through Gettysburg. However, he did notice that this Independence Day was a remarkably quiet one.

He'd put Captain Schilling to bed and forced him to eat and drink plenty of water.

Luckily, the house had not been looted; or even broken into, so provisions were in plentiful supply.

As he continued to observe the street, he was relieved to see a troop of Union cavalry make a cautious appearance and he realised the Confederates must have gone.

The enemy had retreated. Lee was beaten!

"*Yahoo*," he cried, waking up his charge, "Cap'n, we've won, the Union's won the day."

Helmuth dragged himself to wakefulness, "Won what?" He asked.

"The battle."

"What battle?"

"The one you were wounded in."

Helmuth's fingers stretched up to touch his head, which still ached horrendously, "*I was in a battle?*"

"Yes, you were wounded three days ago. I found you wandering from the dressing-station at your church."

"*My* church," seeing the look of concern on Andy's face, Helmuth continued, "I'm sorry, but I can't remember anything... Except...."

"Except what?" Queried Andy after a pause.

"Not what. Someone."

"It wouldn't be a very pretty lady, would it?"

Helmuth managed a smile, "Yes, a beautiful lady in a big house."

Andy's grin broadened into a smile, "That would be Caroline, your wife back in England."

"What would I be doing in England?"

"You're a rich man there, with a beautiful wife and a big house."

Helmuth shook his head, "It's all so much of a puzzle," he said.

Andy patted his officer's shoulder, "Don't worry about a thing, we'll all work to put the pieces together again, I promise."

Chapter Sixteen

"I managed to get steamer tickets for Tuesday," cried Fred Schilling as he burst into his hotel room in New York.

Amelia looked up from the book she was reading, "Oh, Fred, this is good news, I shan't be happy until I'm home."

Fred was concerned for his wife as he knew it would take some time for her to recover from her experiences on the Hanover road. He came to her side and began to comfort her.

Amelia snuggled into his embrace and tears began to trickle down her cheeks.

His lips gently brushed her badly bruised face, "There, there, my lovely. You'll soon be home and perhaps on Christmas Day we'll have a child of our own."

"Is it right to bring a child into a world so full of trouble?" Asked Amelia, echoing the words of the uncountable number of others who had experienced the reality of war and the inhumanity it leads to.

"Of course we do. Think how delighted Julia will be to have a playmate."

"Yes... Perhaps..," Amelia didn't sound convinced.

"Blanchwell, think of it, back to *Blanchwell*."

"My mama, *I want my mama*," Amelia began to sob heavily, causing her whole body to shake.

"Of course, you want your mother," he hugged her harder, "then there's Arabella too, how fine it will be to see them all again."

Amelia sniffed and her tears began to dry up as thoughts of home raced through her mind driving away much darker concerns.

"Think how much you - *no* we have to look forward to," encouraged Fred.

Amelia smiled and then her face became haunted again, "Fred, you must never tell *anyone* what happened to me... On the road... With...," she couldn't finish.

Fred pulled her as close as he could, "It shall never be mentioned again. *We* shall never mention it again."

"I may need to talk... Sometimes....," Amelia shook her head with some vigour.

"Then you shall, my love, you shall whenever you feel it's time to."

"That helps more than you can know," Amelia nodded and smiled as broadly as the damage to her face would allow.

Then Fred's jaw tightened, "And I must see Sir Charles as soon as possible, for the Western Supply Company is nothing other than a fraud."

*****

Grace looked longingly at Major Gideon Sturgis, but she knew that she was to lose him soon. Her special surgeon had saved his leg and now he was to be taken to a hospital near Chicago – or so she'd been told.

"I don't know what I'll do without you," his smile was much more cheerful now.

"You may write to me, if you wish, let me know how you are progressing. I'm Grace Schilling."

"Schilling? Of Gettysburg?" The major became fully alert.

"Yes, we're a long-established family here."

"You have a brother, Fred, do you not? And a sister-in-law by the name of Amelia."

Grace's considerable jaw dropped, "How on earth could you possibly know that?"

"I met them on the Hanover road, on the first of the month."

"Did they go safely on their way?"

"Yes, with a little help from me."

Grace cut-off his words, "There was another person, a Union deserter but dressed in civilian clothes which didn't fit him."

"He was there too."

"What happened to him?"

Sturgis was about to tell the truth, "Oh, he's..," and then he changed his mind, "...run off again."

Grace leaned closer to whisper, "Is the gold intact? The villain didn't take it with him?"

The word *gold* burned itself deep into Sturgis' brain, "Oh, yes," he spoke coolly, "yes, it's intact all right."

"Half of it's mine, you know," she whispered conspiratorially, "in gold eagles too."

"No doubt you and your husband will be pleased about that," nodded Sturgis.

Grace smiled coyly, "I've no husband….. Not yet."

The Rebel Cavalier pulled on a surprised expression, "What? A smart, pretty and gracious lady like yourself? *Unmarried* Why… I'll be darned if I've ever heard such a thing. What are your Yankee men thinkin' of?"

Grace favoured the Rebel officer with a satisfied smile and then went to have get rid of the filthy smock she was wearing, wash and do up her hair.

*****

Lady Marian Martin looked around at her luncheon guests, and her face was lit by her broadest smile, "I'm so pleased you've all had time to accept my invitation, for it is some while since the *Coven* met."

Elizabeth Esprey clapped her hands gently, "Oh, Marian, it's such a relief to leave the theatre behind and enjoy some civilised company for a change."

"Indeed, yes," said Caroline, smiling weakly, "we should never allow so long a time to pass between our meetings."

"Hear, hear to that," put in Jane Turner, who couldn't make up her mind whether Caroline was pining for her husband…. Or, for Richard.

Sarah Nicholson nodded politely. She wasn't sure that such exalted company was the right place for her, though the other women had been very welcoming.

Caroline's mind was fixed firmly on her husband, of whom she'd had no news yet. However, she'd been surprised to learn that a great Union victory had been won at, of all places, Gettysburg.

"Any news of Helmuth," asked Jane seriously, hoping her friend's husband *was* safe, thus keeping Richard safely at home too.

Caroline shook her head, her mouth a straight, severe line, "Afraid not, I'm worried in case he was… Hurt in the recent big battle."

"Jervie says most people in a battle never see anything of the actual fighting," Elizabeth said comfortingly.

Caroline managed a smile, "True, my grandpa' said war was mainly discomfort, dampness and tedium."

"I've decided to serve champagne," Marian thought it best to change the subject of the conversation.

"Oh, how lovely," cried Mrs Esprey as the fizzy wine was her favourite.

Sarah never drank alcohol and so was about to place her hand over her glass but then decided otherwise, "Please," she said to the footman.

"How is Mrs Nicholson senior," enquired Jane.

"She is coping very well, Elinor keeps her busy and her mind off her loss."

"And you?" Marian enquired softly.

Sarah managed a weak smile, "I'm strong and the children I teach help enormously to make me even stronger."

The fish course arrived, haddock in a parsley and chive sauce which stilled the conversation.

Sarah picked a small piece of fish and carried it to her mouth and found it to be wonderfully tasty. Then she felt a sudden rush of guilt. How dare she sit sipping expensive wine and enjoying a fancy fish-dish when her husband was fresh in his grave?

She was about to drop her cutlery and flee to his graveside to ask his forgiveness. However, Jane Turner broke her chain of thought.

"Good fish."

"Mrs Cruddace must be the best cook in the county," suggested Elizabeth Esprey.

"The haddock arrived from Shields just this morning," informed Marian, "I'm told it was swimming in the North Sea yesterday."

"Having two fishmongers in town and the railway to supply them is such a bonus.".

Caroline smiled and nodded, "Yes, indeed it is."

Sarah took a further piece of fish and found it even tastier than the first one. What would John have thought? She asked herself.

"You're very quiet, Sarah," said Marian.

"Sorry, I was just thinking of my husband, wondering what he'd think of his widow taking her ease in a fine house, with fine ladies, eating an excellent meal with expensive wine."

The other four women looked on with interest, their heads tilted to one side waiting for her to answer her own question.

Sarah suddenly smiled broadly and her eyes sparkled, "He'd be very proud of me. I know he would, he'd think it a wondrous thing and against all convention."

"Well said," commented Caroline, who had taken to heart her friend's words.

"Enjoying a meal doesn't mean you've forgotten Mr Nicholson, for this you'll never do," added Jane Turner sensibly.

"No, we women never forget," said Elizabeth somewhat morosely, remembering some of the men who'd once starred in her life.

Lady Marian Martin rose from her chair, put an arm around Sarah Nicholson and kissed her cheek tenderly.

"Well done, my dear, *very well done*," she said.

*****

Even though the battle had been fought and won, Grace Schilling continued to attend the hospital at the Lutheran Church. This was partly because she had no wish to give up being *useful*, as well as desiring to develop further her friendship with a certain Confederate Major.

"Why, Miss Schilling, I'm pleased you've called, for I'm off to-morrow," greeted Gideon Sturgis.

"So soon?" Grace was upset for she thought she'd be able to enjoy the cavalryman's company for some time yet.

"Yes, the surgeon's happy with my recovery and; thanks to you, I still have two legs."

Grace dropped her head, for she deemed this to be very bad news. She was getting along famously with the major and he seemed to like her, which was unusual as she knew that most men didn't.

"Nonsense, you're much too weak and can't walk yet, even with a crutch. I shall see about this."

Gideon Sturgis shook his head, "I'm afraid nothing can be done. I'm to go to a hospital in Chicago and as soon as

I'm well enough I'll be imprisoned in the Stock Yards there."

"Oh no you won't. Stockyards indeed, I'll not have it."

Just then an officer of infantry arrived, "Saying your goodbyes to this handsome fellow-m'-lad?" he asked of Grace.

"Certainly not, as he isn't leaving."

"Orders are orders, Miss, he's off to Hanover Junction in the morning and he'll be in Chicago in less than a week."

"Something can be done, surely," cried a distraught Grace Schilling.

"He could give his parole," suggested the Union officer, "Though he'd need someone to vouch for him."

"I shall," cried Grace holding on to a thin thread of hope.

"There's no room at the exchange camp, so he'd need to live with you. Got any men folk at home?"

"Certainly, my brother is there and we have a black servant with us too."

"You willing t'give your parole," asked the officer of Major Sturgis.

"Sure, I don't much fancy so ordinary an address as *Care of the Stockyards, Chicago, Illinois*."

"Are you to be trusted?"

"I'm a West Pointer, sir. Class of '61."

The Union officer nodded his head, "Then this is good enough for me," he replied.

*****

Fred Schilling was taken quickly to see Sir Charles Martin at the office of the *Martindale Iron & Coal Company*.

"Why, Fred, back so soon?" Greeted the baronet, somewhat surprised.

"We got the first ship we could, Sir Charles. I was in a tearing hurry to make sure we didn't agree a contract with the *Western Supply Company.*"

Charles Martin looked puzzled and his heart was seized by the cold hand of dread. "Oh, why?" He asked as casually as he could.

"Why, sir, they're a fraud."

"Though your report indicated they were to be trusted."

Fred looked puzzled, "No, sir, I expressed my doubts most carefully."

Sir Charles reached into a drawer of his desk, scrabbled about for a moment and then brought out Fred's letter from America. He pushed it towards his young protégé, "Here, have a look for yourself."

Fred; not believing what he was hearing, swooped up the document, however, he was soon wishing a pit full of demons would open before him so that he could leap into it.

"This isn't mine, Sir Charles. I did *not* write this. This isn't my handwriting," the young engineer was shocked.

Charles came around the desk and patted the young man on the shoulder, "Caroline did say that the hand was far too neat to be yours."

"*Are we committed?*" Fred looked up sharply, in an instant his whole world appeared to have been reduced to shards.

"No, we haven't signed anything and we shan't now."

Fred Schilling's breath came more easily.

"However, we have produced many more *railroad* tracks than we currently can possibly sell. Thought we'd stockpile them ready to meet the demand."

"Oh, dear. How this has happened, I don't know," said Fred waving the counterfeit letter about his head.

"Did you post it yourself?"

"Yes," then Fred shook his head, "No, *no* I handed the letter to the desk-clerk at the *Metropolitan Hotel*."

"Then there's the break in the line we're looking for."

"*Dammit*," cried Fred, furious with himself, "I can't apologise enough, I should have known better. The whole scheme was far too pat to be true, but I still blundered."

"Not your fault, how would you know that the clerk had been bribed."

They sat together in silence for a while and then Fred said, "Though I hear they're returning Mr Bellerby's bones."

"A good ploy, wouldn't you say, for how could we doubt them once they did as promised."

"Well," said Fred, after a pause, "Caroline must be pleased, anyway."

Sir Charles Martin shook his head and thought to himself, *I believe I can see the hand of Wright in this.*

*****

Major Gideon Sturgis took his ease in the parlour of the Schilling house in Gettysburg, Pennsylvania. He was now wearing borrowed civilian clothes and his every need was seen to by Miss Grace.

He couldn't help thinking how lucky a coincidence it had been coming across Fred Schilling and a barely clothed Mrs Schilling on the first day of the battle, for it had eventually led him to this haven of safety.

Though Sturgis had fought bravely in the war, after Gettysburg he realised the Confederate States of America was doomed. There would be no further invasions of Union territory, he was sure of that. There was no doubt in his mind that his compatriots would hold out for a year or two longer, but, little-by-little, the South would be squeezed until there was no fight left in her.

The mystical finger was writing a warning on the wall for all to see, and he for one was going to take heed of it.

To top things off, the day after Gettysburg, Vicksburg on the Mississippi had been lost too, which freed this great waterway for the use of Union forces. As well as slicing the Confederacy into two.

Sturgis also knew that he would be expected to take part in the prisoner exchange scheme but reckoned were he to play his wound-card effectively he could remain where he was – with an unmarried woman who also was rich.

"Yes, much better to stay safe and comfortable here," he said to himself before ringing for the maid to bring him coffee and chocolate-cake.

*****

"So, how was Helmuth when you last saw him," Caroline asked anxiously.

"Very well," replied Fred Schilling.

"Tired though, for his regiment had been trailing the Rebels for seventeen days by the time he turned up at Gettysburg," added Amelia.

"He could only stay with us for a few minutes, but insisted we leave for New York as quickly as we could," continued Fred.

"I suppose Grace became awkward," suggested Caroline.

Fred laughed, "Amelia eventually brought her around."

Amelia's face lit up, "I really enjoyed drenching her with a full pitcher of water."

Caroline joined in the merriment, for even on the short acquaintance she'd had with her sister-in-law, she'd found her to be extremely tiresome.

"Once Helmuth had left, we managed to avoid the battle and return to the peace of Blanchwell," said Fred.

"And you are fully recovered from so shocking a journey?"

A shadow passed across Amelia's countenance, "Travelling across a battleground is something I'll never forget, however, I was brought up to be strong and resilient and with Fred's help," she put her arm around her husband's waist, "memory of it will fade."

Caroline looked with concern at Amelia and wondered about the bruises on her face, "You weren't hurt in the battle at all……," her voice dried up as she felt how tense the atmosphere in the room had become.

"Amelia fell heavily aboard ship," Fred put in quickly.

"Though my injuries are much improved now."

"And your Little Stranger?" Queried a deeply concerned Caroline.

The smile returned to Amelia's face, "Doctor Cowley says all is as it should be."

Caroline sighed deeply, "Then everything is perfect, or would be if only Helmuth were back amongst us."

*****

Every morning, once the battle had ended, Andy Jackson took Captain Schilling for a walk along the streets of his home-town. He hoping that familiar sights would trigger the return of his officer's memory. Though however hard he tried the landmarks and buildings remained strangers to Helmuth, who stood shaking his head in confusion.

"Don't ya remember anythin', Cap'n?" Andy was becoming desperate.

"No…. Nothing, though you tell me I once lived here, I have no recollection of it. The woman you say is my sister, I'm sure I've never seen her before."

They came to the edge of town and looked up to Seminary Ridge where an ant hill of men was starting to clear up the detritus of battle.

"You don't remember no fightin' up there?"

Helmuth shook his head, "No…. No, I don't believe I do."

"Colonel Kellogg, you don't remember him neither?"

"Never heard of him."

"What do you remember?" Queried an exasperated Andy Jackson.

Helmuth's reply was immediate, "I can only recall the beautiful lady and the big house."

Andy thought for a minute before he said, "Then we'd best go to find her."

"You know her?"

"Sure I do, you remember Miss Caroline Bellerby who became Mrs Helmuth Schilling."

"Can we go tomorrow?"

"Gotta persuade Miss Grace first – she's got the gold dollars."

*****

Caroline had just returned from a long ride around the Blanchwell estate when she was met by a servant carrying a silver tray upon which stood two letters.

Her heart gave a bound and was filled with joy, which was rapidly replaced by foreboding.

"Two letters, one at least should contain good news," she comforted herself.

"From America, ma'am, both of them are," said the footman, smiling as he did so.

Caroline grabbed them and tore open the first.

Gettysburg,
Pennsylvania,

7th July 1863

My Dear Mrs Schilling,

I am sorry to have to inform you……

Caroline was sure that her heart had stopped beating, but she forced herself to read on.

….that your husband, Captain Helmuth Schilling was wounded in the great battle recently fought here.

However, I am pleased to tell you that, physically, he has not been harmed apart from a gouge in his head, the result of a close encounter with a sniper's bullet.

Though he is physically whole, he has lost his memory and is unable to tell us anything of what happened to him on that faithful day.

He is currently lodged in his own house with his sister Grace, the black servant Jackson and a Confederate officer who has given his parole.

As the exigencies of the service call me away, I can only say how proud I was to serve with your husband and hope that his memory will return and that he'll soon, thereafter, rejoin you in England.

Your Obedient Servant,

Colonel Josiah H. Kellogg,
Commanding the 17th Pennsylvania Cavalry.

Caroline fell to her knees and began to cry in relief. Helmuth wasn't dead. He would be coming home to her.

"Can I help you up, ma'am," asked the footman.

"Yes, please, it would be most kind," she smiled.

Once on her feet again she remembered the second letter, taking it up she saw that it was from Grace Schilling.

My Dear Caroline,

I have little time to spare, being deeply involved helping at the field-hospital which has been set up within the College Lutheran Church.

I'm sure you'll have heard by now that Helmuth is safe but is unable to remember anything of his past life.

The black slave, who insists on trailing around with my brother, is begging for funds to return him to England. However, at the moment, this is impossible, as there is no suitable person to accompany him.

In addition, should Helmuth depart I would be required to give up to the authorities a paroled Rebel officer of whom I entertain high-hopes.

I am sure that Helmuth would not approve of my losing the best chance for my future happiness, were he fit enough to do so.

As this dreadful war will soon be over everything will return to normal and I shall hopefully have become a bride by then.

Your faithful and obedient sister,
Grace

"*Wait until the war is over*, indeed, I should say not," muttered Caroline crossly as she stuffed her sister-in-law's note back into its wafer.

*****

"Miz Grace, we got'ta get the Capn' home," Andy Jackson was almost begging.

"This *is* his home," Grace was determined to keep her brother exactly where he was.

"But he'll recover, sure as sure is, *if* he goes back to Miz Caroline."

"I'll be the judge of that, and I insist my brother stays here until he is fully fit to travel four thousand miles."

Andy nodded slowly, he understood what Grace's problem was were Helmuth to depart for England. Major Sturgis would be sent to a Union prison, as he couldn't be left living with a single lady with no male relative present. He also reckoned that Helmuth's sister had certain designs on the handsome and lively major.

*****

Sir Charles Martin sighed contentedly as he climbed into bed alongside his wife.

She cuddled into him and said, "You sound happy."

He kissed her gently, "Yes, to think, a mere few weeks ago the town was in turmoil, workers were at each others' throats and John Nicholson ended up dead. And now…"

"Everything has returned to normal."

"Apart from poor Sarah losing her husband."

"She has great strength though, a remarkable woman in many ways," judged the baronet.

"Anyway, no one can have any complaints about the organisation and running of the second Martindale Gala," remarked Marian.

Charles laughed at the thought of it, "Yes, and do you know the part I liked most?"

"The parade organised by Mr Villiers?"

"No."

"Mr Vasey falling into the stream after some over-indulgence?"

"Close, but not even that."

Marian narrowed her eyes, "I know, the final of the cricket."

Charles began to laugh heartily, in true delight, "Yes, it was wonderful. The colliers and ironworkers argued over and over again about which of them was going to win the *Nicholson Trophy*....."

Lady Marian began to splutter with laughter too and then said, "And it was won by the unfancied team from the Town."

"Who'd have thought that Colonel Esprey was a demon bowler?" Asked Charles, his eyes twinkling, "Or that Mr Hodge would be a true sentinel at the wicket?"

"As well as scoring sixty-two didn't he?" Recalled Marian.

"Yes – not out, he went in at number four and remained there for the rest of the match."

"How glum were the ironworkers?" Marian tittered

"The colliers looked as though they were about to burst," Charles added to the merriment.

"And then, the next thing we know, a combined deputation of pitmen and ironworkers came to complain that Hodge wasn't a Martindale townsman and, therefore, ineligible to play."

"Colonel Esprey pointed out that the Reverend Hodge had lived at the rectory for several months and was married to a recent inhabitant of the town," Charles smiled at the memory of it.

"This set the miners and ironworkers off arguing amongst themselves, it was all so amusing," Marian cried with laughter.

Charles sighed happily and eased back into his pillows, "You know, a few weeks ago I thought I'd never laugh again."

"Yes, but we are lucky, *lucky* people."

He turned, kissed her and then replied, "there are none more fortunate."

She returned his kiss, though more urgently and eventually straddled his body with her own.

"Oh, my Marian," he cried, "thank-you for loving me."

"How could I do other?"

*****

Geoffrey Hodge, the Vicar of Kirkby, entered his residence with a spring in his step at the thought of spending the rest of the evening with his dear Prudence.

She greeted him at the threshold and thrust her right cheek towards his lips.

He kissed her where indicated, as was their practice.

Then she presented her other cheek and waited until he had also favoured this one with his lips too.

"My love," she spoke as softly as she could, even though her heart was thumping.

"My dearest," he returned before he moved on towards the drawing-room.

She held on to his jacket, "Geoffrey, you must come and gaze upon my latest painting, it is of our garden."

The vicar smiled, "Perhaps I could take tea first, after which with a full stomach, I'll be more able to run a critical-eye over your latest *mistress-piece*."

At that moment Prudence lost her grip on her husband's coat and watched in dismay as he continued into the drawing room, where he was fond of taking a glass of sherry before he ate. She sped after him.

Hodge entered the room and noticed that the french-doors were standing wide-open and a brisk breeze was blowing in, upsetting several of the fixtures and causing devastation to some of the carefully arranged notes for his next sermon.

"Prudence," he called.

"Yes, my love," she returned on entering the room, "Oh, my, why did you open those doors? Look at the state of your papers. Oh, dear me."

"They were already open when I entered the room," pondered Hodge before he suddenly said, "To-day is the servants' day off. Who else could have opened the doors. Intruders perhaps. Is anything missing…."

"Be calm, Geoffrey, there must be a simple explanation."

"I shall venture into the garden…," began the vicar, picking up a poker from the fireplace.

"Ye want these in here, Mrs Hodge," called the gardener's boy from just outside.

Prudence hurried across to the open doorway, "Yes, Tom, thank you kindly. Perhaps you'll bring them in."

"*Ah*, you see, there's a rational reason for everything," said Geoffrey.

Tom entered, his arms full of freshly cut blooms, but he dropped several as he tried to salute his master.

"Never mind that, my boy, hand them over to the mistress."

The young gardener's assistant did as he was asked and as soon as his back was turned towards the vicar he winked slowly at Prudence.

The vicar's wife gave him one of her brightest smiles which grew wider the more she thought of the long, vigorous; though rough and ready, romp she'd just enjoyed.

"He's a good boy is Tom," remarked Geoffrey Hodge, "very trustworthy."

"He is both good and seemingly tireless," Prudence added.

*****

"I see your resources have been wasted," said Tom Widmark, waving documents in front of his employer.

Hannibal Wright looked up and smiled, "Not every game can be won in the first innings," he replied shortly.

"But it's cost you thousands of dollars."

"I have millions and even more on the way."

"Though was it worth it to ruin a minor landowner in a town no one's ever heard of and couldn't care less about if they had?"

"It's for my own amusement, a little game I like to play. Due to no cleverness or ability on his part, Sir Charles Martin is the only man to have had the better of me."

"So, it's personal."

"Yes, to some extent. He brought disgrace upon my only child and thwarted my ambitions. He's gone soft on his workforce too. Provided them with a range of unaffordable benefits.

"You said it worked for him, though, higher production leading to cheaper goods and a greater volume of sales."

"Yes, but another recession will come along soon enough and if he's not aware of it quickly, it'll bring desolation to Martindale, his miserable, bastard town."

"You'll be doing your best to bring this about?"

"Without a doubt, Thompson, without a doubt."

*****

Geordie Cook led a nervous looking Losser into the office of the Martindale Colliery and had him stand in front of Frank Turner's desk.

"This is Losser," he introduced.

"Losser?" Queried Frank.

"Aye, another o' those asylum boys, y'knaw, where they can't even be bothered to give the lads a name," informed Geordie.

"So he has no name?"

"No, but we call him John – John Losser, that's his new name."

"You happy with that son?" Asked Frank.

"Yes, sir."

"But he still likes to be called Losser," informed Geordie.

"Aye, well that's all right by me, I suppose," said Frank.

"Now then, Losser here thinks he would be able to work down the pit. I've told him how dirty and dangerous it is, but he's set on it," informed Geordie.

"Is it really what you want?" Queried the agent.

Losser looked uncertain and then he asked timorously, "Do I get paid? Geordie sez I would."

"Yes, you'll get the rate for the job."

"But will *I* get it?" To Losser it all sounded too good to be true. He'd worked very hard in various factories and works in Liverpool but had never ever received a penny-piece.

"Why, yes, who else would get it?" Answered Frank.

Losser's normally severe countenance was lit up with a huge smile, "I'll do any job ye like."

"Well, ye're a bit big for face work, but there's plenty around here to keep you busy," said Frank and then turning to Geordie, he suggested, "Start him on the bank-top, do you think?"

"Aye, couple o' weeks there and maybe see if we can train him up to be a lamp-house man or even a blacksmith. Do you like ponies, son?"

"Never had much t'do with them, sir."

"You'll soon learn, come in on Monday next."

Losser left the office happier and more excited than he had ever been before in his entire life.

*****

John Fisher couldn't help but notice that Roddy Villiers had taken a further rasher of bacon and had asked for another *two* eggs. This was unbelievable, as the expense of this gorging was going to come from his own pocket.

"I gather you haven't found a suitable home near the theatre yet," commented the schoolmaster, his eyebrows raised high.

Villiers sighed as he welcomed the maid who brought in his extra breakfast, "No, nothing yet," he replied.

"Nothing good enough is available. Has it darling?" added Bobbity Villiers who had also devoured a good breakfast.

"It's just that this house is tied to the school and I fear what the School Board would say were they to discover that I've taken in a lodger."

"*Fie*, shame on you, John," Roberta smiled doe-eyed towards her husband, "No one can object to relatives staying with you."

"Especially close ones," added the actor.

"I'm not so sure about this, just the other day the Reverend Lander was saying…"

Roberta's expression cut him sharply off, for a fire was burning in her eyes and her brother knew it needed putting-out as quickly as possible.

"Yes, of course, I'll be happy to have you stay here for as long as you like."

Roderick Villiers had watched and listened to the ebb-and-flow of this conversation as he dipped a sliver of fried bacon into the yellow softness of an egg yolk. He was quite aware that his brother-in-law wished to be rid of him and he could understand why. However, the School House was very convenient for him. Not too far from the theatre, the meals served there were much improved and, best of all, it was not costing him a penny-piece.

"It's funny, but before I dropped off to sleep last night, there came to me the idea for a new play – one in which the central character can only be played by yourself," informed the actor, his voice deeply serious.

Fisher's ears opened wide, "The leading part?"

"Of course."

"Really," the school-teacher had good reason to doubt the word of the actor as he had been fobbed off with minor, meaningless parts several times since his triumph in *Macbeth*.

"Yes, I've already a title for it," Villiers closed his eyes and his voice became reverent, *The Romantic Magister*."

John Fisher's eyes lit up, "I would play the Master?"

"Who else has the experience," cried Villiers strongly.

"What's it about? I'm not to be a Greek slave I expect."

"*Ha*, the very thought. No, you shall portray a Noble Roman of good family."

"A Patrician?"

"Of course, you will be a famous philosopher, the teacher of the children of a powerful Senator."

"What about myself? Am I not to take part," put in Bobbity, her eyes narrowing meanly.

"Of course, your husband is a man of vile temper who treats you... his *beautiful* wife abominably...," by now Villiers was extemporising desperately.

"And the wife *is* beautiful...."

"Not too beautiful, I expect," put in Roberta with some iron in her voice.

This was becoming increasingly difficult for Villiers to maintain, though he soldiered on, "I thought, perhaps,

Arabella Brass, she is a very attractive young woman, but no one could call her beautiful."

Bobbity considered for a moment, "Yes, this is true, Bella isn't beautiful. Though could *I* not play the role myself? I'm made for it."

Villiers gulped at the thought of this, but as the whole scheme was a figment of his imagination and he had no intention of making it real, it didn't much matter.

"How absurd, there was I casting my mind around for a suitable candidate when the obvious choice was sitting directly opposite me at the breakfast table," the thespian shook his head at his own silliness.

"I shall be delighted to play the female-lead opposite my brother," said Roberta.

Even though some of the gloss had been taken from the project; for Fisher much preferred Bella Brass for the part, he nodded sagely, "An excellent idea, brother," he said with great satisfaction.

*****

After church, Grace Schilling was walking arm in arm with the handsome and charming Major Sturgis. How pleased she was to show him off to the town; especially to those who considered her to be an eternal spinster.

"You know," said Sturgis, "I don't think I have detected even a hint of animosity directed towards myself, even though my side did some damage while they were here for three days."

Grace squeezed her companion's arm, "Why should there be? You yourself did no damage and beside which you've given your parole and I know you will not break it."

"No graduate of West Point could bring himself to do such a thing."

"Were all of your Year so honourable?"

"Of course, but the damndest thing...," Sturgis bit his tongue, "I must apologise for my use of soldierly language."

Grace shook her head, "It is only to be expected of a true fighting-man and I am not at all upset. You were saying?"

"When I was wounded we were engaged with the Michigan Cavalry Brigade which was led by a classmate of mine."

"Really? And who was that?"

"Brigadier-General George Armstrong Custer."

"A *general*! And he's your age?"

"They call him the *Boy General*, or so I've been told. Fancies himself as the American Murat," the fact that Sturgis was disgruntled and somewhat envious told in his tone of voice.

"I gather you don't like him?"

"He's an awful show-off, hopeless in class and always in trouble."

"And yet he's a general."

"He's been extremely lucky and if it hadn't been for the outbreak of the war he would probably never have graduated at all," Sturgis was disgruntled.

"Perhaps he has hidden talents," suggested Miss Schilling.

"Hardly, he came sixty-first out of a class of sixty-one."

"Then he must be an awfully fierce-some fighter to be able to make up for it."

Grace was beginning to irritate the Confederate officer, "Lucky, that's all he is *lucky*. One day; mark my words, his luck will run out."

"Not until this dreadful war is over, I trust," commented Grace.

*****

"Susan, are ye there?" Shouted Joseph Dunnett as he entered the cottage of Mrs Russell.

The lady in question came running from the scullery, her eyes alight and her arms extended.

"Oh, Joe, they've let you out, Oh, thank the Lord."

The gamekeeper took her into his arms and pulled her close.

Susan began to cry tears of sheer happiness, "Oh, I so feared for you, I so feared for you," she sobbed.

"Aye, I must say I've never been in so sorry a place."

"How did ye get out so soon?"

"Sir Charles saw to it, He kept pesterin' everyone from the Lord Lieutenant o' the County to the prison gate-sweeper. Had young Tom Harrington on-side an'all, or so I believe."

"Mr Harrington? Him what's a Member o' Parliament?"

"Aye, but he's a 'somethin' of State' now as well, or so Sir Charles sez."

Susan Russell hugged Joe tighter and tighter, her head snuggling into his chest.

He smoothed her hair and enjoyed the smell of freshly baked bread that exuded from it. She was no beauty, but by God, he thought to himself, she'll do for me.

"D'ye want t'stay the night wi' me," she whispered.

"Aye, I do. But best not."

As he finished speaking he could feel her body trembling and tears began to soak into his chest.

"Naw lass, naw, I do *want* t'stay, I do – but let's wait till we're wed. We'll call an' see the Minister about it tomorrow."

Now he felt her body relax and she moulded herself to him, hugging him tighter and tighter, almost; he felt, to the edge of suffocation."

*****

Elysia Scott-Wilson pulled her stallion to a halt beside the River Wynter and dismounted.

"All that jogging about perched on a lady's saddle must have made you juicy," suggested Jonnie Corsica as he too got down from his mount.

"You're an insolent wretch."

"And you, my dear, are aching for my insolence to proceed further."

"How dare you…"

He laughed, "Unless, of course, that swine Kent has been servicing you in my absence."

"He may have been," replied Elysia sulkily.

"Though now we've left him well behind us and it's very quiet and down here, hidden from sight," said Corsica meaningfully.

"Kent's mounted on *Wulf* and he's the slowest horse in my stable."

Corsica had been through this kind of thing with her many times before, he tied his animal to a low hanging branch and advanced with determination.

"Come any closer and you'll be sorry," warned Elysia.

"Will I now."

Elysia brandished her riding crop, "I'll cut your face open – that'll spoil you for the ladies."

"You might toy with it," Corsica disregarded her threat and moved closer.

"I'll slash your cheek – both cheeks and then laugh to see the blood flow."

Jonnie Corsica threw back his head and roared with laughter too, "Oh, you always have to make a game of it," he said, his voice low and strong.

"Not this time, Mr Corsica. I…," she began, but then he lunged forward and pinned her arms to her sides.

"Get off me, get off at once, you're holding me too tightly, I can hardly breathe."

"I could squeeze the life out of you now if I wanted to. I could do anything to you I wished."

Elysia flung back her head and laughed in his face, "Why, you impudent foreign cur, you have no power over me whatsoever. I could destroy you on a whim."

Corsica held her in a python like grip, "Sure you could, but I'd bring you down with me. Anyway, I'm far too useful to you. Who else would or could carry-out your dirty work? *Kent maybe!*" He laughed at the idea.

Finding herself fully pinioned Elysia attempted to kick her assailant's ankles, but her heavy riding skirt prevented her from causing him much discomfort, so instead she spat fully in his face, her eyes blazing with a combination of frustration and desire.

"Why, you," spluttered Jonnies Corsica as he threw his prisoner to the ground and then climbed on top of her.

"You'll have the breath out of me, you swine," she complained as she tried to roll away from him.

"Made things worse for yourself, haven't you," suggested Corsica as together they rolled into a patch of oozing mud.

"*Get off me, get off me at once,*" shouted Elysia as she felt her skirt being lifted.

Corsica ignored her, he knew what she wanted and as far as he was concerned she was going to get it, he thought as he forced his way between her thighs.

Elysia's mouth became very dry, in complete contrast to her vagina which she knew was becoming very receptive to her lover.

"*Ahh*, sighed Corsica as he moved into her.

"*Ohh... You animal...,*" she cried as they thrashed about together in the mire.

A hundred yards away Virgil Kent crawled to the top of an overlooking rise and took cover behind a shrub that gave him a good view of what was going on between his mistress and Corsica.

"She's a bitch and nothing other than a common whore," he whispered to himself. Not that he was surprised, all the servants; apart from those with the innocence of young children, suspected that Mr Corsica was the Marchioness's lover.

Winterbourne itself was full of her Ladyship's doings, though she was popular enough with the locals, for she supported widows in distress, gave a sovereign to every baby born there and only recently had paid for renovations to the organ loft of the parish church.

On the other hand, any tenant who became more than a quarter in arrears with their rent soon found themselves evicted and out on the open-road.

Kent shook his head, he had the evidence before his eyes here, but it could do him no good.

He'd returned from Martin Hall after instructing the children there how to ride, but he'd been unable to make any progress with Cissy Jackson.

Not that he wished to for himself, as she was such a wraith of a girl, there was hardly a curve to her body and her breasts were virtually non-existent.

However, her ladyship had disappointed him as he hadn't been promoted to under-butler.

Virgil Kent looked back into the valley and saw that the legs of the Marchioness were now wrapped around Corsica's back and they were both coming near to a long and muddy climax.

"Time to be off," he said to himself as he worked his way backwards down the slope, hoping to be mounted and well away before his employer and that dangerous factotum of hers caught sight of him.

*****

"Grace," Helmuth had managed to remember his sister's name, "I must go to England. Andy tells me that my wife is there."

"She is, but you aren't fit to travel."

"I'm well able to travel to any corner of the earth," insisted Helmuth.

"He sure is," supported the ex-slave.

"What business is it of yours," replied Grace sharply, before she turned to her brother again, "You cannot travel alone."

"Mr Jackson will attend me."

Grace laughed, "No, Jackson will be unable to..."

"I am going and Jackson will see to it that I come to no harm," Helmuth cut off his sister.

"You have no money," returned Miss Schilling.

"I'm sure you're well aware of my financial standing, I've enough to sail around the world many times," Helmuth looked hard at his sister.

Grace shook her head and then changed tack, "What of me? What of poor Major Sturgis?"

"What of you?" Helmuth couldn't see what her problem was.

"I cannot be left *alone* with a bachelor gentlemen sharing my house."

Helmuth shook his head, "No perhaps not, I can see that."

"You would not leave your sister in so compromising a situation, I trust," Grace almost begged her brother.

Captain Schilling thought for a moment and then said, "In which case, you shall have to accompany me to England."

"What about the Major, he has given his parole, he cannot travel across the Atlantic, nor can he stay here. He'll end up in prison."

Sturgis spoke for the first time, "I'm sure the Stockyards of Chicago are more comfortable than they sound."

"Oh, no. *No, no, no.* I'll not have it," Grace's voice became shrill as she faced the possible loss of a husband.

"Grace, please, this is not the behaviour of a lady. What would papa have said?"

"My father is dead and I soon shall be if Major Sturgis is sent away," Grace threatened her brother.

"There is a simple solution," Sturgis put in calmly.

The siblings ceased their argument and both looked towards the speaker.

"What would that be?" asked Helmuth.

Sturgis slipped from his chair and down onto one-knee, "Miss Grace Schilling, will you marry me?" He proposed.

Grace's hands became clasped together as if in prayer, "You mean it? You really mean you want me as your bride?"

"Of course, I love you, you're the woman who saved my leg and kept me away from the war and imprisonment," he said as he rose to his feet.

"Oh, yes, Gideon, yes, I'll marry you," she cried as she threw herself into his arms.

Helmuth found it difficult to believe that any man in his right mind would willingly take Grace as his bride though he understood what Sturgis' ulterior motive was.

"I have you permission, sir?" Queried the major, drawing himself up to full attention.

"By all means," returned Captain Schilling without hesitation.

"Will the army authorities agree to this proposal?" Grace asked.

Her brother doubted there would be any problem with a paroled prisoner taking a wife and if it meant that he himself could join the beautiful lady in the large house, so be it.

*****

Walter Matheson, a leading Pennsylvania lawyer, looked up from his desk as his cousin; Colonel Jefferson Stanley, entered the room accompanied by a Union Army captain.

"You anything to tell me?" Questioned the lawyer.

"Quite some, Walt, but let me introduce Captain Wiley Reeks of the Judge Advocates Department first."

Matheson nodded a greeting at the military-lawyer and then suggested, "Why don't you gentlemen take a seat and tell me exactly what happened to my son."

"This boy's got it all filed away, so I'll leave it to him," Colonel Stanley spoke first.

The captain opened the leather document case he was carrying and pulled out a thick sheaf of papers.

"Sonny, just speak it out, you can leave the documentation with me when you go," ordered Matheson.

Captain Reeks took a deep breath and then informed, "Well, sir, your son's body was discovered to the east of the main battlefield, where the cavalry actions on the third day took place."

Matheson's eyes were lit by new hope, "So, he died fighting, you reckon?"

"He was in a civilian suit, sir," Reeks spoke neutrally.

"You mean he was running for it?"

"There's no fully corroborated evidence of that.....," began the captain.

"He could have been visiting friends in the town and was caught out of uniform, but still bravely met the Rebels head on," Colonel Stanley was desperate for a story – any story which would satisfy his powerful cousin.

"Do you reckon this to be a possibility?" Asked Matheson of the soldier-lawyer.

"No sir, most unlikely as it seems the body had lain there for longer than the others – surgeons said the *riga-mortis* in his case was in a more advanced state."

"Now, captain, that don't prove nothing...," began Stanley.

Matheson cut off his cousin sharply, "Tell it how it is, captain, I know full-well what the character of my son was."

"In addition to a single bullet through his heart...," continued the captain.

"Poor boy would have died instantly," once again the colonel interrupted.

"He had suffered considerable facial wounds," Captain Reeks drew a breath of relief after having managed to complete at least one sentence.

"Facial wounds? Knife, maybe?" Queried Matheson.

The captain shook his head, "Very serious wounds, one of you son's eyes was seriously damaged, the sight of it probably unrecoverable."

"Rebel viciousness, I expect," commented Stanley.

"The wounds were inflicted by something with many blades, or forks," informed Reeks, seriously.

"A fork, perhaps? The Rebs will need to carry them," said Stanley, though doubtfully.

"Or a steel comb," suggested Reeks.

"Who the hell takes a comb on to a battlefield and uses it as a weapon?" Wondered Colonel Jefferson Stanley aloud.

"*A woman*," Walter Matheson put a whole barrel of meaning into his words.

"There's no evidence…," began Reeks, but again the military lawyer was interrupted.

"*No*, there is a woman involved here, I just know it," said Matheson, "and this would have been typical of Dred."

The room was stilled for a full minute before the Pennsylvania lawyer spoke again, "What about the Schilling fellow, the one Eldred didn't get on with. He who made my son his office-boy. What did he have to say about it?"

"Captain Schilling was wounded on 1st July and has completely lost his memory," informed Reeks.

"That's overly convenient, don't you think," suggested Stanley.

"His wound appears to be a genuine one," added Reeks.

"Schilling's wound may be above-board – though his loss of memory, perhaps not," considered Jefferson Stanley.

"Further investigation is required, do you not believe so, captain?" Suggested Matheson.

"I've many other cases…," began Reeks.

Walter Matheson's face became grim, "You'll follow up my son's case. Colonel Holt is an acquaintance of mine going back to Buchanan's administration, he'll expect you to give Eldred's killing your full and *complete* attention."

"Sir," Reeks could say nothing else for Colonel Joseph Holt was the Judge-Advocate General of the Union Army.

"Pester Kellogg and anyone else in the 17th Pennsylvanian who has information. Check on the Schilling family in Gettysburg, see if there are any women who knew of my boy. Be thorough. You understand?"

"Yes, sir," again the military lawyer acquiesced.

The tone of Walter Matheson became even grimmer, "I'm soon to become Judge President of a District Court of

Common Pleas. I want anyone involved in the death of my son in front of my Bench in double-quick time. Even should it be somewhere miles outside my authority."

"But...," again, Wiley Reeks tried to protest.

"You have no more important case than this one," Matheson looked very hard at Wiley Reeks, "*Understand?*"

"Yes, sir, I shall not leave it until I have the murderer of your son standing before you in court," Captain Wiley Reeks had no choice other than to carry out his orders.

*****

Caroline Schilling, arriving at her breakfast table, pounced on an envelope which lay waiting for her and tore it open.

She recognised the handwriting as that of her husband and began to read eagerly.

Gettysburg,
Pennsylvania,
10th August 1863

My Dear Mrs Schilling,

In my present uncertain state I feel unable to address you as Caroline and I hope you will forgive me for this.

As I believe Colonel Kellogg has informed you, I was wounded in the great battle fought here a month or so ago. As a result of the injury I sustained there I have completely lost my memory

All I know of my previous life is what I have been told by my sister and Mr Jackson.

The situation here is still fraught, though I have been discharged from the Union Army and intend to travel to Blanchwell as soon as it can be arranged.

Since my wound, my only memory is of a beautiful lady living in a large house. I have been told that this lady is yourself. I look forward to renewing my acquaintance with you and hope that you will love me as much as; apparently, I did you in the past.

Your husband,

Helmuth Schilling,
Captain, 17th Pennsylvania Cavalry.

"He's alive, in one piece and coming back to me," breathed a very relieved Caroline to herself.

As he had no recollection of her previous coolness towards him, she had the opportunity to make a fresh-start. She was determined to seize this chance with both hands and all her heart.

"Not a single day will go by when I do not shower him with kisses and tell him over and over again that I love him deeply," her words were reinforced by the strength with which they were spoken.

This is a work of fiction and every character in it is fictitious and cannot be connected to any person living or dead.

Printed in Great Britain
by Amazon